UMINGMAK

Stuart Hodgson and the
Birth of the Modern Arctic

"Totally engrossing stories of the various aboriginal organizations and their views of Stu and the Territorial government . . . A true picture of the evolution of government in the North."

ROBERT (BOB) PILOT, C.M., KStJ,
Former Deputy Commissioner of the Northwest Territories

"This enjoyable book is about the author's relationship with Stuart Hodgson and how he progressed through the ranks of the Territorial civil service under Stu. All in all a very good read."

DAVID H. SEARLE, C.M., Q.C.
First Elected Speaker, Legislative Assembly of the Northwest Territories

"This is an interesting read about the Arctic just when it was beginning to change and open up. It's about the 1960s and 1970s, the communities and the people, and about Stu Hodgson who put the North on the map while connecting Inuit throughout the Arctic and the polar world – Alaska, Northwest Territories, Greenland."

PETER IRNIQ, former Commissioner of Nunavut; First Cabinet Minister, Government of the Northwest Territories

"Stu was not always in agreement with young Inuit leaders. But without him I don't think we'd have Nunavut. In a dozen years, he brought the government from Ottawa to Yellowknife, moved the appointed Council to fully elected, and in days of truly primitive communication ("Do you copy? Over") made a point of trying to visit each community yearly to hear the concerns of people."

MONICA CONNOLLY, former editor of *Nunatsiaq News*

"The greatest Northerner of all of them."

CLAIRE M. BARNABE, former Arctic community administrator

UMINGMAK

Stuart Hodgson and the
Birth of the Modern Arctic

JAKE OOTES

TIDEWATER
PRESS

Published by Tidewater Press
New Westminster, BC, Canada
www.tidewaterpress.ca

ISBN: 978-1-7770101-0-2 (print)
ISBN: 978-1-7770101-1-9 (html)

LIBRARY AND ARCHIVES CANADA CATALOGUING IN PUBLICATION
Title: Umingmak : Stuart Hodgson and the birth of the modern Arctic / Jake Ootes.
Names: Ootes, Jake, 1942- author.
Description: Includes index.
Identifiers: Canadiana (print) 20200190342 | Canadiana (ebook) 20200190350 | ISBN 9781777010102 (softcover) | ISBN 9781777010119 (HTML)
Subjects: LCSH: Hodgson, Stuart, 1924-2015. | LCSH: Northwest Territories—Officials and employees—Biography. | CSH: Northwest Territories—Politics and government—1951-1999. | LCGFT: Biographies.
Classification: LCC FC4073.1.H63 O58 2020 | DDC 971.9/203092—dc23

Front cover photo: Stuart Hodgson in caribou outfit at Grise Fiord, Northwest Territories. 1975. Department of Information Collection (1975), Government of the Northwest Territories.
Author photo: NWT Prince of Wales Northern Heritage Centre.
Back cover: NWT Shield by permission, Northwest Territories Legislative Assembly.

Unless otherwise credited, all photos are by Jake Ootes.

Printed in Canada

For the people of the Arctic, who enriched my life,
and for David Holehouse, for his invaluable input.

CONTENTS

FOREWORD

THE 1960S AND EARLY 1970S were a time of evolution, of great change for the North. Indigenous peoples were transitioning off the land into communities without the services that existed in other parts of Canada. Our lands and people were administered by the federal government, but we had little knowledge of the role it played in our lives. Bureaucrats in faraway Ottawa knew even less about us.

That started to change when, on September 18, 1967, a plane from Ottawa landed at the Yellowknife airport. On board were two dozen civil servants of the government of the Northwest Territories led by Stuart Hodgson, the newly appointed Commissioner and Chairman of the Council of the Northwest Territories. The Council, forerunner of today's Legislative Assembly, consisted of some elected and some appointed members, but Stu had dictatorial powers. Fortunately for us, he turned out to be a benevolent dictator.

Two years later, I was honoured and privileged to be appointed President of the Indian Brotherhood (later to become the Dene Nation) by the elder chiefs of the twenty-six communities of Treaties 8 and 11, in accordance with ancient Dene customs and traditions. We had come from a nomadic existence and needed to protect our lands, our culture and our way of life. To do so, I realized that we would have to come to terms with Stuart Hodgson and his territorial administration. It would prove to be a time of learning for all of us.

Stu travelled to meet people on their home turf in far-flung and isolated communities—the Dene, the Inuit, the Métis, the non-aboriginals. He listened to our voices, what we had to say, what we needed, what we wanted. He would order his administrators, in no uncertain terms, to fix the problems. Significant changes started to take place for the Dene people and for all of us throughout the North—improved transportation and communication systems, changes to our way of life. He also promoted the North, arranging visits by The Queen, the Governor General and the Prime Minister and encouraging community and territorial celebrations.

Stu united the North, bringing people together. The people of the High Arctic might not know the lifestyle of the people of Rae, my community in the south, and vice versa, but Stu saw it was important that we understand each other, work with each other. On his travels he would educate and encourage people to take control over their own affairs, to become leaders, first at the community level, then at the regional and eventually at the territorial level. Outstanding treaty settlement for my people, the Dene, was a big issue at that time and Stu recognized the sensitivity and importance of this. While the Inuit didn't have treaties, he also respected their desires. He realized that all of us needed a way to control our own lives and futures.

Eventually the Council became fully elected with a significant number of Aboriginal members from all regions of the North, including me. Stu handed over some of his authority and, over the years, continued to relinquish his powers and oversee the transition to an elected legislative body directly responsible to the people. He recognized the importance of governing by consensus—the Aboriginal way—and this is part of his legacy. The Legislative Assembly of the Northwest Territories is truly unique in the Canadian confederation.

There were many times, especially in the early years, when Stu and I had significant disagreements, different agendas. But one thing was clear. We respected each other. We worked through those differences for the betterment of northern people. When I was elected to the Executive Council, equivalent to a cabinet minister, Stu worked with me and heeded my advice. I appreciate the support and encouragement I received from him.

We have come a long way since the day Stu Hodgson arrived in the North. In the Tlicho territory, my home, we settled a land claim with the federal government, and now have our own government where we follow the customs and traditions of our ancestors. By the time Stu retired we were well on our way. He earned the respect of the chiefs, the Dene, and of the Aboriginal people. He set the pace, he governed. He led us into the 21st century.
Mahsi cho!

James Wah-Shee
Chair, Tlicho National Assembly
Behchoko, Northwest Territories

AUTHOR'S NOTE

TODAY THE PEOPLES OF THE Arctic are referred to as Inuit, Inuvialuit and Dene. During the period I write about they were typically referred to as Eskimos or Indians. While these words are now recognized as pejorative, they were commonly used in the North at that time. I have therefore written the terms Eskimo and Indian as used during the years this narrative takes place. The words Native, Aboriginal and Indigenous have all been similarly used in the context of the time. For the same reason, the spelling and names of individuals, communities and geographic locations are used as they were then, and all measurements are imperial, not metric.

NORTHWEST TERRITORIES, 1970

LABRADOR

QUEBEC

Port Burwell

Frobisher Bay

Pangnirtung

Port Harrison

Saniikiluaq

BELCHER ISLANDS

Cape Dorset

Clyde

BAFFIN ISLAND

ONTARIO

Pond Inlet

Hall Beach

Igloolik

Repulse Bay

HUDSON'S BAY

Griise Fiord

Arctic Bay

Spence Bay

Pelly Bay

Rankin Inlet

ELLESMERE ISLAND

Resolute

MANITOBA

Baker Lake

Cambridge Bay

GREAT SLAVE LAKE

SASKATCHEWAN

BANKS ISLAND

GREAT BEAR LAKE

Fort Smith

Fort Resolution

Yellowknife

Pine Point

Rae

Dettah

Sachs Harbour

MACKENZIE RIVER

Fort Simpson

Hay River

ALBERTA

Fort Good Hope

Fort Norman

Tuktoyaktuk

Inuvik

Fort McPherson

BRITISH COLUMBIA

YUKON

PROLOGUE

PRIME MINISTER LESTER B. PEARSON drew his chair closer to the desk. "Your job will be to bring Canada's Arctic into the 20th century. That part of our country has been ignored for too long. Unacceptable!"

The development of Canada's Arctic was part of Pearson's vision for the country. As Secretary of State for External Affairs, he had been awarded the 1957 Nobel Peace Prize for his role in helping to resolve the Suez Canal Crisis. As Prime Minister, he had introduced the Canada Pension Plan, student loans, a new national flag (the red maple leaf), and universal health care. A month ago, he had dedicated the Centennial Fountain in front of the Peace Tower on Parliament Hill, marking the beginning of Canada's 100th birthday. Now, Pearson was determined to bring the territory north of the 60th parallel into Canada's mainstream by appointing a new Commissioner.

"The Northwest Territories forms one-third of our country," said the Prime Minister. "You will be in charge of one of the largest administrative territories in the world, populated primarily by Eskimos, Indians and Métis with little understanding of government." He stopped to collect his thoughts before continuing. "It is a land so vast it is impossible to describe, with one of the most daunting climates on the globe. There are no roads, few airstrips and telephone service is restricted to a handful of larger centres. So there is no effective way to communicate with the 26,000 people who live in fifty isolated communities spread over 1,300,000 square miles."

The Prime Minister looked at Stuart Hodgson. "Arthur here," Pearson nodded towards Arthur Laing, the Minister of Indian Affairs and Northern Development, "tells me you're the best man for this job. That you'll stand like a rock! That you'll give it your all!"

"I'll give it my all," vowed Hodgson. "I'll move the government from Ottawa to the new capital in the North and stay at least ten years to establish the democratic government envisioned by the Carrothers Commission[1]. But I have to warn you that I know nothing about running a government."

"That is exactly why I'm appointing you."

Laing interjected, "Stu, you will have to show results quickly. It's important to the people of the North that this government demonstrates its resolve to bring self-government expediently." The government's interest in affirming its sovereignty over the vast, underpopulated Arctic went unmentioned. Laing continued, "We'll announce your appointment next week."

The ringing bells in the outer corridor summoned members of the House of Commons to Question Period, ending the meeting.

The Prime Minister rose from his chair and stepped around the desk. "Your undertaking is of historic importance, not only for the Arctic and its people, but for all of Canada." His expression was stern. "I expect big results and more than the best from you." He extended his hand to Hodgson. "In return, I will give you my full support. No one else in this country will have the kind of authority you will. Not even me."

---

[1] The Carrothers Commission, formally known as the Advisory Commission on the Development of Government in the Northwest Territories, set up by the Government of Canada, made recommendations in 1966 on the future of government in the Northwest Territories.

Part One

A LEADER IN THE MAKING

1
APPOINTED

"SO, WHO'S GOING TO BE the new Commissioner? You spend all your time with the people here in Centennial Towers. Heard anything?"

I was having lunch in the ground-floor cafeteria with several members of the Council of the Northwest Territories. Pete Baker represented a constituency that stretched from Great Slave Lake all the way to Great Bear Lake. A resident of Yellowknife, he had a bald head and an enormous, weather-bitten nose, as well as failing hearing and eyesight. Beside him sat Bobby Porritt who lived in Hay River and represented a constituency stretching from Great Slave Lake south to the Alberta border. The fourth seat at our table was occupied by Hugh Campbell, a prim and erect Air Marshal from Ottawa appointed by the Prime Minister to share his wisdom with the northern council.

"We'll know soon enough, I suppose," I said. "Bent Sivertz collects his golden handshake in a few weeks. Who do you think it's going to be?" Having joined the Department of Indian Affairs and Northern Development as Information Officer only the year before, I was happy to ask questions they seemed eager to answer.

"Got to be Stu," Porritt said. "He's got the ability to take the Northwest Territories in hand to solve many of our problems. We recommended him to the Minister." He took a bite of his lunch and in between chews said, "Who knows what these political people will do? Without someone like him, we Northerners will lose our identity and become nothing more than slaves to the multinational mining and exploration companies."

Second-hand tobacco smoke tickled the back of my throat as I asked, "What about a Northerner?"

"Northerners? Well, John Parker's been mayor of Yellowknife and served on the Carrothers Commission. And Ted Horton wants the job. But all he'd do is make enemies, same as he does now with his newspaper." Ted Horton owned and published the weekly *News of the North* in Yellowknife. "We need someone they'll listen to."

He leaned back and his voice became more resonant. "Ottawa hasn't paid any attention to the Northwest Territories for the last hundred years. It's a place of ice and snow and howling wind to them. There is no government, just a few federal civil servants scattered around who do two-year stints to collect three years' pension time before returning south. Up until twenty years ago, not one single school had been built. The North was left to the missionaries, the fur traders, the Indians and Eskimos. It was only five years ago that the government introduced its housing program. The Church runs most of the schools, and look where that's got us. There's no local government in any community other than Yellowknife, Hay River and Fort Smith, and they're white towns. It's dismal in the settlements. The Mountie, the teacher, the preacher or the Hudson's Bay storekeeper ends up being the government." Porritt's cheeks flushed as he stared straight at me. "The native people fend for themselves, which means they must hunt, trap or starve. It's the biggest and toughest territory in the world, three times the size of France, and our federal government here in Ottawa could care less about it or its people, except to suck up money from natural resources or talk about sovereignty. That's probably why they sent the Mounties north, so they can claim a government presence."

Porritt hesitated a few moments, looked around the cafeteria and again at me. His cheeks glowed and his voice now vibrated. "We don't just need someone capable to bring government and decency to the North—we need someone with two fists and the guts to use them against Ottawa. Someone like Stu!"

Pete Baker had been staring around the room, oblivious to the discussion. He set his cup on the table, lifted the saucer in which he'd spilled a little coffee and slurped, reminding me of the old farmhands of the Ottawa Valley. Then he turned his milky-grey, cataract eyes toward me and spoke as if passing on a great confidence. "Trappers and hunters'll starve this year, the way it's going. No moose or caribou. Worst I've seen in all my years." He turned to Bobby Porritt. "Isn't that right?"

Porritt nodded his head. "We're nothing more than a rubber stamp for the bureaucrats here in Ottawa. We don't have any power because all the

decisions are made by people in this building, all answering directly to Côté."
Ernest Côté was the Deputy Minister of Indian Affairs and Northern Development. "We need someone who will change that."

"But Hodgson's new to the North and to government. He's only been Deputy Commissioner for a short time," I said. No one said anything. I knew that wasn't what they wanted to hear.

Porritt leaned forward and pointed the tip of his fork as he spoke. "Hodgson may not know the North, nor have a great deal of formal education—and that goes for most of us who sit around that council table, except the Air Marshal here—but he runs circles around these civil servants here in Ottawa. He's young, unorthodox, fearless and as moral as the day is long. And he's a real man of action. I tell you, he doesn't sit on the can for three weeks before making a decision. He gets things done, by God, and look out anyone who tries to stop him!"

"I suppose Hodgson's link with Art Laing might give him an advantage if he wants the job," I said.

The Air Marshal cleared his throat with a slight cough. "I don't think it's political connections that'll get him appointed. After all, Stu attended the founding convention of the New Democratic Party in '61 and was among those who asked Tommy Douglas to become its leader. I don't think you'd find him in bed with the Liberals. Stu would make a good Commissioner because he's the kind of man who'd put the job above his own ambitions. You've got to have someone who'll take the bull by the horns if we're to build an effective government for the North."

I nodded, getting a feel for the support Hodgson had.

"Stu used to be a rabble-rouser and a fist fighter, but that was when he was a young organizer for the International Woodworkers of America. Now he's more of a talker, a negotiator. He's made a tremendous contribution to our Council already, and he's only the Deputy Commissioner. Change is coming to the North. Only a special kind of person can lead us through the havoc that comes with change."

"What do you mean, change?" I asked.

The Air Marshal didn't mince words. "The Northwest Territories is becoming a hot property for mining and oil and gas exploration. Big money is moving north. Life is changing for the whites who live there, but just think what it will do to the native way of life. It will disappear. They'll lose control of what's about to happen around them."

Porritt touched the Air Marshal's arm as he looked toward the entrance of the cafeteria. We followed his gaze as Hodgson himself bounded in. He strode in like a triumphant brush salesman, his baggy brown pants and olive plaid jacket flapping in the jet stream of his movement. His thick raven-black hair was brushed back as if pressed by the force of his passage, giving him a determined look. His bristling moustache and dark eyebrows added an air of impatience and authority. At six foot two and more than 200 pounds, the former union boss was a commanding sight.

I glanced at the Air Marshal. His left eyebrow moved slightly, saying it all.

Hodgson stood erect while he loaded his tray and spoke to several people in line. They laughed, but there were also sideways glances from others who scorned his brashness and lack of decorum.

He carried on, oblivious to the stares, and took a seat at our table, greeting us with a nod.

The Air Marshal said, "Stu, we were talking about the Commissioner's position. There's a strong possibility the bureaucrats here will block you if you're appointed. Some of them think you haven't taken the right apprenticeship for a job like Commissioner. You never joined their club."

His face was serious. He paused, took a bite of his lunch and looked at the Air Marshal. "They're playing the usual game, but I know how to play it better. Let them think they're winning. That way they won't realize I've already had a meeting with Art Laing and the Prime Minister."

Bobby Porritt beamed.

"I'm the man for the job. No bureaucrat here or anywhere else is going to get in my way to get the people of the North what they deserve. That's a promise!"

2

CHANCE OF A LIFETIME

APRIL 1967

I WAS CLIPPING NORTHERN STORIES from various newspapers. Of particular interest was one in the *Edmonton Journal* [2] about pilot Robert Gauchie,
who had been lost in the Arctic in midwinter and rescued after a fifty-
eight-day ordeal. His first words upon being rescued were, "Who's the new
Commissioner of the Territories?"

I cut the story, stapling on a blue circulation notice addressed to the Deputy
Minister and other departmental officials. I kept a separate file for Hodgson.
Culling newspaper stories kept me well informed on northern events as well
as world news: the US had just fired off a space rocket to select a landing spot
for man's first trip to the moon, Dr. Christiaan Barnard and a team of South
African surgeons had performed the world's first successful heart transplant,
Montreal would come of age hosting the World's Fair, Expo 67, and Canada
was celebrating its hundreth birthday.

I had come to Ottawa after a fledgling career as a newspaper reporter,
first in in Watford, in southwestern Ontario, and later in my hometown of
Renfrew. It was my father who pointed out an advertisement in the *Ottawa
Journal* for an Editor of Debates with the Government of the Northwest Territories, based in Ottawa. In his Dutch accent, he said, "Yake, leave this small
town. There's no future here." I had no idea where the Northwest Territories
was, nor what Debates were, but Editor of Debates sounded interesting.
Despite my lack of formal education, I was offered the position in December
1964, at the age of 22.

At that time, the Government of the Northwest Territories consisted of
five employees, headed by a career civil servant with the commanding title
of Commissioner. He met twice a year with members of the Council of the
Northwest Territories, a quasi-legislative body consisting of five appointed

---

[2] Bob Bell, "Pilot Only a Few Miles from Air Route," *Edmonton Journal,* April 3, 1967

members, all from southern Canada, and four elected members who represented constituencies in the western part of the Northwest Territories. The central and eastern parts of the Territories had no political representation. The Council considered, reviewed and passed ordinances and sessional papers. Their deliberations were recorded and transcribed; I was responsible for editing these 'debates,' equivalent to Hansard, the official record of parliamentary deliberations. The Deputy Commissioner of the Territorial Government, to whom I reported, was Stuart Hodgson.

After two years in that position I was approached by Irene Baird, Chief of Information Services Division for the Department of Indian Affairs and Northern Development, and the first woman to head a federal information division. She suggested I apply for a position as Information Officer. I thought it was a plum job and was flattered to join her staff. When I told Hodgson, he was magnanimous, hosting a going-away lunch where he showered me with praise. He made me feel like a prince, a noble of his court.

The Department of Indian Affairs and Northern Development had more than a thousand employees in Ottawa, 350 of whom worked directly on northern affairs. To the best of my knowledge, none were Indian or Eskimo. What did I know about the North and its people? I was one of four white guys in the division assigned to keep the public and media informed about current programs. We wrote news releases and answered letters of inquiry, mainly from writers and students. In my last year, we received some 12,000 letters and distributed 81,000 pieces of material, primarily booklets, mimeographed articles, maps and annual reports. We prepared and published the department's annual report, the staff publication *Intercom*, of which I was editor, and a general interest magazine, *North,* for distribution to the public.

Irene Baird proved to be a good boss, but she retired a year later, and I found the new director insincere, hypocritical and uninterested in our work. Working in such a large organization meant becoming anonymous and my job satisfaction was minimal. I began showing up for work mid-morning and leaving mid-afternoon. No one noticed.

Rain was pounding the large glass windows behind me when the sharp ring of the telephone startled me out of my usual reverie. Erma Courier, Hodgson's secretary, said the new Commissioner wanted to see me. Erma had an air of efficiency and pronounced my last name properly. Most people called me Oats or Oots, Erma always pronounced it Otis. Could I come right away? I smiled. I could imagine that with Hodgson as Commissioner everything in his fledgling government would be immediate.

Hodgson had wasted no time in putting his own imprint on the office. A pair of flagpoles stood behind his desk—one bore Canada's new red maple leaf, the other a blue polar bear on a white background, a design Hodgson had developed as a tourism symbol for the Northwest Territories. Someone had run a hand over the windowpane to clear the condensation; through the drizzle I could see the Peace Tower on Parliament Hill. The sun was starting to shine on the Québec side.

"Come in, Jake!" Hodgson's voice boomed as he stood and walked from behind the big oak desk. His handshake was firm and confident, not the bone-breaker you get from people who feel inadequate. "Great to see you." His large teeth shone under his triangular moustache. His eyes, almost hidden beneath prodigious eyebrows, were trained squarely on me. "Isn't that something, them finding Bob Gauchie after all this time?"

I nodded.

"The man survived fifty-eight days and only froze his toes. It set a survival record!" He sat down and waved his arm for me to take a chair. "And you know what his first words were to the guys who picked him up?"

"I know," I said, but Hodgson continued, "Who's the new Commissioner?" He grinned. "Isn't that something?"

I smiled, warming to his energy, soaking up his enthusiasm. I realized how much I'd missed working for him.

"Well, we're all set to go. Five more months and the government of the Northwest Territories will be gone from Ottawa. It'll be in Yellowknife, the newest capital in Canada. We leave September 18 with two planes—one for the staff and one for the office supplies."

The intercom buzzed. Erma said a reporter from one of the northern newspapers was on the line. Hodgson took the call and nodded his head several times.

"Sure. We'll shut the offices in Ottawa September 17, fly up on the 18th, and open the offices in Yellowknife at 8:30 a.m., September 19." He listened for a moment. "Yes, I know . . . houses and offices won't be ready, but we'll be there. That's the main thing." He listened for a moment and shrugged his shoulders. "Reaction? Oh, good Lord, you should have seen the wires and telegrams and phone calls I got the day I was appointed. No kidding! Write this down. I just had my forty-third birthday and I'm rarin' to go. I want to be living in Yellowknife by the first day of fall . . . Eugene is ten and Lynne is seven. Wife's name is Pearl."

I watched Hodgson with fascination.

"What's that? The line isn't too good."

Perhaps, I thought, spitting into the mouthpiece is short-circuiting the line.

"My plans? First we assemble a top-rank territorial staff, about thirty. We'll accommodate them in whatever housing and office space we can scrounge. I'm contacting Yellowknife town council to get water and sewer services put in for a new subdivision to go ahead right now. Then we set up departments, personnel and treasury, and build the government from there."

Hodgson was quiet again, then said, "You don't mind being forward, do you? Well, I don't believe in secrets. It's $24,000 a year. And I give it all to Pearl. Honest to God. When I get home, I just hand her my paycheque and let her take care of it." Hodgson chuckled. "Talk to you later."

He hung up the phone.

"Thirty people to run a territory the size of India?" I asked.

"All I need is a core group to get things started. The important thing is to be fast and decisive. When the Prime Minister offered me the job, I swore to him I'd shut the Ottawa office and move everything to Yellowknife within the year."

Hodgson was like a fiery warrior, accepting the impossible challenge in hopes of proving himself to the king.

"The big challenge will be to educate local people about government. Hell, they're hunters and trappers who don't know anything about our ways. I've got to take power up there to them, or they'll be trampled and assimilated, maybe even extinguished as unique cultures. Don't ask me exactly how, but that's what I'm going to do.

"I figure I've got ten years, tops. If I fail, the people and the cultures of the North could well be nothing but history."

There was a knock at the door. "Sorry to interrupt again, Commissioner," Erma said, "but CR has been phoning wanting to know if you want your letter to Mr. Laing about the move to Yellowknife BF'd for a future date."

"July 1." Hodgson shook his head, setting his jowls shaking. "You know, Jake, when they made me Deputy Commissioner, I realized I didn't know diddly-squat about the way government works. Nothing! I walked into this office and all it had was a bare desk, a wooden swivel chair and an empty bookcase. I opened the desk drawer and all it had in it was straight pins and urgent tags. That was it! Then the files started coming at me and no one showed me nothing. I didn't know what CR (central registry), PA (put away), or BF (bring forward) meant. You had to mark each file with one of those, and I knew that if I didn't figure this out, I wouldn't get anywhere in the civil service. So I went to the bottom of the organization and started learning about every job in the building. I talked to the lowest clerk and learned everything he knew about handling paperwork. I'd do that every morning and my own job every afternoon. Within a couple of months I knew everything inside out, because I got to know everything from the bottom up. Not many civil servants can say that. Most of them don't know what it's like to work hard, to struggle. They've got it too easy, and so they stop learning and busting their butts. But not me!"

He paused to recollect, his eyes concentrating somewhere else in the room. "My big break came when Bent Sivertz summoned me to his office and said, 'Stu, I've been scheduled to make two speeches, one in Whitehorse and one in Ottawa. I'm going to Whitehorse, so you have to give the one in Ottawa.' 'Fine,' I said. 'Have you got the speech ready for me?' He said, 'No, make your own speech.' I was just elated at the chance to show my stuff. I figure I have three abilities, Jake: the ability to negotiate, the ability to run a meeting and the ability to deliver a speech."

I'd seen enough of him to know this wasn't empty boasting.

"It was a gathering of the Ottawa mandarins who thought the territorial government was just a teeny little thing that didn't account for anything. But I'll tell you I stood 'em on their ears because they'd never heard anyone talk like that before. I enjoy the fiery orator role. When I finished talking all the chairman could say to close the meeting was, 'Well, you certainly put across the view that the territorial government should be located in the North rather than Ottawa.' They gave me a thundering ovation and I was in my element. After that they didn't keep me waiting outside their doors anymore. All of a sudden I was in great demand. That probably did more than anything else to pave the way for my appointment."

He slapped his hand on the table and gestured. "Two years later and here I am." He looked toward the window, then gazed at me. I sensed he was sizing me up. "You always been interested in newspapers?"

What on earth was he getting at now? It was a formidable challenge to keep up.

"Well, yes. My dream is to buy a newspaper someday."

"Well, listen, here's a possibility for you. I'm going to offer Ted Horton, the owner of *News of the North*, a job. I want you to come up with me and put that paper out for a couple of weeks."

I laughed out loud. "So you're buying him off." The last thing Hodgson needed was a newspaper editor mad at him for beating him to the top job.

Hodgson glared and I realized he was not to be trifled with. Finally he said, "There's a spare seat on the plane. Come along, you can help me and also put out the paper for a couple of issues, see if you want to buy the place. I'll arrange for your ticket back."

The sky had cleared and the sun shone through the windows, warming my back. "I can't just leave my job and take time off from Information Services."

"Don't worry. I'll talk to the Deputy Minister and ask to second you for several weeks."

I felt a flash of boldness. "What's in it for you?"

"This'll be good for both of us. You get a change in routine, a little harmless adventure. And in return, I get your help. The first week or two will be critical. A government is nothing without communications. Who knows, maybe you'll arrange some financing with Ted and buy the thing."

I had an entrepreneurial streak, an independent spirit and a penchant for wanderlust that had been eroded by months of drudgery in the federal bureaucracy. In five minutes Hodgson had given it all back. I knew this was a moment that could change the direction of my life.

My girlfriend, Barbara Lynch, and I had a serious relationship with a tacit understanding that we would marry someday. She had a secure and rewarding position as a secretary at Ottawa City Hall and was also adventurous enough to consider a move to the Arctic. There would no doubt be a place for her within the government in Yellowknife.

I went to see Alex Stevenson, Administrator of the Arctic, and a man I respected. He had begun his career as a Hudson's Bay Company clerk in

1935, working in the Eastern Arctic. After serving in the Second World War he became part of the Eastern Arctic Patrol on the *RMS Nascopie* where his knowledge of the Eskimo language was invaluable, especially during X-ray clinics held on board the ship.

I told him my options and he sat bolt upright when I mentioned Hodgson. "God, that's a man to work for! He's like a breath of fresh air around here. He's cheerful, excited and positive. Just working alongside him for a while would teach you how to get things done. He's like a whirlwind when you see him doing his thing in the bureaucracy here. Just imagine what he'll be like when we unleash him on the North!

"You can trust him to do the right thing. He's a leader who, above all else, cares about people. He acts first and asks questions later; no pussyfooting around. And he'll use those traits to help the people of the North."

Stevenson's admiration for Hodgson intrigued me. I'd heard some people deride him as a simple-minded former union leader and pointed this out to Stevenson. "He has his detractors, but pay no attention to them. His achievements will inspire Northerners for decades to come. Jake, he's going to take power and dignity to them. How he succeeds or screws up will determine where the North goes from there.

"It's a hell of an opportunity. The Arctic is the last frontier and it's about to change dramatically. It's going to be exciting, building a government for the largest territory in the world, in one of the toughest climates. But what Bent Sivertz said is also true."

I looked at Stevenson quizzically. He cautioned me not to repeat our conversation.

"Sivertz was correct when he said that the government will delay until death any move to shift power away from Ottawa. The truth is the North is a colony and is treated as such. The bureaucrats think that sending Hodgson off into the wilderness will be the end of the matter. I think he'll surprise them."

He knew I was bored in the information job and his enthusiasm was exhilarating. His silver hair glistened as he leaned across his desk. "Think about what you have to gain," he said, telling me this might be the chance of a lifetime. Maybe I'd be able to buy *News of the North*. Or, maybe, just maybe, Hodgson would want me to work for him. "Even if you spend just a little time with him, your life will be the richer till the day you die."

3
TODAY WE'RE NORTHERNERS

SEPTEMBER 18, 1967

A FILM CREW RUSHED ABOUT Ottawa's Uplands Airport capturing an event of true historic significance. The Commissioner, together with a group of forty people—employees and families, a newlywed couple and twelve young female clerks, stenographers and secretaries—were departing for Yellowknife, the newest capital in Canada. Hodgson's own family would join him once he was settled. Amid hugs and tears, young employees excitedly waved goodbye to parents and friends. They were leaving behind their homes and all that was familiar for the isolated and unknown Canadian Arctic.

A Scottish bagpiper played "Tunes of Glory" as the aspiring Northerners and the film crew boarded the TransAir DC-7 aircraft. Long abandoned by major airlines, these utilitarian piston-engine planes were the workhorses of frontier carriers like TransAir, reliable but not showy. I chose a comfortable but tattered seat halfway up the aisle.

The stewardess welcomed us on board, announcing our flight would be direct from Ottawa to Yellowknife with a refuelling stop at Churchill, Manitoba. Arrival in Yellowknife would be at 2:00 p.m. local time. With that, just as Hodgson had decreed, the aircraft climbed over the nation's capital. It was followed by another aircraft, a DC-4 that carried books, reports, publications, office equipment and furniture.

A thin fellow clutching a pen and notepad took the seat next to me and introduced himself as Stuart Lake, reporter with the Canadian Press and the person in charge of the film crew. [3]

Lake nodded towards Hodgson. "Has a working man's haircut and talks like someone off the street. Not the kind of man you'd expect in this position."

"Perhaps," I said. "But none of the Ottawa mandarins would be this practical. They'd do a three-year feasibility study, with no concern about the

---

[3] "Moving North", NWT Archives © GNWT, G1999-086-1065

amount of money required, ensure no errors would be made, do two dry runs and then, after five years of planning, move a few employees north, being careful not to deplete the Ottawa headquarters of personnel."

Lake pulled a map from the back of his notepad and spread it out. He pointed to the Richardson Mountains on the western border with the Yukon, and then traced a line east along the 60th parallel all the way to Baffin Island. "Two thousand miles straight across. It's so vast it's beyond comprehension. It's as if the population of Stratford, Ontario, was given a third of Canada to spread itself out in."

"Whose idea was the film crew?" I asked.

He pointed at Hodgson. "A documentary for posterity. Like Moses leading his children into the wilderness. All bright-eyed and bushy-tailed. How many of these poor devils have a hope of surviving a year in the North without going screwy? Cold, twenty-four hours of darkness in midwinter, and the isolation! Those who are not frozen to death will probably be maimed for life by frostbite."

As we flew further north and west, the atmosphere became increasingly excited, noisy and bubbly. Hodgson was socializing, connecting with his staff, stopping at every seat to chat. At ours he said to Lake, "You wanted to do an interview with me on camera? Let's do it now."

Lake called to the cameraman at the back. Hodgson bounded down the aisle and lifted his head at the request of the cameraman. He adjusted his suit jacket, did up the buttons and glanced about, theatrically aware of his audience. He was a natural showman, his eyes bright and intense, his movements animated and compelling. Lake took the microphone, cleared his throat, and said he was with Commissioner Stuart Hodgson on board the flight to Yellowknife. Lake was a seasoned reporter and got right to the importance of Hodgson's move. He said some of the Ottawa bureaucrats thought Hodgson wasn't qualified for a job like this; he heard they may try to block Hodgson's every move. "How will you proceed with this seemingly impossible task?"

Hodgson's face became serious. He faced his staff and spoke in a tone loud enough for everyone to hear over the drone of the engines. His left eyebrow moved up slightly as he said, "No bureaucrat is going to get in my way to do for the people of the North what they deserve. That's a promise!" He spoke with confidence in a smooth, deep voice. "What they don't realize, my mission and direction come from the very top, from Prime Minister Lester Pearson and Northern Affairs Minister Art Laing. There's no doubt they will support me all the way. They've given me a ten-year mandate."

As the interview progressed, I felt a sense of wonder. Hodgson, the personal choice of the Prime Minister, was leading us on the journey of a lifetime. The idea struck a note of romance and adventure. I imagined headlines appearing in newspapers across the country: "Brave Crew Heads Off into the Unknown to Achieve the Unheard Of."

"This is a big day in the story of the last frontier. I tell you, the opening up of the Wild West was nothing compared to what we're undertaking today!" He stretched his arms out and extended his palms to his fellow passengers. "We're making history. The government of the Northwest Territories will be on the ground and operational tomorrow morning! Our task will be monumental. We have to establish a government that will serve the current and future needs of the people of the North.

"We have to set up shop in Yellowknife, get the government functioning, and then develop departments like education, social development, economic development, local government. But the key word is unity. We are going to unite the North, give it a voice that all Canadians will hear. We're starting at the grassroots, and once we have a functioning capital we will build our government throughout the Northwest Territories. It'll be hard, there will be failures, but with dedication and determination I know we will succeed!"

All those within earshot smiled and applauded.

When the cameraman finished, Hodgson came and sat with me for a few minutes. He seemed at ease, not pushed to speak or to answer prying questions. After a few moments he said, "Glad to have you along, Jake. You'll do a fine job on that newspaper." He pulled his frame up off the seat and carried on down the aisle.

My fellow travellers were a study in contrasts. There was Erma Courier, Hodgson's secretary, and Clarence Gilchrist, known as Gillie, a career civil servant and veteran of Northern Affairs who Hodgson had hired as his executive assistant. His wife, Bertha, was a jolly woman with an infectious and uproarious laugh.

Most, like me, were young and inexperienced—the stenographers exuded perfume, hairspray and enough nervous energy to make me feel weary just being near them. Bev and Gordy Day had met six weeks before in an Ottawa elevator, married, and were now on their way north. Gordy was a mail clerk and Bev, a typist with long cranberry-coloured hair, also had a job with the new government. Between them they cradled the most unlikely of pets, a de-scented skunk named Snoopy. Even without benefit of its glands the animal still carried a strong aroma that periodically wafted through the plane.

Cyril Martindale, a middle-aged Englishman with a distinctive Cockney accent, stood in the aisle and said, "Me mum won't believe this! Forty bleedin' years I lived with 'er in London, ten million people. Never been out of the city and what 'appens when I emigrates and starts working for you lot? Get sent to the bloody North Pole, that's wot!" Bertha Gilchrist laughed loudly and everyone joined in.

"Bet you can't wait to get there!" Cyril yelled at me. "Probably already made a date with that Indian princess you photographed around Ottawa."

"I'm spoken for." I turned my head away with a great blush amid a chorus of "sure, sure." But I did think about Georgina Blondin, 1967's Indian Princess, who had come to Ottawa for Canada's centennial celebrations. I had photographed her on the Sparks Street Mall for *Intercom*.

As Hodgson continued to work his way up and down the aisle, giving comfort and cheer to the passengers, I understood why he hadn't opted to send everyone on scheduled commercial flights. Where today a group of individuals existed, tomorrow a team would emerge. These people had signed up for a minimum of a year; those who quit would have to pay for their own transfer out. Hodgson's chatter and bonhomie showed that he understood their anxieties and hopes, and that he could relate to them.

After four hours, the intercom squawked to life and the pilot announced our descent for a fuel stop at Churchill, where we were surprised by a rousing reception. The residents and a hundred Eskimo children attending school in Churchill were there to wish us the best. Hodgson addressed the crowd and Lake's cameraman captured the moment. An hour later, we boarded again, refreshed and ready for the final leg of the journey. No sooner were we airborne than the captain spoke over the intercom, "Ladies and gentlemen, I'm pleased to announce we have just crossed the 60th parallel. You are now in the Northwest Territories." Jubilant shouts and cheers filled the cabin. People clapped, then stood and hugged enthusiastically. We didn't know much about this huge territory, but the fact that we were there seemed worthy of celebration.

I looked down at the ground as it shrank away. We were entering what early explorer Samuel Hearne called the Barrenlands, a vast, treeless tundra, an arctic desert of half a million square miles that stretches from Hudson Bay in the east to the Mackenzie Valley in the west. We would not see a single community between here and Yellowknife, seven hundred miles away. From the air, the ground was a treeless brown carpet scattered with thousands upon thousands of shimmering pockets of water. Such plants as did survive, heathers and shrubs that grow a few inches a decade, were invisible to us, as were the caribou, muskoxen and birds that pried sustenance from the meagre environment.

People settled back in their seats and became quiet, perhaps apprehensive. We were aware, some possibly for the first time, of the enormity of the distance we were putting between ourselves and all we had grown used to.

As we crossed the Barrens and approached the treeline, which curved north and west to the Arctic coast, the landscape changed to scrubby, fall-coloured trees. Then came the greyness of Great Slave Lake, an enormous and tempestuous inland sea three hundred miles long and seventy miles wide. The fourth largest lake in Canada (the third largest being Great Bear Lake, also in the Northwest Territories) Great Slave Lake is also the deepest lake in North America, measuring two thousand feet in places. Shaped somewhat like a goose in flight, it is frozen solid for eight months and serves as a transportation corridor for trucks and cat-trains.

Two and a half hours after leaving Churchill, the aircraft decelerated and began its descent. As the ground grew closer, I made out islands glowing with red and yellow fall colours, soaring cliffs, rushing rivers and the Precambrian rock of the Canadian Shield, some of it four billion years old, exposed for all to see. Skimpy trees barely clung to precipices and rock piles.

"Good afternoon, ladies and gentlemen," announced the captain. "The weather in Yellowknife this afternoon is sunny and clear, with a warm temperature of 60°F and winds south at ten miles an hour. On behalf of TransAir and our crew this afternoon, I wish you all success in your new home—Canada's newest capital city."

We were low now. The plane's shadow skittered across the lake's dark swells.

The cabins of an Indian village huddled on a small point of land. Across the bay lay the dusty little mining town of Yellowknife. We could distinguish the old town, a collection of shacks and shanties built on a finger of rock during the first Yellowknife boom in the 1930s. The new town consisted of a tidy grid of homes up on the rocky flats. The headframes of two gold mines, Con Mine and Giant Mine, guarded each end of town. Trucks and cars whizzed along dirt roads leaving plumes of dust behind. Float planes maneuvered around docks, boats carved white scars across the water and a barge train was making its way towards the shore.

Excited comments flew about.

"Is that it?" asked Bev Day.

"Don't be silly," answered another young stenographer. "You'd never get 34,000 people in a place that size!"

"Ha!" squawked Cyril Martindale. "Who told you 34,000? Yellowknife has 3,400 people, not 34,000." The stenographer paled.

Within a few minutes, with a thud and a bump, we were down. The plane came to a stop in front of a small blue terminal where a large crowd of people awaited our arrival. Two men at the edge of the tarmac pushed portable steps toward the rear of the aircraft. I looked at my watch and switched the time back two hours.

Hodgson beamed with excitement. He made way for the film crew to precede him down the steps, then buttoned up his suit jacket, a sure sign he wanted this occasion to go down in history. Outside, bagpipes came to life and Hodgson was gone, blazing the trail into the bright northern sunlight.

The skirl of bagpipes sounded over the jubilant cheers and shouts from the crowd. The whole population of Yellowknife, such as it was, seemed to be there, filling the tarmac between the terminal and the aircraft. Townsfolk and school kids waved small Canadian and polar bear flags, creating a sea of fluttering red, white and blue. On the roof of the terminal building a radio reporter shouted details into a microphone. Flashbulbs popped everywhere. As we stepped down the staircase, we waved back with equal enthusiasm. It was an emotional moment for both sides.

I strode down a red carpet and shook hands with a receiving line of local dignitaries, the first of whom was John Parker, the newly appointed Deputy Commissioner. Inside the waiting room, other local dignitaries formed a knot in front of the Pacific Western Airlines counter while the rest of us crowded into what little space remained.

At the exit door school kids gathered around Gordy Day and Snoopy's cage, the pet a real source of interest. "Your cat smells funny," one youngster commented.

"She ain't a cat, she's a skunk. Here, you want to stroke her?" Gordy opened the cage and held Snoopy in his arms. The kids backed off.

The grownups clapped as Yellowknife's mayor, Chet Wilkinson, stepped up to the microphone. He promised his town would prove itself worthy of being picked as the capital. After a few more pleasantries he turned the microphone over to Bud Orange, the Member of Parliament for the Northwest Territories, who congratulated Hodgson for accomplishing the impossible. He emphasized that many more impossible feats awaited the administration and its leader.

Then Hodgson stepped up. He clutched the microphone with his right hand and scanned the crowd. His face was serious, but I could see a keen sparkle in his eye. I chuckled at the incongruity of the backdrop, a giant poster of a bikini-clad beauty on a Hawaiian beach.

"Mayor Wilkinson, fellow Northerners!" Hodgson's voice boomed through the loudspeakers. "Believe me, it is great at long last to be home!" He paused to let the cheering and clapping die down. The people of Yellowknife had waited so long for someone with any semblance of power to come from Ottawa that they didn't care about Hodgson's hyperbole. The fact he was neither a fellow Northerner nor as of yet home didn't seem to bother them one bit.

"The people we have brought here today are merely a forerunner of the many who will come." Hodgson drew his audience along with his enthusiasm. "We have come here to build a government that will allow you to make your own decisions about your future and that will give the North strength, dignity and the ability to withstand the changes that are coming."

Spittle flew into the microphone. He didn't notice. He didn't care. It was that determined, onrushing single-mindedness that swept up his audience. "The answer for the North is no different from the answer for the south. It is a matter of having homes, food, healthy families, education and an improved standard of living."

The crowd continually interrupted with delighted clapping. His unpretentious oratory genuinely moved his listeners.

Hodgson brought his voice down to a low, sincere level. He used his outstretched right arm to add emphasis to the rhythm of his comments. "I offer no magic formulas, no medicine or potions, but merely pledge that I will use every means and energy at my disposal to do the best job I can."

Yellowknifers loved every word. A photographer beside me raised his bulky Graphlex Speed Graphic, a large-format camera with a side-mounted flash unit, long out of use in southern Canada. He aimed it at Hodgson and released the shutter; a loud pop illuminated the scene. I wondered if this was Ted Horton, or perhaps someone who worked for *News of the North*.

"The people of the North deserve the best and we shall provide it," Hodgson promised. "We will solve many problems, while others will be created. But at the very least, with the government in the North, we will be closer and more sensitive to the everyday needs of our people." Hodgson stepped back from the microphone and bowed slightly in deference to his appreciative audience, who gave one final thunderous ovation.

I turned to the photographer and introduced myself.

He replied, "Don Taylor from *Tapwe* newspaper in Hay River." We exchanged pleasantries and I asked if Ted Horton was at the airport. It turned out that he was not, and Taylor did not know if anyone from *News of the North* was in attendance.

An announcement was made that buses were ready to take the newcomers to town. I grabbed a seat at the front of a decrepit bus with "Frame & Perkins" painted on the side and watched Hodgson and Parker get into a chauffeured car. It was plain that the title of commissioner conferred status here even though neither the title nor the man was significant in Ottawa.

The road weaved across the rise and fall of granite and muskeg that separated the airport from town. There were little cries of surprise and annoyance behind me every time we hit one of the numerous potholes. The presence of bare rock, in jumbled, fractured piles or monolithic extrusions, was everywhere. There were no grass verges, no meadows, none of the greenery that flourishes in regions where water, soil and sunlight are taken for granted. There was life, but it wasn't a generous, friendly landscape.

"Look at the size of those crows!" someone yelled. Six large black birds wheeled in the sky and several more bobbed up and down to get off the road. They were huge, a foot high, three times the size of their southern cousins.

Their broad, powerful wings spread out two feet. Their thick beaks were like Roman noses, with heavy necks and ruffs of black satin, large bodies and legs as bony as coat hangers. If nothing else, I thought, they provided evidence that life could survive in the North.

"Ravens," laughed the bus driver. "You'll see ravens right through the winter. They're clever, those sonsabitches. Some of them live to be forty years old. You just watch them some time when a few get on the rim of a garbage can. They start rocking back and forth until it tips over. Then they pick through whatever's inside. Cunning! I've seen one bite a dog's tail while another steals the dog's food. Be nice to them. The Indians say they have special powers."

We approached a large box of a building faced with posh fieldstone.

"Is that our hotel?" came a question from the back.

"Hell, no!" the driver laughed. "That's the jail, the Yellowknife Correctional Institute."

The boneshaker bus maneuvered through a portal blasted out of a huge outcropping of rock, a chunk of the same grey rubble that pocked and punctuated the landscape all around us.

"There's your house, Nancy!" said one of the passengers, pointing at a mess of plywood and churned dirt behind a big sign that read "Territorial Housing Subdivision."

"God, we'll be living in hotels for months before they get any of those finished."

Once we reached downtown Yellowknife, Airport Road became Franklin Avenue, the main street of a rough and uncultivated mining town that was now, on paper, the capital of the Northwest Territories. The ugly main drag, scoured free of greenery and other living things by wind and frost, was lined with dusty cars and pickup trucks. Side streets were unpaved so when a vehicle entered or left the main street, clouds of dust filled the air.

A few stores lined Franklin Avenue, their walls dressed in stucco or faded siding, their fronts adorned with a variety of rooflines and false fronts. An old black vehicle, a hearse now used to haul laundry, was parked along the street with a huge wooden sign on top: "Why Kill Your Wife—Let Us Do The Dirty Work." It was parked in front of a clapboard building called Max McCara's Dry Cleaning. Across the street the Hudson's Bay store, a single-storey building, covered one whole block. In the display window, an old guy in a huge grey overcoat slumped in one of the easy chairs. I assumed it was some kind of pre-Halloween mannequin until I saw him rise and fasten his coat, ready to shuffle off.

"Tom Doornbos," said the bus driver. "Strange old bugger, rumour is he's made a fortune hauling water to houses in Old Town with two pails on a yoke and used the money to buy real estate. People say he's loaded, but he always acts like a bum. Wears old trousers he finds in garbage cans."

Across the intersection we came to Sutherland's Drug Store, the post office and the Yellowknife Hotel, a two-storey, white stucco building, the largest on Franklin Avenue.

The driver shut off the engine. In the momentary stillness, we realized we had arrived. As Hodgson had said, we were home.

As our luggage was hauled out of the well beneath the bus, we had our first encounter with some of the North's native people. I suddenly realized the greeters at the airport had all been white.

A large number of Indians hung around the entrance to the hotel, silently leaning against the walls with their hands in their pockets, wearing uniform outfits of windbreakers, shapeless pants and baseball hats. The women wore windbreakers, scarves, print skirts, bobby socks and moccasins with rubber overshoes. Their hawkish noses and narrowed, jet-black eyes were trained steadily on this bus full of newcomers, especially Bev Day and her long cranberry hair.

They didn't seem like insiders either. They seemed as lost and confused as Hodgson's new arrivals. Maybe his fear, that this culture was already losing its grip in the survival tug-of-war, had some foundation.

"The Commissioner's loyal subjects are overjoyed to see us!" Cyril Martindale whispered in my ear. "Now I can see why they didn't send the usual bureaucratic old fart up here to get a government rolling."

We looked at the Indians, they looked at us, and then we turned our attention back to the business of organizing our luggage. They ebbed and parted to allow us to enter the lobby, a dingy cavern laced with two-by-fours painted to resemble gothic beams. Toward the back was the dining room, and on the left a staircase led to the upper rooms. A great noise spilled from the entrance to a beer parlour.

"Christ, this is right out of the Wild West!" said Cyril.

I gave my name to an attractive young woman whose name tag read Grace Chassie.

"The two of you will be sharing a room," she said, nodding at Cyril. "Tonight the town is throwing a welcoming party at the Elks Hall and everyone is invited."

Upstairs the corridors were panelled in mouldering veneer, festooned with hot water pipes and illuminated by ancient light fixtures. A dry, musty smell filled the air.

The air was close and stuffy inside our small room. I flopped on one of two single beds—Jesus, it was hard. A big old black telephone with no dial sat on a side table. The front desk would do the dialing. No privacy here.

"So here we are," Cyril muttered disconsolately. "I feel like I'm bloody stranded in Never Never Land. Let's go home, Toto." The sun setting beyond our grimy window darkened the room. "Why did Hodgson have to come up here anyway? He'd have been better off staying in Ottawa, where all the bloody decisions are made!"

"That's the whole point, isn't it?"

Cyril ignored me. "What a fantasy to think he is going to accomplish anything. Who controls the money?" He looked at me as though I was going to provide an answer. "You think he'll ever win that kind of power from the people in Ottawa?"

"From what I saw this afternoon, he's going to have a hell of a good time trying."

BY 7:30 THE SUN WAS setting over Yellowknife and there was a chill in the air. The Elks Hall turned out to be a boxy, stucco-clad building with a flat roof and one dim light bulb hanging over the main entrance. A few steps up the interior staircase brought us into the main hall, already noisy with a crowd of two hundred.

"We're in the right place, all right," Cyril said. Tobacco smoke billowed down from the high ceiling, shrouding the lights and partially obscuring an unbelievable variety of clothing, makeup and hairstyles. Some people looked as if they shopped in the salons of Paris, others as if they'd just come in from traplines.

Hardwood floorboards glistened from years of use. The hall had rectangular folding tables set around the walls, along with legions of metal chairs. Six bartenders served a crowd lined four-deep at a huge mahogany bar. The Elks Hall wasn't flashy but was probably the finest Yellowknife had to offer.

Cyril and I surveyed the scene. "We're being eyeballed," I said, nodding towards a side table where a wild-looking woman stared at us.

"You've set her in motion. You've got the knack for attracting the ladies all right."

"She's fixed on you, Cyril. Look at her peering through the crowd." I gave her a slight wave and then pointed to Cyril.

She stood up and made straight for us, pressing her way through a circle of people who blocked the way. Her knee-length, pleated chiffon dress, filled with static from the dry air, clung to her, displaying a fair figure. Her untamed hair was mounded on her head and balled up in knots where it fell below her shoulders. I didn't know what to make of this apparition.

"Hello," she said. "What's your names?" She eyeballed Cyril. "I'm the Caribou Queen."

"You're from Yellowknife?" I asked.

"Well, mostly. I live on the Barrens, on the tundra, huntin' and trappin' with my fella."

"You meet a lot of Indians and Eskimos, then?" Cyril said.

The Queen cackled with laughter. "You're like all them southerners who think there's nothing but Eskimos and Indians and igloos and dogsleds up here! The Eskimos are mostly way up on the Arctic coast, and the Indians stick to the bush country. Where we go trappin' out on the tundra there ain't no one! We go out there for some months, and don't see nobody. Come back to town once in a while to see some company." She motioned us to follow her to her table where she picked up a glass, drank the contents in one gulp, and then said, "Let me get you some drinks. They're free tonight."

For several minutes I watched the wall of dresses, bush gear, baggy denim and gold jewellery ebb and flow around the floor. Then, with some rousing curses and vicious elbowing, the Queen returned, triumphantly bearing a huge tray with six glasses of rye and ginger ale. She set the tray down and waltzed around the table, her tresses flying about her animated frame. "Here you go," she said. "One for you and you! One for me! Some for later!" She flopped down next to Cyril. She toasted us, her chair scraping closer to him as he surreptitiously eased himself away from her. If this kept up, we'd soon be sitting on the dance floor.

After I finished my drink I said, "I'm going to socialize." Cyril looked terrified.

I squeezed through the crowd, ordered a drink at the bar and stood off to the side, taking in the scene. Yellowknifers were having a roaring good time, joking and talking, knocking back the free drinks. The newcomers, my travel companions, looked uncomfortable amid this lack of decorum.

"So you met the Caribou Queen!" said a burly man with a smile on his face. A vivid scar crossed his forehead, and one ran down his neck.

"No choice." I stuck my hand out and introduced myself.

"Dale Eckleson. Came north to play hockey on the Con Mine team." He put a finger to one of his scars, by way of explanation. "I drive taxi nowadays." He pointed to the Queen. "She's a character all right. Has a heart of gold, but gets into the damnedest situations. She nearly ripped the pants off a guy at the Con rec hall one time because she wanted his mukluks. The guy was carrying a tray of drinks and they flew all over!" I strained my neck to see how Cyril was managing. He was in conversation with the Queen.

"She has a terrible habit of taking other people's drinks. She came to our table once and took a drink, but it was straight pop. When she realized what it was she spat it out and hurled the glass against the wall. The guys tried to throw her out, but it was like handling a snake—she wouldn't go. There was a huge melee to get her out but this big Swede who kind of fancied her climbed over the upstairs balcony and was all set to jump down on the people trying to subdue her. Just as he was about to leap off his sister grabbed him by the leg and he just hung there, upside down, with everyone looking up and yelling 'Drop him!' We called him The Swingin' Swede after that!"

We stared at the crowd for some time and then Eckleson asked what I did with the government. I told him I was here to put out the newspaper for a couple of issues and possibly take the place over as Ted Horton was going to work for Hodgson. I asked if he knew Horton and if he was here tonight.

Eckleson looked around the room and shook his head. "Horton nearly choked with disappointment when he wasn't named Commissioner."

"Why?"

"Rumour had it that Ted was the frontrunner, and he believed it. After all, he was a former mayor and president of the Liberal Association. So when a writer and photographer from *Weekend Magazine* came up from Toronto, it was Ted they interviewed and photographed. Everyone in the North figured it would be Ted, or John Parker."

"What's local opinion about the newspaper?" I asked.

"Not much of a newspaper really. Kinda crappy."

David Searle, a young Yellowknife lawyer I'd met in the receiving line at the airport, came over. Searle grew up in the North and had recently been elected to the Territorial Council, defeating Pete Baker. He put a stubby cigar to his mouth, blew out a cloud of blue smoke and proclaimed in an expansive tone that there was no looking back. He said the Territorial Council needed to take power, and was thankful that the election last April had provided some new blood. The federal government had fostered a colonial attitude and the Council needed to work towards provincial status and proper autonomy, like the provinces enjoyed. "The people in Ottawa are so cynical. They make a pretence of caring about the people up here, but it's all a flimsy smokescreen for their real ambition."

"Which is?" I asked.

"To suck us dry of every natural resource." He nodded, puffed on his cigar and gazed about the hall. He nodded towards Hodgson, surrounded by a group of Yellowknifers, and suggested we join them.

Hodgson was relating how Yellowknife had been named capital. The crowd listened eagerly, feeling they were being let in on some confidence. "The matter of naming the capital took place at the council session in Resolute in 1965. David's predecessor," he nodded at Searle, "Pete Baker, was so eager to make the motion that he would jump to his feet at the start of each day, intent on nominating Yellowknife before anyone else could say anything. As you know, Pete is myopic and almost deaf. And every day the Air Marshal, seated next to him, would tug on Pete's sleeve and shout, 'Not now, Pete. Not now. You have to wait until it's on the order paper.' Pete was scared to death we'd pick Fort Smith or some other place. So every morning he'd stand up, lift his papers with one-inch type to his nose, address the chair and start to read his motion. Each time the Air Marshal would pull on Pete's sleeve and shout, 'Not now, Pete.' This went on for five days. Then, on the appointed day, Commissioner Sivertz called for motions, the Air Marshal shook Pete and shouted, 'Now, Pete!' But Pete had come down with the flu and wasn't feeling too chipper. He rose to his feet, held the paper to his nose," Hodgson mimed Baker's actions, "but skipped all the pages of explanation and suddenly said, 'I nominate Yellowknife the capital of the Northwest Territories.' Then he dropped the papers and ran out of the Council Chamber." Hodgson's audience listened with obvious curiosity. "Commissioner Sivertz said the motion was in order so the Council proceeded with the vote. Afterward, I went looking for Pete. Found him standing in the shower stark naked, washing out his long johns. He'd shit his pants." The laughter echoed through the hall. "That's how Yellowknife was named capital and the member for Yellowknife missed the vote."

Someone asked him what his priorities were and Hodgson spoke in a serious manner. "I always felt the Territories should be run from within. I'd only just started the job in Ottawa as Deputy Commissioner and realized you simply can't walk into your office, two thousand miles from all the action, take off your southern coat, put on a northern coat, do a day's work, and at the end of the day put on your southern coat again. As of today, we're Northerners, living and working in the North. When you're cold, I'll be cold. When your pipes freeze, so will mine."

Hodgson looked at his watch. "I promised the government would be open for business the day after we arrive, so we'll be operational tomorrow morning at 8:30." He turned to me, "First thing tomorrow I'm swearing in the staff. Take some photos! You'll get a scoop!"

"Sure. But isn't that Horton's job?" He ignored me.

"That picture will be great for the front page: 'First Territorial Civil Servants in the North.'" His hand swept across, making a headline. "I'm going home, hit the sack. Be there first thing in the morning!"

4

NOWHERE TO GO BUT UP

SEPTEMBER 19, 1967

BREAKFAST IN THE MINERS' MESS coffee shop in the Yellowknife Hotel was an enlightening experience. I was seated on a red plastic-covered stool at a 1950s soda counter. Next to me, still in his greatcoat, was the old fellow from the Hudson's Bay store window. "The usual two cups of free hot water, Mr. Doornbos?" said the waitress sarcastically, pouring boiling water into two mugs. Without answering, Doornbos poured ketchup into one mug. Voilà, he had tomato soup. Then he reached inside his greatcoat, pulled out a paper bag of tea leaves and spooned some into the second cup. Frontier spirit, frontier peculiarities. I finished breakfast, picked up my camera and bid him goodbye.

Outside, the warmth and clear skies of yesterday had been replaced by low clouds and a cold northerly wind. Franklin Avenue was abuzz with people hustling along the sidewalks and vehicles turning on and off the main street. As I headed down a gravel side street, I became aware of being watched by a raven atop a power pole, the black sheen of its feathers as cheerless as the sky. The town's Board of Trade had adopted the raven as an emblem, which struck me as odd, as these birds are scavengers. But they are also extremely versatile, opportunistic and intelligent, and feature prominently in mythology, folklore, art and literature. He heckled me with contemptuous clucks and squawks, a mournful portent.

Hodgson's headquarters were as bleak as the ravens and the weather. The two-storey building was a former school, now condemned, a green hulk with blotchy, peeling paint and boarded-up windows. The steps to the front entrance had separated from the building and now canted to one side. Several trucks were parked beside the building and lines of workmen were hauling office equipment, furniture and boxes towards a back door.

I stepped around the corner and nearly bumped into Deputy Commissioner John Parker, who, atop a ladder, was nailing up a one-foot by four-foot wooden sign that read "Government of the Northwest Territories," the first evidence of our presence.

"Momentous occasion," I said, snapping a photo. Parker enjoyed the instant, the humble beginnings of what could someday be a gigantic bureaucracy.

"Where's the legal department?" shouted a workman.

"Curling rink," Parker shouted back. Frank Smith, the legal advisor, had his office behind the bar of the curling rink. Parker looked down and grinned. "That's probably one of the better places we have. Tourism is in a vacant old house and we're using spare space in the library as well."

I walked to the back entrance and gingerly stepped up lopsided wooden stairs that squeaked under my weight. The ramshackle building was as decayed inside as out. An extension cord ran from classroom to classroom providing power for the office machinery. I hopped over cardboard boxes and around pieces of furniture as staff members picked through a mountain of supplies, moaning about what a lousy night's sleep they'd had and bitching about the problems of getting organized. It would be weeks, maybe months, before their houses and apartments would be ready. I wondered how anybody could make anything out of this mess.

"Seen the Commissioner?" I asked Clarence Gilchrist.

"Down the hall! Tell him we've got a bit of bad news. The truck carrying our printing equipment is upside down in a ditch on the Mackenzie Highway."

"Me?" I shook my head. "I'm late and I don't need him to get on my case." I walked along a corridor that had lost most of its linoleum tiles, peering into the window of each classroom until I found the right one.

Hodgson's broad frame faced a crew of employees. Stu Lake's cameraman was busy filming and I stepped behind to take photos. Hodgson stood erect in his dark business suit, his buoyant voice booming through the room, speaking as much for the camera as for the staff. "There is no precedent to guide us. Never in Canada's history has such a huge and difficult task been given to a group of people like us. Our reward will be greater than any pay raise." He reflected on what he had just said and quickly added, "Though of course that too is important. It will be the pride which all Canadians will show toward those who help develop their far northern territory." His body language said as much as his voice. He stood tall, head held high and eyes looking straight at his staff.

At Hodgson's command everyone raised their right hand and took the oath of allegiance to the new government. This must have been a Hodgson invention, because I had never taken an oath of allegiance upon joining either the territorial government or the federal department of Indian Affairs and Northern Development. They all looked at Hodgson with pride and devotion, mesmerized by his promise of a great future.

Hodgson shook hands with each person. When finished he turned to me and said, "Well, you got a real scoop here for the paper. Come to my office for a minute."

He strode down the hallway like a vigilant school principal, his open suit jacket flapping. We passed one of the classrooms with a homemade sign that read "Information Department." Inside, an older man sat with his back to the door, hunched over an Underwood typewriter. Hodgson saw me hesitate. I wanted to go in and introduce myself, but Hodgson tugged on my sleeve and said, "Ted's kind of busy now."

Hodgson's office was in the kitchen. It was cramped, with barely enough room for his huge oak desk and a side chair. Files were neatly stacked and the two flag standards from his Ottawa office stood in the corner. His black leather swivel chair was a stark contrast to the tarnished faucets and cupboards with peeling green paint.

"I hope you're going to send a photo of your surroundings to the bureaucrats in Ottawa," I said. "The sight of you running one-third of Canada from a derelict school kitchen would make their day."

"Hell, if I wait till there are no problems, the North will never get to where it needs to go. You have to forge ahead, Jake, and trust people to follow."

We were interrupted by Erma. She said Rae Parker, a social worker in town, was here to see him. Erma didn't have the chance to say any more before the woman stepped past her into the kitchen. She did not offer her hand and, face flushed, immediately demanded to know what a bulldozer was doing on the property down by the arena.

Hodgson stood, indicating she take the only side chair, which she refused. I wanted to leave, but she blocked the way.

The woman carried on. "It's clearing property that we, the people who lived here for years before you and your crew ever decided to move up here, intended to use for a senior citizens' home."

31

"Ah, that," Hodgson said. "I've got staff camped all over town. They need homes fast. It's now designated for housing for my staff."

"And the senior citizens of Yellowknife can go to hell, is that it? You wouldn't know about this, of course, but an old man died last winter when his shack in Old Town caught fire. We've got federal approval to put sixteen seniors' units on that site. You've got no right to take it."

Now it hit me. On my way here I had noticed about a dozen people demonstrating and carrying placards, one of which read, "Don't Grow Old, Just Fuck Off."

Hodgson remained composed. He wasn't anxious, or upset, not even slightly shaken or cowed, telling her the site was now territorial property and his first concern had to be his staff. He continued standing and stared straight at her. She looked on in frustration, her lips pursed and her brows locked in a frown.

He held up a hand and said he would be out of this building before next spring. He promised he would make this site available for the seniors' home and would also provide funding for twenty units, not just sixteen.

Parker stared back at him, and then at the room about her. She leaned forward as if to walk away. There was a moment of silence. Then she stood straight again and looked Hodgson full in the face. "I'm a social worker and I know what life in the North is like. Northerners have put up with newcomers walking in and giving orders for too long. I hope you'll show some sensitivity to the real problems we face here."

Hodgson raised an eyebrow and waited for her to continue. "You think you've got problems now," she said with a touch of hostility. "You'll get your new offices running nicely and your staff settled into their new homes, and then you'll encounter problems you've never dreamed of. The longer you're here, the harder the problems are going to be and the faster they'll come at you." She turned, and with a slight bow, stepped out the door.

Hodgson sat down. "I've been given a great opportunity to take a territory that's a hundred years behind everywhere else and bring it into the 20th century in just ten years. My job is to make it work until northern people can speak for themselves. Step One has been taken. Step Two is to build departments and hire people to run them. That'll take about two years. Step Three is to teach the people what government is and what we're here for. Step

Four is to get them involved, to join forces with us. And Step Five is to give Northerners control."

Returning abruptly to the present, he said, "Are you going to get that newspaper out tonight?"

"Tonight? I haven't even been over there yet." I had no idea if the newspaper had any staff working today. I could do the editorial work, the photos, the darkroom, the paste-up, but I sure didn't know how to print the thing.

"Do your best! Take this editorial I've written and print it on the front page." Hodgson handed me a piece of paper and then pulled a $10 bill out of his pocket. "Here, buy pizza for the staff. And if there's any overtime, tell them I'll pay for that too."

OVER THE YEARS YELLOWKNIFE HAD had a number of weekly newspapers. The only one to prove successful was *News of the North*. In 1948, when E.R. (Ted) Horton, president of the Alberta Press Gallery and reporter for the *Edmonton Bulletin*, saw an advertisement that a paper was for sale in Yellowknife, he borrowed the money and bought it. He soon discovered it was in financial difficulty but carried on because he couldn't afford to return to Edmonton.

Horton had put a great deal of energy and enthusiasm into the paper, becoming an outspoken advocate for northern issues and serving as mayor for six years. He lambasted corporations like Imperial Oil Limited and Canadian Pacific Airlines for charging Northerners too much and, to garner publicity for Yellowknife, once invited Fidel Castro to judge the local beard-growing competition.[4] Castro did not reply. "If an atom bomb landed on Edmonton," Horton once stated, "it might make *News of the North*, but only if it passed over Yellowknife first."[5]

The newspaper was housed in a dilapidated, wood-frame building, the outside of which was covered in grey asbestos paper, torn off in places, making the building a patchwork of exposed planks and insulation. On the roof, a large rusted sign read, "News of the North and Alberta Horton's Stationery Store."

I stepped into a musty room in which piles of envelopes, boxes and paper were scattered all about. Through a side door and into the back I could see the

---

[4] Ray Price, *Yellowknife*, (Peter Martin Assoicates, 1968), 295
[5] "Canada, Journalism, The North Estate," *Time* magazine, Canadian Edition, April 22, 1966

mess repeated—piles of discarded paper lay scattered on various tables, mixed in between layers of newspapers, magazines, old tools and cast-off machinery parts. Two ancient linotype machines faced each other in dusty silence, long since disabled and gutted. Several old printing presses and a headline machine, with great tides of junk in between, were obviously no longer in use. Every time a machine quit, a substitute of some sort was apparently set up by its side.

I shouted hello, but was met with silence even though, at the rear, I saw a fellow wiping down the rollers on a well-worn printing press. He resembled the expired machinery around him.

"I'm here to help put out the paper," I said, mustering as much enthusiasm as I could. He didn't look up but after a while mumbled, "You don't look much like a backshop worker."

Great! At last he speaks. "What's left to be done?"

"Lots. For starters, throw away the tie."

"Right!" I introduced myself.

"Ray Jantzen," he responded. He made no effort to shake hands for which I was grateful, as his were covered in black ink. "Hardly had any sleep all week and I doesn't get paid overtime. Paper's supposed to be out today." He shook his head. "Never make it, unless you know how to run the darkroom."

"Where's the other staff?"

"I'm it."

"You're it?"

"I'm it."

There was silence. Then he spoke again. "That goddamned Ted. Cheap as hell. I busts my ass and he won't pay overtime." Ray mumbled something else as he began ladling black ink out of a round can and into the tray of the press.

When I asked if Horton might drop by, Ray said, "Hope the hell he stays outa' here. Told me two weeks ago he'd been given a government job. Hardly seen 'im since." He pointed an inky hand at the press. "If she breaks down we're screwed. 'Cause I ain't goin' through another night of repair work." He spread the ink with a broad knife. "Havin' trouble with the electrodes in the platemaker too. And take a look at this." He reached over to a table and handed me a photograph. It was a picture of a float plane upside down in a body of water, but it was so dark it would come out totally black when printed.

"You don't run stuff like this?"

"Yep. People come to expect it . . . along with Ted's thumbprints on the front page. I just want you to know, so you don't think it's somethin' wrong with my printin'."

God forbid, I thought.

"What can I do?"

"Already printed the first three sheets, both sides—that's twelve pages. We've got a total of twenty pages. So two sheets to go, both sides. Then got to fold and collate 'em. Most of the layout's done, 'cept'n the front page."

I asked him what he had for material.

"Ted's left some filler junk."

"Well, I can solve that." Hodgson's editorial and my photos would work nicely. I asked where the darkroom was located.

He pointed to a door. "Messy, but there's chemicals and an enlarger."

"What's the press run?"

"Twelve hundred. Only two newspapers in over a million square miles," he declared. "But we're mostly distributed in town. The other communications up here is CBC Radio. They've got a staff of six in the buildin' across the street." He pointed through the grimy window at a cement block building on the corner. The largest radio network in the world, the Canadian Broadcasting Corporation had a network of radio stations in Yellowknife, Inuvik and Frobisher Bay.

Remembering Hodgson's offer, I said, "Look, Ray, if we finish the paper tonight I'll get you some overtime pay. And I'll buy the food."

At the mention of food he said, "Get me a burger and fries. I'm so hungry I could eat the arse end out of a dead skunk."

I grinned, elated.

"How long have you been in Yellowknife?" I asked.

He had come from Alberta a year ago, was now divorced and lived in a ramshackle little trailer. "When I get some money, I'm outa' here."

What should have been two hours work took all day. Once I had developed the photographs of Hodgson's swearing-in ceremony, I pasted up the front page. Hodgson's guest editorial, typed by Erma on her IBM Selectric typewriter, provided some crisp, clean copy, in contrast to the smudged and faded material prepared by Ted. Next, I shot negatives of the flats and burned the printing plates. Ray fastened one to the printing cylinder and turned on the machine.

"Print, ya' bastard!" he shouted, smoothing the ink in the tray and adjusting knobs here and there. An arrangement of suckers plucked the topmost sheet from the stack of paper, rolled it under the gyrating cylinder and spat it out the other end. Every so often one of the sheets would cling to the cylinder and become covered in ink. "Goddamned static. Press is a pile of shit," Ray would shout, then clean the cylinder and start again. "Have to overprint by a couple a' hundred 'cause we still got to print the other side. Otherwise won't have enough." Now I understood why so much paper garbage was strewn about.

The press was on a slant, so Ray was constantly scooping ink to the higher side. At one point he yelled, "Watch the press!" and handed me the broad knife, running out the back door without saying another word. I didn't take my eyes off the bucking monster, scared it was about to reach some irreversible and destructive climax. If something had gone wrong, I would have been helpless.

Suddenly, I became aware of a subtle change in the pitch of the floor and the levelling of the ink in the press tray. Ray returned and gave the machine a professional glance. "Have to jack the goddamn buildin' up every so often," he yelled. "Permafrost in the ground. Hard to build here in Yellowknife. New buildings are put on piles driven thirty feet into the ground. Keeps 'em from sinkin'."

At five o'clock we stopped and ate our burgers and fries, appreciative of the quiet. I slumped on a broken chair and thumbed through the paper, looking at the quirky editorials and slovenly production with a marked increase in tolerance, due, no doubt, to the investment of my own sweat.

"Keep the hell out off the road at fires!" blared a half-page advertisement from the Yellowknife town office. "Leave firefighting to the people paid to do it and mind your own damn business!" It was a different kind of country, all right, with a different language and a different way of doing things. On one inside page was the picture of a smiling couple in wedding garb with a cutline explaining they were Mr. and Mrs. Frank Campbell Dorrance, whose marriage had taken place in Montreal, and whose parents lived in Montreal and Turner Falls, Massachusetts. There was no reference to a connection to the North or Yellowknife so it was beyond my comprehension why it was in the newspaper. But the newlyweds looked lovely and happy.

I heard someone step through the front door. Ted, I thought. Finally, I get to meet the man. To my surprise, Hodgson bounded in as if he owned the place. He looked around with satisfaction, oblivious to the mess.

"Say, this looks fantastic," he said holding up an unfolded sheet. He shook hands with Ray, ignoring the ink smears. "I've got some people from *The New York Times* coming up in the morning. They want to interview me. I'll bring them around to see this operation. They would love to see how a small-town newspaper operates."

I felt sick. I could just imagine the reaction of some big-city hack tiptoeing through the wastepaper, ink and junk. What would they think of me, an apprentice publisher, and Ray, a cantankerous printer?

"They'll love it," said Hodgson. "I want them to know there's nothing more important to me and my government than communication. And this is all we've got besides CBC Radio. You boys might not realize it now, but I see a time when this newspaper will be holding its own with the very best."

Hodgson treated us as if we were the most respected newspapermen on Earth. He walked into this pile of junk and saw possibilities, tools for his purpose, a vision of the future, not the crap and difficulties that had kept us busy all day.

I nodded my head in silent admiration. He was filled with as many surprises as this strange newspaper office. He knew how to get things done, by God, and he knew how to get folks to help him. He'd sucked me right into printing this newspaper, and now I felt good that I'd achieved what he wanted.

"When you're finished, bring a paper to my place, Jake!" He wrote down the address and drew a map on a scrap of paper. And with that, he was gone.

THE LIGHTS OF FRANKLIN AVENUE faded as I walked down a side street to Hodgson's house. There was a distinct arctic chill in the air; winter was just around the corner. My early morning walk from the hotel to St Patrick's School seemed days ago. Here I was on my first full day in the Northwest Territories and I'd already produced a newspaper.

Hodgson's temporary home was a small, two-bedroom government bungalow, formerly the home of Justice J.H. Sissons, the first judge appointed to the Territorial Court of the Northwest Territories, who had retired and moved south.

"Extra. Extra. Read all about it," I yelled as I opened the back door and stepped inside. The house was filled with federal government furniture: a kitchen table, four chairs, living room sofa, coffee table, several side chairs and a china hutch. The furniture was solid maple, colonial style, supplied to all federal public servants posted in the North. Hodgson stood in his shirt sleeves by the stove stirring a one-quart can from which steam emanated, making the room feel muggy. Wrapping a towel around his hand, he lifted the boiling can off the stove and set it on the counter, inviting me to stay and have some corn. He stepped to the cupboard and brought out a brick of butter, a salt shaker and a table knife. "I've got no pots or pans. They're all in crates coming from Ottawa. We'll eat right out of the can and use it to make tea when we're finished." He handed me a fork.

His new house was being built across the street but wouldn't be ready for four to five weeks. "It won't be long until Pearl and the kids get here. They're visiting relatives in Edmonton."

"What will Pearl think of this? I mean the town and the North and this house and everything?" I asked.

"Oh, she's the best, a real trooper. We've known lean times. When I started working in the union office in Vancouver, she was a secretary there, this good-looking blonde. She wanted a light for her cigarette, so I whipped out my lighter." He held out his hand to demonstrate. "I didn't even smoke, but I did have a lighter. Everybody smokes now. I shouldn't say I don't, but only one a day, at the end of the day. Anyway, that's how I met Pearl. As I took on more and more responsibility with the union, she helped me do it." Hodgson rambled on. "I mean I didn't have the first clue how to write a letter. Pearl taught me how to do all that stuff, from scratch."

I was daydreaming about the newspaper and how to approach Horton, not quite paying attention, when Hodgson made some reference to the fact he had only a high school education before joining the navy. The revelation was a shock. Then I realized that, while his formal education may have ended there, he was a man of incredible experience.

"I've never been afraid of challenges, even when I wasn't sure how to meet them. That's why I advanced in the union. I lasted seventeen years, part of it as financial secretary. There were a lot of challenges. After the war I helped kick the communists out, and in Newfoundland I managed to escape a lynch mob. I've advanced because I'm not afraid of hard work and not afraid to stand up for my beliefs. That comes from my father. All through the Depression he never let go of his beliefs. When I was a kid we went through rough times, but we were taught that family and hard work were the most important things in life."

"What do you get out of all this?" I asked. It was a bold question, but I was curious about Hodgson's motivation. "I mean, why take on such an enormous challenge? Some people would say it's an impossible task."

"I'm excited just to be given the opportunity. And remember this, the North has nowhere to go but up. Anything I do will be an improvement." He was silent for a minute and then continued. "Yellowknife and several other communities do have some amenities although, as you've found out, it's not great. But the rest of the North has nothing—no jobs, lousy houses, no stores, no radio service, no airstrips and no government. My staff may not look big today, but over the next two years those few federal staff now working here in the North, in the settlements, will be transferred to my control. That'll leave me eight more years to build and refine the government. The bureaucrats back in Ottawa think they've sent me up here to build a nice little bureaucracy in Yellowknife. What I really have to do is build the northern people a life raft, a government that will save them when the development dam bursts and threatens their way of life."

Hodgson left the table, poured water from the can into a tea pot, stirred and poured the tea into our cups.

"I was part of that unwanted generation, born in the 1920s, a generation that learned our work on the job. We had to prove our capabilities to our employer and our ability was judged by what we could do. A lot different from today's generation, where people are judged by what they know and by how many certificates and degrees they have hanging on the wall." He picked up a folder of papers. "Look at these. Applications from one end of the country to the other. People wanting to work up here. I need people to head up departments: local government, finance, public works. Take a look! See who you think are good."

"Good grief, I'm not qualified for this sort of thing!" Despite my protest, I felt a glow of appreciation.

"It's the feel that counts. That's how I pick people. I need people I can work with, people I can get along with. You can get the best brains in the world, but you have to make sure they know how the real world works."

ON ARRIVING BACK AT THE hotel, I walked proudly toward the beer parlour, copies of the newspaper tucked under my arm. Stale cigarette smoke and the smell of spilled beer permeated the place. A group of the new arrivals was seated well away from the band.

"Jake," Gillie greeted me as I pulled up a chair. "How's the newspaper business?" I passed him a copy and put the rest on the table. "With all our printing equipment in the ditch, you might have to become the territorial printer for a while."

Gordy Day was talking about Snoopy. When he and Bev had left for work this morning, he had put Snoopy in the bathtub. When the maid came in to clean the bathroom she pulled back the curtain and "damn near fainted." Now the hotel manager was telling him to get rid of the skunk.

Bertha Gilchrist screamed with laughter.

"She's house-trained," Gordy said indignantly. "The only time there's a smell is when she has a dump or piss. Otherwise she doesn't smell."

"Not much," Cyril shouted, and Bertha went off again.

Cyril leafed through the pages of the paper. "Not much of a newspaper."

"It's great if you could see what we had to work with."

Cyril asked if I was going ahead with buying the place.

"It's not worth anything," I said. "It's a pile of junk."

"To you. But to Ted, even the smallest bit of junk might be worth a lot of money. There's a lot an owner considers valuable when he wants to sell a business—fixed assets like presses and other equipment, inventory, goodwill, the name, the reputation, his client list."

"Goodwill? The place is full of scrap."

Gillie said, "Cyril is right. You have to know where Ted is coming from. He'll bring all those items into the equation. And Cyril hasn't even mentioned the premises. Here's what you do. Give him a lowball price for the fixed assets. You have to be the judge of that." Cyril nodded. "Add in inventory, for whatever you think it is worth, and goodwill. Ted will know you have done some homework. He can counter back. At least it gets the ball rolling."

"What about the premises. You mentioned the premises?"

Cyril jumped back in and suggested I offer to lease the premises. "Let him set a price that might be the most appealing part of the whole deal. Try to keep the lease term as short as possible. You can move out if you have to," he said.

Excellent suggestions, but what worried me most was how to pay for the place.

Gillie suggested I pay a premium if Horton would let me pay in instalments with no down payment. Horton couldn't do both jobs. He would have to get himself out of the newspaper, and quick.

"Have you talked to him yet?" asked Cyril. I shook my head. "It's still early. Call him tonight. Tomorrow he'll be tied up again."

His suggestion made sense, so I excused myself and returned to the hotel room, pleased with my progress. I smiled. Perhaps by tomorrow night I'd walk into the bar as the new owner of *News of the North*.

Ted Horton answered the phone after three rings. I introduced myself, apologized for calling so late and then asked if the Commissioner had talked to him about my interest in the newspaper. "Yes," he said ever so slowly. "Stu told me a while back you would be helping out." We agreed to have coffee in the Miner's Mess in the morning.

Thoughts raced through my head as I tried to sort out how to buy the newspaper. My mind drifted back to my school days in Renfrew, Ontario, writing a weekly high school column for the *Renfrew Advance*. Every Friday after school, I brought my copy to Hugh Gilbert, a former editor at *The Globe and Mail* and current editor of the *Advance*, who taught me how to write a newspaper column. After that I was destined to be a reporter. Now in Yellowknife, I was determined to become a publisher. I had to own *News of the North*.

5

IN ON THE GROUND FLOOR

SEPTEMBER 20, 1967

BY SEVEN A.M. A HUBBUB of locals and Ottawa transplants filled the Miner's Mess. Horton sat by the back wall, a stocky, unruly-looking man of about fifty, with a big round head, a grey brush cut that badly needed a trim and a bushy moustache to match. Printing ink stained his fingers.

Insignificant chitchat was followed by questions about my experience. I wanted to get directly to the point so I asked if Hodgson had mentioned my interest in buying his business.

"He never said anything like that to me." Horton shook his head. "Just that you would help put out the paper." He hesitated. "It might have made a difference."

"What do you mean?"

Horton said he'd sold the paper two weeks ago, to a fellow from Frobisher Bay. "He'll be taking over in three weeks. It's a signed deal."

My heart sank. I excused myself politely and returned to my hotel room where I let loose my anger, throwing a book against the wall so hard the spine split. I screamed and threw a pillow across the room. I vented for five minutes, then wondered how I could talk to Hodgson. He was my ticket back to Ottawa, and since he had lots of connections within the department, any outburst would surely end up coming to the attention of my boss.

The sharp ring of the telephone startled me. After four rings I finally answered. It was Hodgson; Horton had reported our discussion to him. "Obviously things have gotten off track," he said. "Come by my office and let's talk. See what can be done."

"Nothing can be done. He's sold the paper."

"Jake, we need to talk."

Hodgson's call focused my energy. "First I need to clean up this room, or they'll evict me."

Hodgson was on the phone when I walked in. He cut the conversation short, motioned me to sit down, looked at me and said, "I have an alternative. Try this on for size. Come and work with us in the Information Department." To say I was speechless was an understatement—first he encourages me to fly up here to publish the paper, look at buying the place, and now he's telling me to stay and work for Horton. "This will be a great opportunity. Someday our government will have a thousand or more employees and you'll be in on the ground floor."

I needed to mull over the idea of working for Ted Horton, so I decided to take a walk through Old Town, where this frontier community had its beginnings. My jacket, mitts and wool hat kept me comfortable as I walked the half-mile down Franklin Avenue, despite the autumn storm bringing freezing temperatures. Back in Ontario, the leaves on the maple, poplar and birch trees would only now be starting to turn from forest green to a blaze of gold, yellow and orange. Here, on the edge of the Arctic, the stunted trees had already lost their leaves and fine, wet snowflakes chilled my face, a warning that winter was about to begin. The place now looked bleak.

Should I forget about buying a newspaper for several years? I had to consider that I needed more experience to run a business. And Hodgson was right—I would never see another opportunity like this again. My parents, who had immigrated to unknown Canada after the Second World War, had inspired my brother and me to work hard and take risks. Was I really ready to settle for life in Yellowknife? This decision would shape the course of my life, and Barb's, for many years, perhaps forever.

Ahead, jutting into Yellowknife Bay, lay a peninsula shaped like a prostrate human form. A causeway connected the body to its head and a huge mound, a miniature Gibraltar the locals called The Rock, dominated the midsection. Shanty homes, warehouses, float planes and docks butted up to a twisting road that hugged its circumference.

It took me fifteen minutes to walk to the base of The Rock in Old Town. Seventy-five wooden steps (I counted on the way up) had been built in a zigzag up the side, and on top stood a monument to the North's bush pilots. Yellowknife's memorial was not the traditional general on horseback waving his sword, but a tapered pillar of stone, topped by the abstract steel form of a delta-shaped aircraft pointing north, its back to the horizon from which the first white residents of Yellowknife had come. Still and lifeless though it was, it all but quivered with the legends of deeds and ghosts of those early bush pilots who flew small, single-engine planes before decent maps and the most basic of radio communications were available. They were the third wave, following the early European fur traders and, later, the combined forces of the missionaries and the Mounties. Hodgson and his young government would constitute the fourth wave.

The hustle and bustle of the wharves and float plane docks surrounding The Rock countered my feelings of isolation. Standing on the crest, I looked over the water and down at the log and plywood shacks and the Old Stope Hotel built along the humpbacked rise of the rock. A float plane came in from the north and landed in the bay.

"Terrible day for sightseeing!" The voice startled me. It was Dale Eckleson, the taxi driver I had met at the Elks Hall.

"I wanted to see the rest of Yellowknife, get a different perspective."

"Trying to decide about the newspaper?"

"Fallen through. Horton has already sold the paper. I'm terribly disappointed. But Hodgson has offered me a job at the Information Department under Horton. It's a tough call because Horton's obviously not an efficient, organized person. I don't know what I can learn from him. I already have a dreadful job in Ottawa. I need to decide what to do."

"Well, don't be influenced by me. I love the place. Where else in Canada do you have prospectors, whores, misfits, bootleggers, smugglers, princes and paupers all having a good time together? We were the first town in Canada to ask parliament to legalize prostitution, you know. And the MPs, who generally use hookers more often than anyone else, turned us down. How could you find a more interesting place?"

Eckleson stared out at the snow falling into the ice-cold waves below. "That's the Con Mine headframe." He pointed south. "It's the oldest producing mine in the Northwest Territories with 250 employees. And that over there," he turned 180 degrees and pointed north, "is the Giant Mine, the largest gold producer in Canada. It employs four hundred people."

"There must have been lots of success stories over the years," I said.

"The town started in 1934, when two prospectors had to wait in Yellowknife Bay for a storm to die down. They beached their canoes, wandered inland and literally fell over a seam of gold. The Depression was on, so of course, pretty soon every prairie farmhand and adventurer was on his way up here. Farmhands in Saskatchewan were getting $10 a month back then, but mining companies would pay them $20,000 for any productive claim they could stake. One guy dismantled his farm tractor and turned it into a power plant for a raft. People travelled to Edmonton by wagon or rail and then took the trail north to the town of Peace River. From there they'd float down the Peace till it joined the Hay River. That took them to Great Slave Lake. They had to cross the lake to reach Yellowknife. There's plenty that never made it. One guy insisted on bringing his pig and cow on the raft with his family— he'd built three different rafts by the time he got here!" Another couple, Alice and Ivor Johnson," Dale pointed to a lumberyard sign, "they're still in town, came with enough macaroni to last ten years. A bit of a community sprouted up right here around The Rock. There was a guy with a foot-powered drill to fix your teeth. A fellow called Gordon Latham had a tent on the island that he called the Corona Hotel. There's a causeway joining the two nowadays, but back then you took a rowboat to cross over. A woman called Bertha Watt rowed the boat over for five cents a person. Once an airplane taxied through the narrows and sliced her boat in half.

"See over there," he pointed to the water's edge, "that's Willow Flats, where Glamour Alley used to be in the '30s and '40s. There was a row of shacks along there used as cathouses. There's this tale about some guys who needed booze really bad one night, so they woke up the woman in charge of the girls. She refused to give them anything to drink and slammed the door in their faces. That made them mad, so the next thing she knew her shack was moving toward the lake. The men had hitched it up to a tractor and were hauling it toward the water. After that they got all the booze they wanted."

Dale's stories gave me a sense of the spirit of this unruly town.

"Max Ward, who started Wardair, was a fixture around here," Dale said. "He started after Second World War with nothing but a Fox Moth and a bank loan. One time a guy chartered Max to fly him out of Discovery Mine, about sixty miles from here. Max loaded his bags. One of them was real heavy, so Max asked him if he had a gold brick in the bag. The man laughed and said 'yeah,' and they took off. Max found out later the guy had stolen two gold bricks. He was caught getting on a ship for Australia. He sure had gall—asked for severance pay from Discovery Mine, did a couple of years in jail, and when he finished his time he asked Discovery for his old job back! Max, of course, went on to develop his holiday charter business."

Dale said that Hodgson had already taken the biggest step by bringing the government up here. "Politics was something that went on in Ottawa; we couldn't do anything but bitch about it. Now, we can get involved. You'll never see anyone more interested in politics than a Northerner."

"That could mean we're in for some challenges."

"Oh, Yellowknife people are generally happy to see you guys up here. It's when you head up the Mackenzie River or out into the Arctic you'll find the going will be different. The Indians and the Eskimos are in the majority there. You've got to remember, they've never had much contact with government except for a local administrator, a Hudson's Bay clerk or a Mountie."

Dale pointed to an old building at the base of The Rock. "Over there, that's where the Moulin Rouge used to be. It was a real big bootlegging joint that opened when the bars closed each night. They played poker and all the rest of it in there. I was driving by one night, looking for a fare, when I spotted a bunch of cops staking the place out. I found a phone and called the woman who ran the place and she just laughed. She said 'Send 'em in—I've got the whole Territorial Council in here!' As it turned out, they didn't raid the place until the next night."

He twisted his head for me to follow. "I'll show you some of the sights so you can see for yourself how nice it is." We walked down The Rock, got into his taxi and headed over the causeway that put Bertha Watt out of business.

The taxi climbed the spine of Latham Island, then past an outcrop of rock where we were confronted by an explosion of unexpected colour. A row of houses, all painted in a multitude of bright, incongruous colours looked over the lake.

"This is Rainbow Valley," said Dale. "The Indians asked the government for paint, but instead the government gave them money to buy their own and let them pick their own colours." Just about every wall, window frame and door was a different colour, adding a defiant note of life to the craggy rock and grey lake that tried to overwhelm the little community.

"The Indians you see in town are from here, or from Dettah, that's the Indian village on the other side of the bay. As a matter of fact, the name

Yellowknife is derived from the Indians here, from the knives they used. Their blades were made from the naturally occurring copper found further north, near the Arctic coast."

"What does this all mean to the native people? I mean the coming of government, the gold mines and the development here. How do they feel about all this action going on?"

"Who knows? I certainly don't have a lot to do with them. They don't work in the mine and they live off by themselves. You'd have to talk to them."

Dale swung the taxi around and headed back to Old Town, across the causeway and then up to New Town.

"The state of buildings and services in Old Town eventually became inadequate, and there wasn't a lot of room, so New Town has become the centre for community services. It contains the main business section and most of the private homes."

While Yellowknife was a typical town in some ways, it certainly was not like any other capital city. This was a frontier town, on the edge of a huge wilderness filled with unknown peoples and cultures living in isolated communities. It was quirky and apparently fiercely loved by all who stayed more than the token two years. I began to feel some affection for this exuberant little community. As I relaxed in the warmth of the taxi, I remembered the words of Alex Stevenson, the Administrator of the Arctic: "Think about what you have to gain. If you have a chance to see all the changes that are going to happen, be there!"

MAY–JUNE 1968

BARB WAS AS ENTHUSIASTIC ABOUT our pending new life on the Canadian frontier as I was. We were married in Renfrew on May 4, 1968, and immediately left by car, travelling west across northern Ontario, Manitoba and Saskatchewan, then to Edmonton where we turned north to Yellowknife. We hit construction at High Level, Alberta—the northern extension of the Mackenzie Highway, littered with giant potholes, thousands of curves and many miles of mud and gumbo. The driving was treacherous and occasionally downright dangerous. As we were only able to drive at thirty to forty miles per hour, the drive from Edmonton to Yellowknife, a stretch of eight hundred miles, took three days. But this was our honeymoon and we were elated that the government had paid for our move.

In Yellowknife, Hodgson and his staff had moved out of St. Pat's school into a new three-storey building located next to the Elks Hall. In addition to executive offices for Hodgson, Parker and Gilchrist, the building included office space for the newly created departments of information, public works, and personnel. With the exception of Cyril Martindale, who had decamped for parts unknown, employees had moved out of the hotels into government housing. Barb and I were provided a two-bedroom apartment. The fledgling government was taking shape.

I dove into my responsibilities as Assistant Director of Information, working in a large open room along with Ted Horton and two other staff members. Not surprisingly, the office looked like the back shop at *News of the North* with old newspapers and files everywhere.

After a month, I had had enough and stayed after hours to make the place presentable, throwing away old newspapers and stacking files off the floor onto desks. I was proud of my accomplishment, but Ted did not take kindly to my efforts, grumbling about missing files and misplaced papers, so that evening I hauled my desk and chair out of the office and down the hall to an empty cubicle the size of a broom closet. I nailed my public relations certificate from Carleton University on the wall and moved a two-drawer file cabinet in to serve as my telephone stand. There was no door and any visitor would have to sit on a chair in the hall, but this was my private space.

No one commented on my move, certainly not Horton, who was no doubt pleased to be rid of me. Hodgson passed by, did a double-take, smirked, then bounded down the hall. My territory was staked.

I PREPARED A PROPOSAL TO establish a printing bureau, a design and type-setting unit and a public affairs division to manage public and press relations. Horton read the document with little enthusiasm and didn't act upon my ideas. I was disappointed and knew I would have to speak to Hodgson. No matter what the consequences, I was determined that Yellowknife was not going to be another Ottawa. But not today. Today, June 27, Hodgson was to be front and centre at the opening of the session of the Council of the Northwest Territories.

On his way past my office, Hodgson commanded I join him to check on the preparations at the Elks Hall. When the elevator door opened, we found two startled children standing inside. The button for each of the three floors had been pushed. As this was the only elevator in the Northwest Territories, it was a novelty and kids had become a nuisance.

"How come you're not in school?" I said. One of the boys boldly proclaimed that the Commissioner had declared a holiday for the opening of the government.

When the elevator came to a halt on the ground floor Hodgson said, "I'm the Commissioner and I only declared a half-day. Now get to school or I'll have you picked up for truancy." The kids turned red and scrambled out the door.

Outside, several ravens were perched on the roof of the Elks Hall. The wind messed up their satin ruffs and made their scrawny legs fight for balance. They cocked their heads and croaked insolently at us as we walked the few feet to the Elks, fought the wind to yank open the door and stepped inside.

Workers had set up tables and chairs and, at the back of the hall, had hung a portrait of Queen Elizabeth. Stenographers lifted reports out of boxes and placed them on tables.

Hodgson waved Binx Remnant, the Clerk of the Council, over to join us. Binx was tall and skinny, with large spectacles and hands that tended to flutter, an officious workaholic whose loyalty to Hodgson and the system was absolute. Hodgson told him to move the tables for the members of the press to the other side of the hall. Binx nodded. He then asked if the velvet rope to cordon off the council area had arrived. "On this morning's plane," Binx responded.

Hodgson went on. "Everything's got to be perfect! The table linens should be ironed! No creases!"

"It's being done."

"And the guest gallery? Have you got name cards?"

"Taken care of."

"Good man." Hodgson strode to the wall where The Queen's portrait hung. It was too low for his liking and he instructed me to get a hammer. That chore completed, Hodgson continued around the hall while Binx and I dutifully followed.

"Jake! Stand at the back! See if the mace is visible. People need to see the mace!" Hodgson had no intention of leaving until he had checked everything from dustballs under the tables to the functioning of the coffee urn.

"Binx! Have you got a copy of the invitation list?" Binx plucked the list from a pile of papers. Hodgson scanned it and said, "Jake, go back to the office, phone all of them to confirm their presence!" Binx remained impassive. I knew he would have taken care of that detail, but we knew not to question Hodgson's command. "Remind them the opening is 2:00 this afternoon! They must be in their seats by 1:45!" Hodgson tugged at my arm and addressed us both. "This has to go off like clockwork, without hitches or surprises!"

I left Binx to cope with Hodgson.

SITTING FRONT AND CENTRE IN the Elks Hall, right in front of the purple velvet ropes that cordoned off the council area, three older women chatted animatedly, their fingers clicking knitting needles, bags of wool by their feet. They reminded me of citizens knitting in front of the guillotines during the French Revolution.

The public gallery had been set up with a hundred chairs, all in perfect rows. The Queen's portrait hung straight and the linens looked as if Binx had ironed them right onto the tables. Pageboys stood before the velvet ropes to show council members and dignitaries to their seats. A big sign taped on a side table identified the press area. The contrast between the rumpled old Elks Hall where one got drunk on Saturday night, and this formal, stately chamber was stunning.

Art Sorensen, the northern reporter for the *Edmonton Journal*, said the place looked like a miniature House of Commons.

"That's what it's supposed to be," I told him as I wondered just what Yellowknifers would make of the Hodgson touch.

"Hodgson could charge admission," said Sorensen as we were joined by Bill Meyers, with the CBC's Mackenzie network, and Colin Alexander, the new owner of *News of the North*. Alexander was thin, with a high forehead and a twittery demeanor. I felt a tinge of spite as I shook his hand. I sensed his hesitation; no doubt he knew of my efforts to buy the newspaper.

At a time when most Canadian legislatures were concerned with issues of balanced budgets, transportation, housing and job creation, Territorial Councils still fretted about the smuggling of polar bear hides to the south, supplying eyeglasses to Eskimo and Indian hunters, making it legal for a spouse under twenty-one years of age to join his or her partner in a drinking establishment, allowing a minor to drink in his own home, and stopping the sale of all salacious magazines and newspapers.

The members who made up this Council would prove to be different. Even though it was not yet a truly representative and responsible government, the territorial election in 1964 had extended the franchise to all of the Northwest Territories and increased the number of constituencies from four to seven. Young and well-educated, with an abundance of northern experience and knowledge, the seven elected members were clamouring for control over their own resources and demanding status as Canada's eleventh province.

David Searle, the member for North Slave, as a Yellowknifer, lawyer and President of the Yellowknife Liberal Association, had the credentials to be one of the leading lights. So did Duncan Pryde, a Scottish-born orphan who had gone to sea at fifteen and arrived in Canada with the Hudson's Bay Company three years later. For eleven years he had managed four of their trading posts, learned the Eskimo language and was in the process of writing an Eskimo dictionary. The Eskimo people who lived around the posts he managed called him the White Eskimo or *Tagak* (Skinny).

Pryde was the definitive adventurer who almost died trying to visit his constituents in the Western Arctic. He had intended to take his canoe a total of 1,100 miles along the Arctic coast, down the Mackenzie River, and across Great Slave Lake. But, before he reached the river, he ran into gales, fierce cross tides, twenty-foot waves, a ten-foot barricade of ice that threatened to slice his powered craft to pieces and finally a barrier of fresh ice that forced him to go back a hundred miles and forget all about the trip.

Simonie Michael, who represented the Eastern Arctic, was the first Eskimo to be elected to public office. An orphan raised in an igloo, Michael had been a dishwasher, janitor, mechanic, carpenter, interpreter and businessman. Like Duncan Pryde, he struggled to visit his constituency. To visit the Belcher Islands in Hudson Bay, he had to fly from his home in Frobisher Bay on Baffin Island to Montreal, then to Ottawa where he could catch a plane to Roberval, in the far north of Québec, from where he could fly the final seventy miles to the Belcher Islands. On at least one occasion, he didn't make it. Stormy spring weather blew up in Roberval and he had to go home, the same long way around. He had travelled more than two thousand miles without seeing a soul on the islands.

Lyle Trimble, the member for Mackenzie Delta, was a stern and swarthy ex-Mountie from Aklavik. He was a conservative, clean-living missionary who left the RCMP when he married a local Eskimo girl. Elected as the Mackenzie Delta representative in 1964 at the age of twenty-seven, he was now the longest-sitting council member.

Robert Williamson, the member for the Central Arctic, was an English-born anthropologist from Rankin Inlet who sported a flowing beard, wore a silk ascot and smoked a stubby pipe. Williamson had worked on the Mackenzie River barges and as a carpenter before making anthropology his career. He now ran the University of Saskatchewan's Arctic Research Centre in Rankin Inlet.

Don Stewart was a tall, smiling man who had arrived in the Territories as an airline radio operator in 1946. He entered the Council as the member for Mackenzie South, fresh from a judicial inquiry into an alleged conflict of interest between his position as mayor of Hay River and his ownership of a construction company that had contracts with the town. The judge found that Stewart had done nothing more than act "as an energetic mayor" and refused to disqualify him. But Stewart didn't pay the court costs as ordered, so could not run for mayor. He campaigned for the Territorial Council instead and had lost so little face in Hay River that he beat local hero Bob Gauchie, the rescued bush pilot.

The seventh elected member was Mark Fairbrother, who won a by-election to replace William Berg, a Fort Simpson game outfitter killed in a plane crash shortly after the general election. Fairbrother was also a member of the village council of Fort Simpson.

The five appointed members were Air Marshal Hugh Campbell; Chief John Charlie Tetlichie, a hunter and trapper and Chief of the Fort McPherson band of Loucheaux Indians, the first Indian to sit on the Council; Dr Lloyd Barber, Dean of Commerce at the University of Saskatchewan; Gordon Gibson, a flamboyant former member of the British Columbia legislature known for his business acumen; and John Parker, the Deputy Commissioner.

We were startled by a loud pounding at the main entrance, and a bellowed cry of "Order!" The maelstrom of excited chatter ceased as we all stood up with a scraping of chairs. The crowd hushed and heads turned as the clock on the back wall chimed two o'clock. A procession led by two RCMP corporals, dressed in ceremonial red serge and brown Stetson hats, marched flags down the centre aisle. Four paces behind, and in perfect step, an RCMP sergeant, also in red serge, carried the impressive five-and-half-foot territorial mace high on his right shoulder. Frank Smith, Legal Advisor, decked out in a black suit and white bow tie, followed. And then Binx flew in, dressed in a black suit but sporting a black cape that made him look like a raven attempting to get airborne. Behind Binx marched RCMP Inspector Harry Nixon, the newly appointed honourary aide-de-camp to the Commissioner, dressed in a ceremonial blue officer's uniform. Three paces behind Nixon marched Hodgson, showing no sign of nerves or tension, clearly proud of this day and of his position.

The pounding of the Mounties' boots echoed off the walls until the procession stopped in unison at the front of the hall. The flag bearers placed their standards into the floor stands, turned 180 degrees and came to attention. At this point the sergeant shouldering the mace turned sideways, stepped in front of the table, turned and deftly placed it in its cradle. Binx and Frank Smith took their positions at the staff support table. Inspector Nixon stepped onto the podium while Hodgson took up his position at the lectern.

All eyes were on Hodgson, who was clearly enjoying the spotlight after weeks of painstaking planning. Everything about the scene bore Hodgson's stamp—he was holding court, surrounded by his subjects and his advisors. He faced the crowd, grasped both sides of the lectern and bowed his head. You could hear a pin drop. And then he intoned the prayer that would open the session.

As he spoke, Art Sorensen nudged me, nodding toward the entrance. Tom Doornbos, who made his own tomato soup at the Miner's Mess restaurant and snoozed in the easy chair in the window of the Hudson's Bay, shuffled into the hall, picked a seat and sat down even though the whole crowd was standing. He arranged his ancient greatcoat and bulging shopping bag to his satisfaction. A red tuque, pointed skyward as if starched, remained on his head.

The prayer over, Hodgson's voice suddenly boomed over the superfluous microphone, making the speakers squeal. The reporters scribbled, the CBC reporter turned on his tape recorder and the Debate recorders bent to their work.

Hodgson spoke clearly and emphatically so that his sentences would be easily understood by everyone. He frequently let one hand rise to the level of his face to cradle and mold his message with fingers that sculpted every syllable. He made direct eye contact, aware that people were taking him seriously, impressed with the fact he was taking the occasion, the Council and his duties seriously as well.

"I take great pleasure in being able to stand before you in our new capital today, on what is indeed an historic occasion, to officially open the 37th Session of the Council of the Northwest Territories.

"I have always believed that people, with their needs and aspirations, must be the most important consideration that any government has if it is to function democratically as the servant of those it purports to govern. Those of you who know me and have worked with me know this is a conviction I've held all my life."

Hodgson spoke as though he had no prepared notes. His eyes were not on the lectern but roved the faces of his audience and occasionally scanned the ceiling. His grammar was rough but his skill as a speaker more than made up for any lack. His physical size added to the impression that he was reliable and dedicated, as did his strong, deep voice. He inspired confidence—a general marshalling his forces.

"Since we arrived in Yellowknife on September 18, 1967, I have had ample proof of the great value inherent in being located among the people." Loud murmurs of approval and desk thumping interrupted his speech as council members endorsed Hodgson's point of view.

"Creating the machinery of government in the North is perhaps our easiest task. The challenge will be to involve people of the North in taking part, in taking responsibility for fair and effective government in all regions and communities. This is not a concept that is part of the tradition of the North. In fact, our form of government is alien to many in the Territories. For this reason much of my work in the coming years will concentrate on encouraging and educating those Northerners who are ready to take on this great challenge which is, I believe, the greatest challenge and the greatest privilege ever accepted in the free world."

Hodgson continued his opening address for an hour. It was a speech from the throne that outlined the work to be done: twenty-four bills, eleven recommendations, and nineteen sessional papers. When finished, he called for the first order of business, the adoption of a flag for the Northwest Territories. The idea of a heraldic symbol for the Northwest Territories was entirely Hodgson's, and was based on the adoption by Canada of the maple leaf flag in 1965. National newspaper advertisements offering a $1,000 prize had generated three thousand submissions ranging from a striking set of abstract designs from Cape Dorset to a drawing of Queen Elizabeth stranded on a snowbank. The winning entry had royal blue bars on each side with the Territories' coat of arms in a white middle section. Anxious to avoid the kind of rancorous debate that surrounded the Canadian flag, councillors took just sixty-seven seconds to adopt the recommendation of a three-member committee. Hodgson beamed at the quickness of the business at hand and called for a twenty-minute break.

The CBC's Bill Meyers slung his tape recorder over his shoulder, stepped over to Hodgson and asked about the mace. Hodgson explained that Vincent Massey, Canada's first Canadian-born Governor General, had commissioned eight Eskimo stone carvers from Cape Dorset to create the mace, which was presented to the Territorial Council in 1956. The mace was made entirely of northern materials with narwhal tusk for the shaft, whalebone from Fox Peninsula, natural copper from the Arctic coast, muskox horns from Ellesmere Island, gold from the mines in Yellowknife and porcupine quill work from the Mackenzie Valley. The Eskimos initially called it *Pingwartok* (the Plaything) but when they understood its importance they changed its name to *Anaotalok* (the Great Club).

While Hodgson carried on the interview with Meyers, I joined David Searle by the coffee bar. He was telling Duncan Pryde that he and Bobby Williamson had decided to run for Council at the same time. "I was appointed Crown Prosecutor for the Territories to travel with Judge Sissons and met Bobby Williamson in Rankin Inlet. He and I used to kill a bottle of scotch in an evening and chat over where the North should be going. We were concerned there were only four elected members of Council, and five appointed, and that the Eastern, Western and Central Arctic had no representatives at all. We were concerned this was just a rubber stamp of the federal government and that the territorial government wasn't responsible. It was contrary to all principles of democracy. So one wintry night we decided to run for Council." I realized they would be a rambunctious and determined bunch.

Pryde took a slurp of his coffee and jabbed a weather-beaten finger toward me. "You've come 'ere to set up government in Yellowknife," he said. "Only problem is that doesn't do much for people two thousand miles away on the Arctic coast or on Baffin Island. Rome wasn't built in a day, I know. But when our Commissioner stands and says what a great job he's done setting up government, it's 'ard to keep me mouth shut." Pryde didn't mince words. "Who's got the most benefit so far out of 'avin 'odgson and the government in the North? The people of Yellowknife! Who's getting rich off the presence of the government? The people of Yellowknife! Wot's the government done for the rest of the Northwest Territories? Nothin!"

Pryde's derision took me by surprise. It was true that, as of yet, no benefit had been bestowed on the rest of the North, but I already knew that, if this land was to become part of the Canadian mainstream, the North needed Hodgson. He had proven to be a man of his word and I was confident he'd do the impossible for the rest of the North. He was the right man, in the right job, at the right time.

Hodgson pounded the gavel to call the members back into session.

"Back to work, gentlemen," said Searle. "Who's up first? Oh crap, it's Trimble." He dropped his voice to a whisper. "Everyone on Council gets along well, but Trimble, well, everything has to come within narrow boundaries before he can go along with anything. He regards himself as the opposition and is interested in raising hell. But he can make an entertaining speech, I'll grant him that."

Hodgson banged his gavel again. Quiet returned to the hall as he called the next agenda item—replies to the Commissioner's address. Hodgson looked about. "Mr. Trimble?" The council member rose; his colleagues leaned back in their chairs, all set to enjoy the show.

Trimble had a frank face that spoke of silent strength and unyielding convictions. "I compliment you on the splendid pomp and ceremony which attends the opening of our session, sir," Trimble said, directing his gaze first to the Commissioner and then to the audience. Hodgson smiled and inclined his head, pleased he'd made an impression.

Trimble buttoned his jacket and returned his stare to the Commissioner. "Your address, sir, indicates the tremendous strides being taken to bring government, good government, into the Northwest Territories. We know you and your staff have experienced many problems in taking this action. We see the conditions under which you are compelled to work. I believe you have done the right thing, and I further believe my respect for the courage and determination demonstrated by yourself and your staff is shared by everyone in the Territories."

A ripple of nods and murmurs of assent passed around the council table.

"The fifth Council is history," Trimble intoned, his voice low, level, measured. "But during the life of that Council, a revolutionary change was set in motion. The Northwest Territories is on its way to the autonomy of provincehood, and neither hell nor high water, nor a few associates I would like to mention, can stop the momentum which has fired the imagination of people everywhere."

Sorensen and Alexander wrote furiously, recording Trimble's words. Hodgson sat impassive, his hands on the desk in front of him, his face immobile. He was not only weighing Trimble's words, but also sizing up the strength of the various alliances and rifts among his colleagues.

"The members of the fifth Council, both elected and appointed, served their country well. I am proud to have been a member of that Council. I possess even greater pride in being part of this, the sixth Council, because I know that when this Council finishes its course there will be no doubt but that the people of the Northwest Territories are well able to manage their own affairs."

Trimble spoke the very words Hodgson had said to me. But Trimble had a much different timetable than Hodgson.

As Trimble continued, his voice rose steadily up the scale. "Why do we want to be an autonomous province instead of a territorial dependency? Why do we talk of the desire to manage our own affairs? It is because for so many years this Council has been treated like a little child, like a little Pinocchio, and denied all semblance of rights and responsibility." It was an apt simile of long-nosed marionettes dancing under Ottawa's manipulative strings.

"And with what result?" Trimble demanded. "Those problems that we can see so clearly, and that we know can be solved, are ignored by our masters in Ottawa and perforce by us too, because our masters will give us no spending money. We can raise only a quarter of our budget of eight million dollars, mostly from liquor sales. The rest has to come as a charitable handout from Ottawa."

Trimble paused and rolled his eyes heavenward, seeking divine inspiration. At that very moment the massive furnace, whose motor had valiantly tried to keep fresh air flowing, let out a pained, nerve-jarring squeal. Laughter broke out among the audience.

"Heavenly signal!" said Art Sorensen.

Trimble's face remained impassive while he paused slightly, took his eyes off Hodgson, panned the council members, then the audience and continued. "To take over the administration of the Territories, and to set up the machinery of government in the comfortable confines of Yellowknife is not the most difficult task you face, Mr. Commissioner."

Hodgson's eyebrows fell a degree as he waited for Trimble to continue.

"To provide the administration the people of the Territories deserve, and expect, is something else again. Those of us who live a thousand or two thousand miles from here want to see an administration that addresses the fact there are citizens living in tents and shacks in 60-below weather; people with no source of income except for the tiny carvings they create; people whose mortality rate is twice that of Canada's average; people who face death every time they leave their settlement; people with no real medical help, no access to modern communication or transportation facilities."

Trimble's brows lowered over his impassioned eyes. His voice rose in intensity. His hand rose in front of him and he pointed at Hodgson, like an inquisitor of old marking a suspect citizen. "The Northwest Territories today is receiving the same treatment from the Canadian government as the original inhabitants of this land received so many years ago, and where are those original inhabitants today? At the bottom of the heap as far as this country is concerned."

Trimble leaned forward and pounded the table in front of him, spittle starting to break from beneath his lip. "It is unthinkable to me that this nation feels no shame that our vast territory is home to people who have no clothing save what they make from the creatures they catch, who starve to death when the caribou change their migration route, who cannot reach a hospital if they break a limb, who cannot communicate with each other except by word of mouth at chance meetings on the tundra and who have no understanding of, nor role in, this country or this century. Yet such, and worse, is the case."

Trimble glanced around the chamber and picked up the glass in front of him for a drink of water. He continued, but in a lower tone. "Your new administration governs more than Yellowknife—it governs the entire Northwest Territories, a region of stunning diversity in cultures, races, terrain, climate and resources. Everywhere one looks there is deprivation of the worst kind. The people are just emerging from the Ice Age. They're totally unequipped to deal with a wage economy and the abuses of the white man. The Eskimos have sixteen words for snow, but not one for government—they know nothing of it."

The councillor paused once more. He leaned forward, rested both hands on the table in front of him and fixed Hodgson with a challenging stare. "We want to know if you, Mr. Commissioner, and your staff in Yellowknife, are up to the test. I'm referring to the test of going the extra mile, of going beyond setting up government in this safe enclave called Yellowknife. Are you willing to face the danger, and the shame of seeing for yourselves what truly exists out on the eastern tundra, high in the Arctic islands or far down the Mackenzie River?

"I conclude, Mr. Commissioner, with the same comment that I made in my reply to your opening address. We stand in awe at your accomplishments in bringing the government to Yellowknife. But we fear your predecessor, Mr. Sivertz, was perhaps right when he talked of the new commissioner being shipped off to the bush with no staff and no money, simply to remove the embarrassment from Ottawa's sight. We hand you the challenge, Mr. Commissioner, of showing Ottawa that the Northwest Territories will not stand for this treatment, and of proving your new government has the courage to tackle more problems than those few that exist in Yellowknife."

And with that, Trimble sat down. The hall erupted into applause as onlookers in the public gallery, except the snoozing Tom Doornbos, endorsed Trimble's words. Several council members rose and walked over to shake their colleague's hand.

I looked over at Hodgson, half-expecting him to look angry, or disgusted, or defensive, but instead I saw an almost imperceptible nod of agreement, as if he were saying, "Right! We'd better get out there and see what we can do."

Part Two

REACHING ALL NORTHERNERS

7

WAKE-UP CALL

SEPTEMBER 1968

ONE DAY IN EARLY FALL Hodgson said he was going to Rae and wanted me to come along with a notepad and camera.

Rae is sixty miles west of Yellowknife and seven miles down a side road off the Mackenzie Highway, a two-hour drive. On the way out of town, a sign instructed us to "Stop, Look and Listen," a reminder that the road was at the north end of the airport runway.

The drab rocks and landscape no longer glittered with the gold of autumn's leaves, and the waters of the myriad lakes no longer danced and sparkled. The same pink-and-licorice seams of rock that swam through Yellowknife also snaked through the bush and muskeg on the way to Rae, lifting scrubby conifers toward the sky and forming swamps and evergreen stands, now frozen solid and covered in snow. Everything was white.

"How's Barb enjoying her job?" Hodgson asked.

Barb had obtained a position as secretary to the Director of Public Works. "Very much," I replied.

We had been silent for a spell when Hodgson suddenly blew the horn and stepped on the brakes. Five or six white balls of snow suddenly fluffed up on the road.

"Ptarmigan. They come to this area to escape the harshness of winter further north. Part of the grouse family," said Hodgson. "They never leave, just come south in winter because there's more light here than further north. Turn from white in winter to grey and brown in the summer." They resembled white pigeons with fluffy feathers and feet padded like snowshoes.

Hodgson changed the subject. "Let's hope we can get this relocation dispute sorted out." I didn't know what he was talking about but knew his comments would become self-explanatory if I let him ramble. He said people at Rae were getting sick from the drinking water. The water treatment plant didn't work properly and never would because the lake was too shallow and silty.

"Why can't they truck water from elsewhere?"

"The community needs a new school, but two years ago the consultants for the Northern Affairs department said the community was unfit for future development. They said Rae is too swampy to exist and suggested the school be built at a site fifteen miles away. The population is expected to double in the next ten years, so the consultants felt that people should move to the new site when they want new houses. I want to talk to the chief to see whether it's a good idea."

"Who's the chief?"

"Jimmy Bruneau. He's one of the last hereditary chiefs and is the senior leader of all the other Dogrib bands in the outlying communities."

"Hereditary?"

"Chiefs who inherit their position because their father, or some other relative, was chief. Bruneau was there when the government party came to Rae in 1921 to get signatures on Treaty 11. Wasn't chief then, but he was there."

Rae was the biggest Indian settlement in the North, with about five hundred residents. In the spring, about six hundred additional Dogrib Indians from the three smaller settlements within a hundred-mile radius would come to Rae after the winter trapping season. Many of the summer population lived and slept in tents and tepees, with all daytime living, cooking and eating carried on outdoors.

The last bit of road brought us up a slight incline bordered on both sides by stubby trees and undergrowth. Once we reached the top, a view of the whole settlement opened up before us.

About ninety small log houses were situated between us and the shore of Marion Lake. We drove perhaps a quarter of a mile, pulling up in front of a carefully crafted wood-frame Roman Catholic church with a tall, dominant steeple. There were no roads among the houses, just well-travelled pathways. One pathway crossed a narrow wooden bridge then climbed a gentle rise, past some ornate crosses and picket cribs that marked burial places.

Most dwellings were cabins, built of small, skinny logs hewn from the spindly trees around the settlement, with porches, lean-tos, kennels and sheds affixed in a random process. Dried-out caulking of moss and tattered tarpaper partially covered their exterior, and rusted steel chimneys spewed acrid smoke onto corrugated metal roofs. Each residence had an outdoor privy and a litter of rusted fuel drums, firewood and assorted domestic garbage. There was no evidence of electricity.

Dogs lay here and there tethered to chains. Kids played everywhere. Past the settlement and across the large lake, scrubby spruce, poplar and birch stretched southward to a distant ridge of yellow granite cliffs.

I wondered how sixty miles of gravel road could so totally separate my world in Yellowknife from this scene. These Dogrib Indians still lived the traditional way, off the land, hunting and trapping. It was a culture that included the majority of Northerners and I knew nothing about it, nor did Hodgson. I felt self-conscious, unsure of our relevance to this community.

Hodgson was already out of the car, and the instant I joined him, my ears and nose told me more about Rae than my eyes ever could. As I closed the vehicle's door, I picked up an image of noisy children, barking dogs, pungent woodsmoke and inadequate sanitation that no photographic image could ever convey. Ravens perched on the rooftops, watching our every move.

No sooner did we greet the first of the residents than we were face-to-face with the Chief. There was no mistaking his rank. He wore his treaty suit, an outfit bestowed on Indian chiefs when treaties were signed. The style was ancient, like a British naval officer's uniform from the 19th century—dark blue, double-breasted with large brass buttons, a wide yellow stripe around the cuffs and down the pant legs, and a bowler hat rimmed with a red band. He clenched a strong, big-bowled pipe in his mouth.

Chief Bruneau's taut, skeletal, ancient face, his translucent skin and wise eyes, silently said, 'We've been here ten thousand years, who are you?' He had a young man at his side, a fellow in his early twenties, slim, about six feet, with black hair down to his shoulders. He wore heavy-rimmed glasses, jeans and a moose-hide jacket with fringes. Behind them a group of villagers had gathered, silent in their dark jackets and baseball hats, gazing intently at us. Most of the elders had weathered walnut skin, deep facial creases, unsmiling mouths and opaque dark eyes.

There was no move to shake our hands. Hodgson showed respect to the eighty-four-year-old Chief, waiting for the young interpreter to lead the proceedings. In a guttural monotone, without taking his pipe from his mouth,

Bruneau intoned some opening words. "The Chief welcomes you to our community," said the young man. His fluency said he was no stranger to our white world and culture.

The Chief intoned another monologue and waved at the lake as he spoke. The young man translated, "Dogribs have lived in this area for a long time. It is good land. We have plenty of fish to feed our dogs, and plenty of dogs to work our traplines. Many people live here in tents because there are not enough houses."

The translator then said the Chief would like to show Hodgson his community, at which Hodgson nodded. With the translator between them, the three walked toward the bridge, an interesting tableau. Hodgson towered over Bruneau and the young translator's dress suggested a generation destined to become impatient with both worlds. I fell in among the retinue of elders and villagers.

We crossed the creek and climbed past the whitewashed and weather-bleached grave markers to the shacks close to the boulder-strewn shore of the lake. Boats were pulled up on the beach, and dogs jumped and lunged as we passed. Ravens hopped up and down on rooftops, agitated by our intrusion.

"These homes are too small." Bruneau stretched his arm out to a shack. "About three families live in each house, some with as many as twelve people."

I looked in awe at the unsubstantial dwellings. None were bigger than fourteen by sixteen feet, if you discounted the porches and kennels. Most were distinctly smaller than that.

Bruneau pointed to a forty-five-gallon steel drum and said each house had water delivered by truck once a week. There should be more but that's all the water plant could suck from the lake.

As we walked, I realized that my spontaneous judgment of the community as scruffy and decrepit was a product of my own naivety. True, they needed more and better houses, but the Indians simply had different priorities—they needed fish to feed their dogs and dogs to hunt and trap. Dog shit and fish heads were no more disgusting here than discarded newspapers and rusty bicycles would be down south. This place was a typical Indian community of the North—a place surviving on its own wits and determination in the absence of any help from outside.

Around the point we got a clear view of the back bay and the decaying water treatment plant. Hodgson asked, "What about the sanitation problem? There's been some problem with sickness from the water?" He let the young man translate. No one said anything, and then Hodgson continued. "The drainage is no good here. The wastewater runs straight back into the lake where you get your drinking water." He said no more and there was further silence. Finally, Bruneau said, "I asked for a new school. The government says it will look after us and educate our children. But it will not build a new school here, only on the other side." Bruneau pointed to the far end of the lake.

Hodgson nodded. He was slow to respond, just like the Chief. "The government, the Ottawa government, has plans to build the school over there because the ground is better."

"But we live here," said Bruneau, his face immobile, his voice remaining monotone.

"It's better sanitation there. Your children won't get sick as they do here when they drink the water. More houses can be built there."

The Chief didn't respond. Bruneau was silent, scanning the horizon with his milky old eyes while his moccasins, covered with rubber overshoes, scrunched the ground.

He intoned his words and the young translator said, "The Chief does not want any of his people to be forced to move, but he will not prevent anyone from leaving if they so choose." Hodgson's body and features relaxed.

We continued our tour and finally came full circle to the central area where the car was parked. Hodgson turned to face Bruneau. "Thank you for showing me your community," Hodgson said, trying to melt the ice that seemed to weigh down smiles and hearts. The Indians remained impassive. "I will do everything to help. The people of the North have been governed by Ottawa for a long time. I have brought the government to Yellowknife so that decisions can be made in the North."

The translation came in a steady chant and the elders and residents of Rae listened, their eyes staring at Bruneau and Hodgson, their faces grave.

"My job is to help all Northerners and, over the next two years, the government in Ottawa will give more authority to my government in Yellowknife so decisions can be made in the North. I want to pass that authority down to the people in the communities, so you can eventually take control of decisions at the local level."

There wasn't a single smile. Hodgson's words died in the windless air. Stony, silent faces gazed at him. The translator stood silent too, watching the revered Chief.

If Bruneau said farewell, it was with an extra firm chomp on his pipe. He turned and headed through the crowd, which dispersed behind him.

The young translator remained and said, "The Chief sees you as an agent, an Indian Agent, as in the original colonial title. Through Treaty 11, the Chief has always dealt directly with the federal government. Also, the Chief has always included the people. As you can see, all the people were here so they are informed of what the Chief and you talked about. But you told the Chief you and your government are in charge and suggested the Chief deal with you. Your way is not our way. We signed peace treaties, not treaties giving our land away. And now the federal government says Indians are to be the responsibility of the territorial government. The Chief doesn't see it the way you do." And with that, he too walked off. It was a wake-up call.

8
A GOOD MATCH

DECEMBER 21, 1968

THROUGHOUT THE FALL AND EARLY winter the light dwindled by ten minutes each day. On December 21, the shortest day of the year, Yellowknife had five hours of daylight, from ten in the morning until three o'clock in the afternoon. Those five hours were bleak, with constantly overcast skies.

The thermometer fell lower and lower, becoming colder by ten degrees per month. The first snowfall in late September had remained on the ground and the thermometer now hovered at -40°F. We were in an arctic deep freeze, and the weather played havoc with transportation systems. A Pacific Western Airlines flight had made an attempt to land three days ago but returned to Edmonton when it couldn't locate the runway. The ferry crossing the Mackenzie River had been pulled out of service a week ago, but it would be three weeks before the river froze over enough to allow an ice bridge to be constructed. Grocery stores were already running low on supplies. We were cut off from the outside world; the darkness and bitter cold played on everyone's mind.

My despondency was the result of more than just the weather—my tolerance for Horton had fallen to zero. He was sloppy, failed to lead his staff and provided no vision for the future. Other departments were increasing in size and momentum while we were not keeping up with the demands for typesetting, design, printing services, press releases and the public relations needs of those departments. They would soon set up their own service bureaus as an alternative, instead of relying on our centralized operation.

Hodgson summoned me to his office. He stood before the window, gazing through the ice fog that was swirling up from the vehicle exhaust on Franklin Avenue. He gestured to the four-storey headquarters building under construction across the street. Rumours were flying around Yellowknife that it would become a white elephant. "I'm going to name it the Arthur Laing building."

The federal election, held the previous June, had brought changes and many new faces to power in Ottawa. Pierre Trudeau had replaced Lester Pearson as Prime Minister and Jean Chrétien, a young self-assured politician scrambling up the ladder in Ottawa, had taken over from Arthur Laing as Northern Affairs Minister. I wondered if the change in political masters would have negative implications for Hodgson. Would he still have his direct pipeline to the top? It was Pearson who had promised him a free hand and Laing who had provided the support. Now both were gone, replaced by a pair of relative unknowns from Québec who could introduce an element of instability and uncertainty. Would Hodgson still take over responsibility of the central Arctic in 1969 and the Eastern Arctic in 1970? Who knew if these new political masters would share his vision for the North?

Hodgson turned from the window and, with obvious concern, asked how I was getting along with Ted.

I was relieved that he raised the issue and told him Horton was incapable of providing the services the government needed. I said I was as frustrated as I had been when I was an information officer with the department in Ottawa. I needed specific projects such as producing a magazine, an annual report, a promotional brochure, a radio program. I wanted specific orders, direction and guidance. I had hoped for someone to show the way, reward me, and discipline me when needed. "I'm only twenty-six and I think I can do a better job than Ted." I spoke the way I felt. Hodgson showed no surprise. "I appreciate what you have done for me." I hesitated. "I'm sorry. I'm carrying on." I felt I had said too much already, but this was my chance. "What about moving Ted and giving me his job?" I said audaciously.

Hodgson stared straight ahead, massaging his right ear. He said he understood but couldn't change things right now. "Besides, you're not ready."

I looked at him quizzically.

"You need more experience. I had expected Ted would provide that but it's obvious that's not the case." He let out a sigh and rubbed his face. "You need to learn the real secret of being a good manager. The principles of good management are often very muddled and not understood."

"What do you mean?"

"Well, a good manager will consider the consequences of what he does. I think the first test of a good manager is the ability to think and act for himself."

"Well I can do that."

"Let me finish," he held up his hand, signalling me not to interrupt. "He should be able to originate ideas and plans, and solve problems without always going to his superior." Hodgson hesitated for a second. "A good manager can work independently and needs only the barest minimum instructions to carry out his job. His principal duty is to provide leadership. Unfortunately, very few men are natural-born leaders. Some learn the lessons of leadership in university, others on the job. Wherever learned, there are some basic rules which apply everywhere."

I appreciated his advice and pulled out my notebook to write it down.

"I learned this stuff in the union and some of it from the company bosses, watching them and, in most cases, learning how not to do something. And I read a lot. Some things I memorized and every chance I got I'd tell others the secrets of management until I thought they were my own invention. They're not, of course, but by repeating them I'm reminded every time to do things the correct way. Write this down," he said. He spoke slowly and carefully so I could keep up. "Lead by example—show a man, as well as tell him, how to do a job. Accept responsibility for the people under you and accept the blame if something goes wrong. And make sure to give them the credit if something is done right." Hodgson spoke as if rehearsing a speech. "Don't ask someone to do something you're unwilling to do yourself. If there's a dirty job to be done, be prepared to do it. Be firm but fair with your employees. Show concern for their needs and try to meet reasonable requests. Treat your junior employees with patience and understanding and back them to the hilt."

I was reminded of an incident back in Ottawa. I had inadvertently placed a set of colour keys for a printing project on the floor beside my wastebasket. The next morning they were gone, disposed of by the janitor, and days of work went down the drain. I was humiliated. Hodgson had calmly suggested I go to the Ottawa dump to see if possibly, by some miracle, I could find them. I immediately realized the impossibility of the task and the foolish nature of my quest but, after pondering my circumstance, a wonderful idea came to me—why not go to the Queen's Printer's office and ask if they could replace the colour keys? They did and I proudly proclaimed the solution to Hodgson. "How was the dump?" he chuckled. He hadn't admonished me but made me solve my own problem.

"Don't pamper them and remember, familiarity breeds contempt," Hodgson continued. He paused to let me catch up with my notes. "And most important, praise employees in public. If they have done a good job tell them so in front of the other employees. Discipline them in private or you will humiliate and demoralize them." He hesitated and asked, "Did you get all that?"

I nodded.

"I learned my own lessons in the tough, no-nonsense plywood mills of Vancouver and as financial secretary of the Vancouver Local of the IWA, the biggest local in the Pacific Northwest forest industry, and the most rebellious in the whole union. As I said, half of what I learned about how not to do something was from the company bosses. For instance, we all believe that bosses should act swiftly and be all-knowing but lightning-fast decisions can be wrong. Don't set unachievable deadlines so that people face impossible time pressures,and stop correcting flaws. Pay close attention to how you treat everyone. Don't interfere with their personal time by holding meetings on weekends just to show your own dedication to the job. Don't play favourites with your subordinates. If you promote an underperformer or incompetent because he or she fawns over you, the co-workers will think he or she is your favourite." He stopped for a moment. "Loyalty is another important quality. And it has to be demonstrated by all of us to our superiors."

"You don't have a superior."

"Well I do. I answer to Art . . . Cretain now," Hodgson mispronounced Jean Chrétien's name. "And my loyalty has to be to him. Now one more thing, and that's about education. There's a lot to be said for a solid, formal education, but for a lot of good leaders, their formal education stopped at high school or even grade school. Although a good education usually helps a man who wants to be a good manager, I don't believe it is always essential. Many great leaders taught themselves. You'll have plenty of time and plenty of people to learn from. You have learned from Ted. We can all learn from others. I have gained so much from the Air Marshal over the years. He is a master at leadership, had to be as Chief of Air Staff."

Hodgson stopped talking and turned to look out the window. Finally he spoke again. "Why don't we do this? I'm going to promote Clarence to become the Assistant Commissioner. He has already become too busy to do many of the things I need done. You become my executive assistant and work directly for me. You can do all of my correspondence, organize trips, take notes, prepare reports and do follow-up work. You can attend meetings with me, go on trips to the communities and organize functions."

My heart pounded. Yes! This was the opportunity I needed, I wanted, to have someone experienced take me in hand and mentor me, and now I would have Hodgson's guidance. Hodgson saw the smile on my face. I didn't comment. I just savoured the moment.

"We're a good match, you and I. You're a good listener and you're a good communicator. I don't mean just in the writing skills but in the relations you develop with people. I need that. I need someone who can keep his ear to the ground and find out what's happening, what other people are saying." He continued to muse out loud. "Someone I can bounce ideas off. This will be good for both of us. I'll tell Ted you've been seconded to me to do special projects."

"Horton won't object," I said. "Thank you. Thank you. I appreciate you doing this." I could barely contain myself. This position had prestige and influence. I would be up front and not back behind the scenes. I had just been handed an incredible opportunity to learn.

"First thing, I want you to arrange a trip through the High Arctic this winter. The time has come for the people of the North to meet their commissioner. I want to know what is going on out there. Let's see what you can do."

9

ARRANGING A GRAND TOUR

FEBRUARY 1969

JANUARY TURNED TO FEBRUARY AND, while daylight returned by ever so slight amounts, the temperature continued to drop. Then, for eight weeks, the thermometer remained at a miserable -40. I was arranging Hodgson's grand tour of fifteen far-flung communities of the High Arctic, a significant challenge as telephone service did not exist. Their only connection to the outside world was an antiquated air radio system.

Our two-week tour would cover over two thousand miles, taking us to some of the most desolate areas of the world, during the dead of winter. We would depend on the generosity of the communities for eating and sleeping arrangements, no small undertaking.

The tiny settlements, some with as few as seventy people, were scattered hundreds of miles apart and were run by area administrators, federal employees selected by the Department of Indian Affairs and Northern Development who were soon to become responsible to our government. Area administrators received ten months of training at the pretentiously-named Northern University—in reality, an operation with no campus, only a part-time director and no authority to confer degrees. During my time with Irene Baird, I had been allowed to attend in order to become more familiar with northern matters. It was one of the few times I appreciated being an employee of that department and meant that I had a previous connection with some of these individuals.

Now I had to contact each one, advise of the Commissioner's visit, request a community meeting and arrange accommodation and meals for the twelve members of our party plus air crew. I relied on the telephone operator in Hay River, located 120 miles across Great Slave Lake. Microwave towers, resembling oversized drive-in movie screens, linked Yellowknife to Hay River, where Canadian National Telecommunications had its long-distance exchange.

Armed with a list of administrators and contact numbers obtained from Northern Affairs in Ottawa, I set to work. I dialed zero on my black rotary phone to reach the operator, briefed her on my project and asked if she could help. She connected me by landline with an operator in Edmonton, then an operator in Montreal, and then north again to a shortwave radio system. The first call was to Arctic Bay on Baffin Island.

I asked the operator to stay on the line. "Yes, dear," she replied, reminding me of my youth.

"Hello? Arctic Bay?" I said.

The response was garbled. What I did make out was, "Repeat. Over."

The operator cut in. "You have to enunciate every syllable."

"Okay." I started again. "Hel. . .lo . . . Hel. . .lo . . . Arc. . .tic . . . Bay . . . Can . . . you . . . hear . . . me?" There was silence.

The operator came on. "You have to say 'over' when you're finished."

I repeated my initial message and ended with "Over."

A reply came back. "This . . . is . . . Arc . . . tic . . . Bay. Over." I made out the words, but they faded in and out due to atmospheric turbulence. I was reminded of an old war movie, with a desperate hero behind enemy lines sending a crucial message on hopelessly inadequate equipment. I continued in the staccato style. "Commissioner. Party of twelve and two air crew coming February 28. Want community meeting. Over."

"Roger. Over."

This seemed to be going pretty well. "Will . . . o. . . ver. . .night. Over."

"Re. . .peat. O. . .ver."

I did and received the same "Re. . .peat. O. . .ver."

The operator came on. "You will have to spell each word. A for Alpha, C for Charlie, D for Delta, and so on. I did so and silence ensued. I wondered if the line had been disconnected but I eventually got a reply of "Ro. . .ger . . . O. . .ver."

I then transmitted my name and ended by saying, "Over and out!" I was to become quite proficient at using the phonetic alphabet.

The process took great patience. Some calls were easy, others excruciatingly difficult but I enjoyed the challenge and the experience. I was in the thick of the action doing work with meaning and purpose. This was life on the frontier.

On the morning of the second day, Hodgson startled me, sticking his head into my cubicle and asking for an update.

"Some of the area administrators don't think you should risk touring the Arctic at this time of year."

Hodgson grinned. "Ten months of the year it's winter, so now's the best time to see what their problems are."

"They say it's dangerous."

Hodgson looked me square in the eye. "This is important, and I won't be put off."

"Yes sir. It's not me. I want you to know what some are saying."

"We don't have the luxury of travelling the North on the timeframe of the area administrators. They'll try to put us off because we'll be a pain to them."

My phone rang, interrupting our conversation. "Operator?" I yelled as I battered the button on top of the telephone. My feet bobbed up and down. "I don't believe it, I've been cut off again! It's as hard to get the Hay River operator as it is to reach Igloolik."

Hodgson nodded consolingly and said I was doing a great job. "They may try to talk you into having me delay this trip but you and I both know we have to do this."

I smiled appreciatively, my annoyance evaporating. This job was teaching me patience and determination. Once again I picked up the phone and dialed the operator, launching into my routine with the exaggerated clarity of an orator. I transmitted my message in as few words as possible and ended with "mark airstrip for pilot." I checked Pond Inlet off my list. They knew we were coming, even if there had been no chance to ask about food and accommodation.

Hodgson had instructed me to follow up each phone call with a letter but, as most of these communities got mail once or twice a year by sealift or the occasional charter aircraft, it seemed an exercise in futility. Regardless, I confirmed each phone call with a letter and discovered there was method to Hodgson's madness. Months later he asked me to contact postal officials to complain about poor mail service throughout Canada's Arctic using those letters as proof.

My attention was diverted by a fellow in his early forties, sporting a bushy beard and a huge wolfskin parka, swaggering down the hall. He stopped at my cubicle. "Can I help you?" I asked.

"Who are you?" he said.

"I know who I am, but who are you?" I answered.

"Daryl Brown. I'm the pilot who's going to take Hodgson on this hare-brained jaunt around the Arctic."

"Jake Ootes. I'm arranging the tour."

"Maybe I can talk the silly bugger out of the whole idea," he said. *Great, a cantankerous pilot.* We stared at each other.

"Well, I'll tell you that the Commissioner is quite a determined person. This trip is an important part of preparation for the takeover of the Eastern and High Arctic next year."

I escorted Brown to Hodgson's office, where the Commissioner led us into the boardroom.

"We're using Wardair's new Twin Otter, right?" Hodgson asked. Wardair had the first Twin Otter certified for northern use. It had already proven itself a powerful and reliable aircraft and its short takeoff and landing capability made it ideal for remote and northern areas. Brown nodded.

"With skis?" Hodgson asked.

"We'll use balloon tires," Brown replied and then pointed out that this was the wrong time of year to be going. "No one's done such a jaunt before. You're taking your life in your hands. We could get lost in a whiteout or freeze to death just walking from the plane to the community."

Hodgson glared at him.

"And my base manager, Fred Dornan, told me himself that finding fuel up in the communities will be a bitch. Finding accommodation for everyone will be really tough. And God knows if there'll be anything to eat."

"Well, you tell your boss we'll take care of the accommodations and food. We'll eat whatever is offered. It'll be your job to get us there and get the fuel. If you have to dig it out of snowbanks, then damn well dig it!"

"There are no airstrips in these places. We'll have to land on the sea ice or some esker or flat spot near the community," Brown continued. Hodgson ignored him and, turning to me, asked how far I had gotten with my part of the project.

"I've reached eight communities. Some meals might be thin and accommodations a little rough. Some I don't know."

"Ha!" Brown said. "You won't be so cheerful after two weeks of chewing *muktuk* and seal meat. Better take your own teapot too. Theirs are full of caribou hair and stuff!"

"You just do the flying." Hodgson turned back to me, throwing out instructions. "Bring a frozen turkey for each administrator. And get a whole bunch of those miniature liquor bottles. We'll give some to the administrators and community priests. Keep a few for ourselves!"

"The liquor store is all out," I said.

"We run the liquor system. Phone them up. Tell 'em I want them."

I handed the itinerary and passenger list to Brown. "We'll be gone for at least two weeks and visit about fifteen communities," I said.

"Twelve people! You know you'll be crowded."

"We were told the plane could carry fifteen."

"That's not counting the turkeys, sleeping bags and luggage you're going to cram in. And the miniature booze bottles."

"Don't worry. There'll only be nine to begin with," Hodgson said. "We're picking up three more in Resolute. These people are all very important. I've invited a photographer, some newspaper people and a reporter with the CBC."

Brown frowned. "I'm telling you this ain't going to be a pleasure jaunt. We'll be flying for hours and hours on end, through the middle of nowhere. And there's no toilet on board. I piss in a little bottle I keep in the cockpit. What are all these women going to do?"

Hodgson didn't flinch. "Get used to it! I'm going to visit every community in the North at least once a year. No one's going to help northern people take control of their own lives if I don't go out there. John Parker and Clarence Gilchrist can take care of the administration here." He poked his index finger in Brown's direction. "You don't have to fly us if you don't want to. I'm sure Wardair can find another pilot. But despite your asshole attitude, I've checked you out and everyone in the business says you're the best."

The two glared at each other in a brief, angry tussle of wills.

I waited for Brown to rise and walk out. Instead, he glared back at Hodgson and said, "You'd never make it without me. Some other asshole would probably get you killed. Then we'd have to go out and find a new Commissioner. Start all over again."

Hodgson smiled.

10

THE TOP OF THE WORLD

THE ARCTIC DESERT STRETCHES FOR almost a million square miles across the top of Canada, sweeping in an immense diagonal curve from the Mackenzie Delta in the west to within a few miles of Churchill, on the Hudson Bay coast, then across to Arctic Québec.

Six hundred miles north of the Arctic Circle we were still not there. The day before we had flown four hours north from Yellowknife, overnighted at the Distant Early Warning (DEW) line facilities at Cambridge Bay on Victoria Island, then flown four hours straight north to Resolute where we refuelled. Now destined for Grise Fiord on Ellesmere Island, we were as close to Moscow as to Ottawa.

"We'll end up with saddle sores before this trip is over," said Ed Cowan, Canadian correspondent for *The New York Times*. The seats in the Twin Otter were nothing more than steel tubing that supported imitation leather seats and backs. Each was hinged so the back and the legs could be folded down and the whole thing pinned up against the cabin wall to make room for freight. Five single seats ran down the left side and five double seats down the right side of the cabin, a tight fit with little leg room. A small compartment at the back accommodated our luggage and fifteen frozen turkeys. Heat from the engines was pumped through a distribution system that had people at the front roasting while those further back froze. I prayed I wouldn't need a bathroom for the next several hours.

The cockpit door was open. We could see Daryl Brown and his co-pilot, Bill Monaghan, who, rumour had it, was an heir to the Otis elevator fortune. Seated in the front two seats of the aircraft were Pat Carney, business columnist for *The Vancouver Sun* and Syd Thompson, a former colleague of Hodgson's and president of the Vancouver local of the IWA. Air Marshal Campbell and Kay Vaydik, a news reporter for the CBC in Yellowknife, were seated behind them. Walter Petrigo, a Calgary-based photographer for *Time* magazine was in the next seat, the one in front of Ed Cowan and me. Down the side aisle were our secretary, Mary-Ellen Davies, seconded from another department to record the meetings, and Hodgson. We would be joined by three more people when we returned to Resolute .

As trip organizer, I looked after accommodations, meals, luggage transfers and scheduling. I was also to record as much community data as possible including population, names of community leaders, local problems and the number of houses. Menial tasks perhaps, but in my eyes this trip was the dream of a lifetime. What young Canadian would ever experience this fantastic journey to this unique part of Canada with these amazing people?

We flew through a colourless, eggshell sky at two hundred miles per hour, ten thousand feet above sea level. The Twin Otter could easily have flown much higher but lacked pressurization and oxygen for the passengers. The pallid shadow of the plane crossed frozen straits and fjords, jumped over the cliffs and spires of the ancient islands below. The snow-covered islands and icebound channels bore no resemblance to the scrubby fir and muskeg of the Yellowknife area. Land and sea were fused in frozen immobility. "Looks like the bloody moon," Cowan muttered.

The chatter in the cabin subsided as the Twin Otter banked. We had crossed Jones Sound, an icebound channel of the Arctic Ocean between Devon Island and its northern neighbour, Ellesmere Island. On the battered and jagged southern coast of Ellesmere lay Grise Fiord, the most northern inhabited community in the world, and one of the coldest, with average daily temperatures of only 2°F. The plane, tiny against the unmoving majesty of the ice below, dropped until we could see ripples and gorges where unseen tides chafed sea ice against the island's shores. Huge pressure ridges in the ice reared up like battlements along the shore; the southern ramparts soared three thousand feet above the strait. Cradled below was a meagre crescent of flattish beach that was home to about ninety people. It was not yet noon, but the day seemed to be caught in a lingering opalescent half-light, augmented by a few electric lights glowing inside small houses.

In this polar desert, the sea ice shone white, with hues of the purest blue emerging from beneath the surface. "That's beautiful!" Cowan said, breaking the spell. "And so tiny! I was expecting more houses, a church, some large building. Something more."

I was enthralled by the view. "These people roam the arctic sea ice like the Bedouin roam the deserts."

The plane turned away from the settlement and continued to lose altitude. About a mile out from the shore, I spotted a bunch of red fuel drums which marked what the locals considered to be the most favourable landing spot.

Brown pushed the stick down for a landing then suddenly cursed loudly enough for everyone to hear. We surged forward with a roar of the turboprops and climbed again. One of Monaghan's shoulders rose in a shrug, and then I was able to see Brown's predicament. The homemade runway was choked with milling, waving Eskimos waiting to welcome us.

Brown began a new approach. I held my breath as the plane decelerated. Our shadow fell closer and closer to the cracked ice until finally we were down, bumping along what must have been the only smooth patch of ice in the entire sound. Brown brought the plane to a stop and, in unison with my cabinmates, I exhaled a sigh of relief.

THERE WAS COMPLETE SILENCE AS the door of the plane opened and frigid air filled the cabin. I thought of Pat Carney, who wore a fashionable blue leather pantsuit that would provide little insulation against the piercing wind and cold. But Carney was an experienced northern traveller and I suspected her suitcase was packed with arctic clothing—parka, wind pants, fur mitts— into which she would change at the earliest opportunity.

Hodgson bounded out of the aircraft, his already large frame bloated by a parka, fur mitts, wool hat and fur boots. He snapped his parka hood onto his head, grinned with pleasure and towered over about fifty animated Eskimos milling around the aircraft steps.

The older men were dressed in caribou skin clothing, knitted hats, fur mitts and sealskin boots called *kamiks*. The younger men wore jeans and duffle parkas like ours. The women's parkas were similar to those of the younger men, with an additional A-framed covering that formed a sack on their back. A baby peered out from one woman's back, as ready as a young seal pup to survive in a harsh land.

Each resident stepped up and shook the hand of this big stranger. Hodgson was in his element, chatting and smiling. His enthusiasm and statesmanship were infectious and we all joined in, one glove off to greet these people.

Unlike the casual motion to which I was accustomed, the Eskimos shook hands efficiently, lifting up once and pressing down once, appropriate in this harsh climate. Their smiles and gestures radiated friendliness.

Their language was rhythmic and multisyllabic. "*Tunngasugit. Nunaptinni. Qujannamiik tikinnavit*," or "Welcome to our community. Thank you for coming." On and on the words flowed.

I snapped two photographs, the cold metal stinging my fingers. I unzipped my parka and slipped the camera next to my body to keep the mechanism from seizing and the film from breaking.

One fellow stepped up and, with a New Zealand accent, introduced himself as Maurice Cloughley, the schoolteacher and part-time area administrator. "Visitors are a rarity, especially this time of year. We're just out of the dark season," he said.

I asked Cloughley if he had been able to make out my telephone request for a community meeting.

"All set to go. First we will have lunch at my house." Accommodation wasn't a concern since we were scheduled to spend the night at Resolute , the nearest community to Grise Fiord, but still some 250 miles distant.

When the formalities of welcoming us came to a close, one of the Eskimos walked to a long wooden sled I later learned was called a *komatik*. Traditionally made of bone tied together with pieces of leather or rawhide, this one had runners made from heavy piece of lumber and a frame of wooden crosspieces tied together with nylon rope. Snowmobiles, increasingly common in larger communities, were still beyond the reach of the residents of Grise Fiord, and the komatik remained the only available mode of transport.

A pack of frisky dogs at the head of the komatik lunged and yelped, anxious to be off, stretching the fan hitch that allowed the lead dog to run out front while the troublemakers stayed back within easier reach of the driver's whip. Our host indicated that Hodgson should get on.

"Let the ladies ride! We'll walk," Hodgson said.

Pat Carney, Mary-Ellen Davies and Kay Vaydik were bundled onto the sled beneath layers of caribou hides, and the komatik took off in a swirl of powdered snow. I zipped my parka up to my chin and tightened my hood. I'd never been as cold as I was when we walked the one mile to the community. I was convinced that frostbite had started to rot my face; it felt as if someone were rubbing it with rough sandpaper. My toes went numb as the snow squealed and cracked under our boots. The air seared my nostrils, the smell of the cold distinctive, as our breath created plumes of mist. We looked like walking chimneys. This had to be the most physically intimidating environment in the world.

As villagers and visitors moved toward the tiny community, someone spotted movement near the hills. *"Umingmak! Umingmak!"* A herd of muskox bounded across the rocky uplands, their woolly fringes flying at their sides like heraldic blankets on the warhorses of old. Smaller than buffalo, muskox stand about four feet high, are four to six feet long, and weigh approximately six hundred pounds. Closely related to sheep and goats, the muskox resembles a small woolly mammoth with bulky black, grey and brown fur unevenly trimmed below the knee.

At the shoreline we picked our way between ridges and mounds of ice thrown up in careless palisades along the beach. These eerie mounds kept a supernatural watch over us as we approached the community of Grise Fiord—a dozen houses, a shed for the diesel generator that supplied electricity, a small rectangular box of a building for a community hall, a one-room school and a little white building with a sign that read, "Grise Fiord Co-op."

I dared not stop to take a photograph for fear of freezing solid on the spot. Instead, I quickened my pace and led the others toward the Co-op. Once inside, I huddled close to the oil-fuelled stove, catching my reflection in the window. I looked like Father Time, with frost covering my eyebrows and the fur on my hood pure white.

The store's inventory included several pairs of pants, a couple of shirts and a few tins of food. The rest of the shelves were bare. Stacked in the corner was a mound of dried, flat sealskins behind which rested a six-foot long gnarled narwhal tusk. I asked if it was for sale. *"Ayee,"* said the Eskimo, pointing to the $150 price tag. Lord knows how I expected to get it home in our jam-packed airplane, but I asked him to have someone take it out to the plane. "Ayee," he nodded.

When I took out my camera to photograph the inside of this little store, the warm air hit the cold glass and the lens fogged up instantly. After it had defrosted, I stepped outside and took several photographs of the community. A crescent of houses, referred to as matchboxes, straggled down to the silent, motionless sea ice. Designed by the National Research Centre in Ottawa, each matchbox was a rectangular box with a flat roof, a door, one window and no interior amenities. Many of them had steel tubs up on their roofs storing half-butchered seals out of the reach of sled dogs and other animals. Empty barrels, caribou carcasses and stretching frames with polar bear hides stood outside the houses. Wind-tousled sled dogs were tethered to posts.

Cloughley's house, while far from grand, was much larger than the matchboxes. We entered via the ground floor, a suspended basement with a furnace where we took off our coats and boots. Wafting down the staircase was the tantalizing aroma of roasting meat. Upstairs, the home had some of the comforts of the south including power, running water, nice china, prints on the walls and rugs on the floor.

In the sitting room, I took a seat by the picture window to observe the scene. Down on the beach, Daryl Brown, Bill Monaghan and some Eskimo men were digging aviation drums out of a snowbank, excavating the precious fuel that would ensure our departure. To my astonishment, a child rode a beaten-up bicycle down the snowy path, its tires removed to allow the rusted rims better traction on the ice and snow.

"What's the temperature out there?" I asked Maurice.

"Thirty-eight below . . . but there's an eight-mile-per-hour wind, so it will feel like about -50." How could these people survive in such a place?

Cloughley's wife, Katie, served us a meal of roast caribou, powdered mashed potatoes and canned peas that was one of the most welcome of my life. We ate with our plates on our laps, consuming the food with heartfelt appreciation.

Hodgson, sitting next to me in an easy chair, leaned nearer and muttered in a stage whisper, "Make sure we give Maurice one of those turkeys when we leave!"

Walter Petrigo set his plate down on the coffee table and walked over to look out the window. When he put his hand on the back of the sofa, about four inches from my head, a vicious electric spark jumped from his fingers to my shoulder. "Whoo!" I said, almost losing the plate off my lap. Maurice explained that the friction of leather shoes on the rug built up a static charge in the dry air. "Trash the leather shoes, Walter. You're a walking dynamo!"

"How do you get your supplies?" someone asked.

"Annual sealift. The federal government provides an annual food ration and an order form which lists all the canned, dried and packaged foods available. I check off what we'll need for the coming year. Then my order arrives by ship from Montreal, along with the goods for the co-op and whatever else the community needs. The rations have to do us for a full year until the next sealift. No possibility of going to the corner store here."

"That's if the ship can get through!" Katie shouted from the kitchen.

"Most of the time the ice is gone between mid-July and mid-August," said Maurice. "But the smallest delay can wreck the shipping schedule. One year the teacher here went a whole year without supplies. Luckily we can get caribou and seal meat from the hunters. But we never get any fruits, vegetables or salads."

We were silent, imagining life in this remote settlement.

"We're getting a fair bit of light now. In early November the sun disappears below the horizon and doesn't reappear until February. It's dark for three months straight. The only light is from the stars, the moon and the Northern Lights reflecting off the snow, if it's not overcast. It's some experience. Makes you realize you are literally on top of the world."

"How much snow do you get?" asked Kay Vaydik.

"The further north you go, the less precipitation. It only snows two or three times a year here though, of course, it's so cold the stuff never goes away."

"So how do people survive?" someone else asked.

"Off the land, mostly. They spend almost their entire lives hunting whales, walrus, seals and polar bear, sometimes roaming as far as Greenland. They hunt on the sea ice between Ellesmere Island and Greenland. There are no jobs as we know them, no money, little to buy and less to buy it with. Their lives revolve around finding enough to eat and enough skins to make clothing and shelter. They might make a few dollars selling a polar bear skin, and that buys a rifle with shells and some canned food."

"This has to be the most isolated place in the world," Kay Vaydik said. "What happens if someone breaks a leg when they're out hunting, or even in the settlement?"

"We have to charter an aircraft to medivac the person to Frobisher Bay, six hundred miles south. It's a dangerous life. They could be a hundred miles away by dog team, and there's no way of letting anyone know if they're in trouble."

Ed Cowan asked how the people had come to live on this lonely beach.

"The government moved a number of families from northern Québec both here and to Resolute in the early 1950s. There was a shortage of game in Port Harrison, and it was felt the game here was plentiful. It took six weeks on the government medical ship *C.D. Howe* and was a complete change of routine for the Québec Eskimos—they'd gone from eating fish, small game and tundra berries, with occasional food from a store, to depending on polar bear, walrus, whale and seal with no store with which to trade or buy goods. They were joined by three families recruited from Pond Inlet on Baffin Island, who it was believed could familiarize those from Port Harrison with the High Arctic environment. The original understanding was that if, after two years they were not satisfied, they could return to their homes at Port Harrison."

"Have any moved back? Who would handle that?" I asked.

"Good question. It's never been raised as an issue with me."

After lunch Hodgson rose from his chair and nodded for us to be on our way to the community hall, plainly anxious to get on with his job.

THE SKY HAD BEGUN TO recede into early afternoon twilight, casting a pallor on the mountains above the beach. Out on the sea ice, the Twin Otter was just a speck, a lonely gull resting on a comfortless perch. It was our life-line, without which we would be stranded in this small community.

The community hall was a flat-roofed, rectangular plywood box, twenty by thirty feet, furnished with rows of wooden benches facing a table at the front. An oil stove burned full tilt in the centre of the room. I stepped into the hall to the notes of a harmonium organ and was surprised to see Hodgson sitting at the old instrument, a foot-powered relic hauled in years before by some missionary, playing a wheezy version of "Lara's Theme," from the movie *Doctor Zhivago*. The lapels on his black suit flapped and his well-groomed hair came loose here and there. Wearing a suit on this trip wasn't practical, but it was his way of showing respect.

About sixty adults and kids arrived, perhaps the entire population of Grise Fiord. Cloughley had chuckled when I asked if anyone would come. "You are the biggest thing to ever happen in Grise Fiord and it's the first time anyone like Hodgson has come to hold a community meeting. Not that they really know who the Commissioner is, you understand."

There was a crescendo of excited noise as Hodgson moved to the table and motioned for Cloughley to join him. Cloughley rose, said a few words of welcome, explained who the Commissioner was and turned the meeting over to Hodgson, who spoke a few sentences before realizing that the Eskimos did not understand. He asked if someone could translate. One young man smiled, and Hodgson asked him to come to the front.

"I intend to visit Grise Fiord once a year. Today I want to hear what your problems are and to have the government, my new government, help." Without any expression on his face and no emotion in his voice, the young Eskimo translated Hodgson's opening statement into "*Ausuittungmunngauju-maqattaraluartunga arraagutamaa. Sunanik naammanngittunik nunapsinni tusarumagama.*" It was a fascinating language, soft and even, combining four or five ideas into one descriptive phrase instead of relying on the short words we use in English.

"How many of you know what government is?" Hodgson asked, and waited for the interpreter to translate. No one raised a hand. The Commissioner took a breath and said, "Government is something people use to make decisions about their community and their lives. In Canada there are three levels of government. One is the federal government that deals with problems affecting all of Canada. The second is the type of government that affects a province, or a territory like the Northwest Territories. The third is a type of government that affects a community like Grise Fiord."

"Ayee, ayee," came the reply after the translation, followed by much nodding.

"Today your community is run by Mr. Cloughley, who is the schoolteacher and also the part-time administrator. He makes most of the decisions." Again they all nodded and intoned "ayee."

"I want to bring changes to the settlements so the people make the decisions. Someday I want you, the people of Grise Fiord, to have more say in your own affairs. I don't want to build a government that depends on me. This land belongs to all of us as Northerners and, as Canadians, we must help each other. The people of the south paid to have this hall and your houses built here through their tax money. But you can make more decisions for yourself. That is called local government. Government is like a snowmobile, sometimes you pull the rope and it doesn't start. But you can't fix it unless you know how it works.

"When you feel ready, when you tell me you feel you could take on new responsibilities, I will be prepared to give them to you. Then, when I come to see you, instead of you asking me what I'm doing, I would ask you what you are doing. This simply means government by the people." His deep, smooth voice established trust. His eyes reached everyone.

Off to the side, an Eskimo sat at a small table, jotting down notes in syllabics, the 19th century writing system developed by missionaries. It was a simple system using easily remembered circular and triangular symbols, taught by rote in Sunday schools.

Hodgson spoke for half an hour after which he asked if there were questions. We all waited for some polite comments on Hodgson's words and his vision of local government. Finally a man stood. He was very dark-skinned, with a weathered, round face that gave no clue to his age. He fingered the identification tag that hung around his neck. The letter E and associated numbers indicated that he was an Eastern Arctic Eskimo. Many Eskimos, who traditionally used one name, had been assigned surnames during baptism that were frequently modified or misspelled by subsequent southern officials, resulting in widespread confusion. Disc numbers were introduced in the 1940s to locate members of this nomadic culture and make bookkeeping easier. Most questioners referred to themselves by their disc numbers.

The young man translated: "Some families have all boy children, others have all girls. It has been our custom to exchange children when they are eight or ten years old because each family needs boy children. The problem is the children then feel they have two sets of parents. What should we do?"

The basic problems of daily life were much more important than concerns about government. Hodgson's solution was to exchange children earlier, so they would grow up with just one set of parents. He told the community that he would ask the territorial judge to visit Grise Fiord and confirm these exchanges in law.

"We get a new movie only about once every six weeks when the airplane comes in, and it costs lots of money."

"How much?" asked Hodgson.

"Twenty-five dollars." Hodgson asked what kind of movies they liked. Westerns, the young translator explained, the people liked westerns from the '50s because, while they didn't understand the words, they could follow the storyline of good guy versus bad guy, bank robberies, train chases and the hero winning the woman.

"We watch the same movie every Friday and Saturday night for six weeks. We'd like to be able to get more movies."

Hodgson pointed to a startled Kay Vaydik and said she would head up a committee to solve the movie problem.

And so the meeting went on. Hodgson was tireless, listening attentively to every word, offering immediate solutions or committing to writing back with answers. He solved problems in minutes that federal bureaucrats had let fester for years and likely never knew existed. This one meeting illustrated how this gigantic portion of Canada was so poorly served by a federal government that had left it in isolation.

It wasn't all talk. Frequently there was silence between questions while the Eskimos chain-smoked. This penchant for quiet deliberation between comments and questions seemed to be their way. Smoke floated down from the ceiling as Hodgson patiently waited for the next person to rise.

"We would like telephone service. We can pay $3 a month."

"I have a question," said one man. "I've been paying taxes, but I've no idea what taxes is or what it's for. I'd like to know that."

"When will the big government pay us for our work?" asked another. "We were asked to fill bags with polar bear bones and send them to the Canadian Wildlife Service in Ottawa. We were promised $10 a bag. But we've never been paid."

Hodgson motioned me over and whispered, "Give me a $10 bill!"

He turned back to the man in the audience. "I'll pay you for one bag now," he said, handing the man the money. "Tell Jake here how much you are owed and the territorial government will pay you. The government in Ottawa can then pay the territorial government back."

My head reeled from keeping track of the concerns. I was pleased to see that Mary-Ellen had efficiently recorded all that was said in shorthand. On our return to Yellowknife, she would provide a transcribed record and I would prepare letters of demands and instructions to the departmental directors for Hodgson's signature.

Darkness enveloped the community and Daryl Brown whispered in my ear that we needed to leave for Resolute soon. "Why the rush?" I asked.

"The darkness," he replied.

"Can we take off in the dark?"

"Yes, no problem."

"And Resolute has a runway with lights?"

"Yes," he said.

"Then we are staying until the Commissioner is ready to leave."

The people of Grise Fiord wanted to raise issues in their own time and deserved the Commissioner's attention, no matter how long it would take. They had concerns, problems to be solved, and every right to demand better treatment. As the one man said, he paid taxes but did not know what they were for. Here was the perfect example of why Prime Minister Pearson picked this deceptively untutored unionist to forge a future for the North. Hodgson cared.

When the meeting was over and we were back on the plane, Hodgson said, "These meetings are their meetings and if they want to meet all night, so be it! I am not going to cut them short. Ottawa barely knows these people exist. The danger is that our people in Yellowknife will become just as apathetic. I have to get these people started on the road to self-government. That way they'll have more control over their own fate and be able to speak for themselves. The North we see today will be completely changed ten years from now. These people will experience changes they never dreamed of."

Hodgson was silent for some time, then said, "Now you see why you and I are going to be on the road a lot over the next few years. We'll get to know the Arctic like the back of our hands, Jake! Nobody, I mean nobody, will be able to talk about something or someone in a community that I don't know about."

AS THE NORTHWEST TERRITORIES ACT required one meeting of the Territorial Council be held each year somewhere in the Northwest Territories, I had visited Resolute in 1965 as Editor of Debates. During my two-week stint there, I had published *Arctic Antics*, a daily news-sheet with a masthead that read, "The only newspaper on top of the world," appropriate as we were only sixty miles from the Magnetic North Pole. My columnists then were several experienced journalists: Ralph Armstrong of the *Edmonton Journal*, Jonah Kelly of CBC Frobisher Bay and Barry Kelsey of CBC Yellowknife.

Resolute had changed since my previous visit. Just as Yellowknife had become the centre of government for the Northwest Territories, so Resolute had become the hub of extensive oil and gas exploration in the High Arctic, the only community with regularly scheduled flight service from the south. From our plane it looked like a cold but busy place with an untidy clutter of oil storage tanks, drilling equipment, metal shacks and various types of small aircraft spreading out from the nucleus of the airstrip.

Resolute had its beginnings in 1947 when Canada and the United States built a joint weather station and airstrip. This was followed by a Royal Canadian Air Force base made up of military personnel and meteorologists. In 1953, Resolute, like Grise Fiord, became a relocation spot for families from northern Québec and Pond Inlet. The Eskimo community now numbered 119 people and was located three miles from the airfield, with a rudimentary road connecting the two. While the Eskimos were allowed on the base and could use its facilities, including the Arctic Circle Club, a federal government policy of non-fraternization prohibited base personnel from visiting the Eskimo community.

Upon arrival our luggage was looked after by base personnel who directed us to a bright orange complex, a series of interconnected corridors resembling a giant octopus. Snow, bulldozed off the roadway, was piled seven feet high up the side walls. The complex included dormitories with sleeping rooms, washrooms, a cafeteria, offices and a bar. Many permanent residents didn't leave it for months on end. After room assignments, we gathered in the cafeteria for a dinner of steak and fish with all the trimmings, as well as fresh produce—an incredible luxury on the Arctic frontier.

Hodgson asked what I thought of the meeting today.

"I think you're the first to extend them the courtesy of a community meeting, to ask what they need and what their problems are. I doubt if any federal official of significance has ever been there, let alone asked what they need. They have nothing. No phone service. No radio. A movie they show over and over. No scheduled air service. Nothing. It was a real eye-opener, especially when you hear people refer to themselves by disc numbers."

Hodgson nodded in agreement. Looking at his watch, he left for the airstrip to await the arrival of the scheduled Nordair flight from Frobisher Bay. He was to meet Jean Fournier, special assistant to Jean Chrétien, along with Simonie Michael of the Territorial Council and Dennis Decker, the regional engineer from Frobisher Bay, who would join us on the tour.

In his bass voice, Syd Thompson announced, "I'm going to lie down for a while. Have my wits about me for this Arctic Circle Club." The rest of us proceeded to the bar.

The Arctic Circle Club was located at the far end of the complex. In the hallway outside the entrance several young Eskimo children hung about waiting for a parent to take them home. Inside the place was jammed, noisy and smoke-filled. The only women, beside those in our party, were Eskimo. One was quite drunk and staggered toward the bar where one of the white guys put his arm around her shoulder. Several other Eskimo men and women were seated at various tables.

A waiter came over and said that those of us crossing the Arctic Circle for the first time needed to be properly inducted into the Arctic Circle Club. "Weldy? Come give me a hand!" waving over a bearded fellow by the bar. Weldy Phipps was the owner of Atlas Aviation and was reputed to be the hardest living, highest flying, most ingenious and just plain toughest pilot in the whole Arctic. The call sign on his Twin Otter aircraft was WWP (Whisky Whisky Pappa); "The Alcoholic Twin Otter" was painted on the door.

The waiter left and came back with a mop and a bone about a foot and a half long and an inch and a half in diameter. The audience, realizing what was about to take place, became quiet. The waiter sat himself on a chair in the centre of the room, arranged the mop on his head and brandished the bone like a sceptre.

"What is your wish, O King?" Weldy intoned. "Who should we initiate first?"

"That one!" roared the King, pointing his sceptre at Mary-Ellen.

Poor Mary-Ellen turned white and squirmed as Weldy pulled her from her chair. She was made to kneel before the King, where Weldy fitted her with a blindfold.

The King intoned some regal mumbo-jumbo while Weldy stepped to the bar, returning with a pan of crushed ice with some grapes thrown in. The room was very quiet now.

"First," the king announced, "She who presumes to enter our kingdom must eat ice worms and seal eyes."

Mary-Ellen fished around in the ice box with her fingers. Finally she grasped one of the grapes and brought it to her lips, but wouldn't eat it. The king roared threats and curses until she finally put the grape in her mouth, only to spit it out directly onto his shirt. The audience roared with laughter.

"The second test!" shouted the king. "Our presumptuous adventurer must kiss the royal *oosik*!" He held high the oosik, his sceptre.

"What's an oosik?" chorused about a dozen people.

"Walrus penis!" roared the king.

Mary-Ellen's final indignity was drinking from a bottle of rum that the king maintained was well-laced with saltpetre, alleged to curb sexual desire.

"Welcome to the Arctic Kingdom!" shouted the theatrical waiter, as he removed Mary-Ellen's blindfold. And as if on cue, the crowd chorused, "Welcome to the Arctic Circle Club."

"Who do you think should be next, brave lady?"

They inducted two more of our party while I pressed back in my seat, hoping the revellers would run out of grapes and rum before they could pick on me. I was glad Syd Thompson was not there. He would probably have put a couple of kinks in the royal oosik if they tried anything with him. After the inductions our group huddled closer together, to laugh about the event and to ward off the unfamiliar that surrounded us. We were becoming a family.

The jukebox blared and the din made it difficult to hear. Every conversation was a shouting match. An Eskimo man, his round face puffed up with drink and anger, tripped on Kay Vaydik's chair, hitting the floor with a slurred curse and an almighty thud. I sat there, too stunned and stupefied to do anything. Other than those at our table, no one in the smoke-filled room seemed to care as the man rose to his knees, raised himself and then staggered out the door, almost paralyzed by alcohol.

The incident cast a pall across our table. "Not quite the pristine glory of Grise Fiord, is it?" someone commented.

When Syd Thompson finally joined us, I shuffled my chair to one side so he could take the seat between me and the Air Marshal. While they shared qualities as leaders, they were from the opposite side of the social fence—the union organizer peered out from under his craggy eyebrows, took one look at the immaculately attired Air Marshal, and made for another seat on the far side of the table.

"What time are we to leave in the morning?" Daryl Brown growled.

"Seven," I announced.

I heard Mary-Ellen ask Brown about the rule of not drinking before flying.

"Bullshit!" said Daryl.

Just then Hodgson, his moustache still bearing flecks of frost, breezed into the room with Simonie Michael, Dennis Decker and Jean Fournier. We hauled more chairs around the tables while Hodgson introduced his guests.

Fournier, a young chap with dark hair and dark eyebrows, gave a thin smile and a nod, showing himself much too polite to upbraid Hodgson for his miserable French pronunciation. Fournier had an intelligent look and a quiet, reserved manner that suggested he'd been sent north to observe, not interfere.

"And this is Simonie Michael, member of the Northwest Territories Council for the Eastern Arctic." Michael nodded in an unassuming manner. Ironically, it had been he who had successfully argued that barring Eskimos from the Arctic Circle Club was discriminatory, leading to the consequences we had just witnessed. I concluded that the federal government had once again neglected its northern citizens by failing to address alcohol issues. Hodgson had already established the position of Alcohol Education Officer and appointed a capable educator by the name of Harold Huggins. I made a mental note to advise Huggins of the situation here.

Pat Carney complimented Hodgson on inviting Fournier along on the trip.

"It's a whole new bunch in Ottawa," Hodgson replied. "I have no idea what agenda they have for the North, what plan. With Jean along I will have an opportunity to chat with him about our needs."

Syd Thompson, showing his contempt for any who would lord it over the working stiff said, "They likely have a plan to cream royalty revenues off the energy and mining companies up here, and that's as far as it goes. They don't plan to hand that money directly over to you. On that you can bet all your polar bear hides."

I started to relax, my mind wandering until I heard Walter Petrigo say something about "false hope." He was questioning the value of Hodgson "playing Santa Claus" for northern communities, walking in and providing adoption plans and the like.

Hodgson's manner changed as he lowered his brows and fixed Petrigo with a powerful stare. "Nothing personal, Walter. But don't tell me I can't solve these people's problems," he said in a rigid, controlled voice. "If I can't give them a radio phone for hunting trips, who can? They can't afford one. If I can't do these things, how will they ever have faith in the power of our kind of government? I'm 'playing Santa Claus?' Well, you can call it whatever you want, I'm here to get results any way I can!" I had some sympathy for Petrigo's position, but also understood Hodgson's approach. He didn't brook any naysayers.

I stood up and asked who'd like another round. With no formal duties to perform this evening, Hodgson allowed himself one alcoholic drink, his favourite gin and tonic, instead of his standard ginger ale. Upon my return from the bar, the conversation had changed. Hodgson stirred his drink and smiled, flooding the group with his customary good humour and confidence while recounting the story of the HMS *Resolute*, one of the ships sent to search for the Franklin expedition. For some reason the ship was abandoned and drifted out into Davis Strait. The following year, the ship was picked up by a United States whaler and, after repairs, the Americans returned her to Britain. One hundred years later Britain used some of her timbers to make a gigantic desk which was presented to President John F. Kennedy. "The desk is now in the Oval Office of the White House," said Hodgson, pleased as punch with this tidbit of history. "Speaking of ships, did you know that one of my titles is Admiral of the Fleet of the Northwest Territories?"

Thompson snorted, "Stu. Heh! Heh! You may well have the title, but no fleet!"

THE CENTRAL HEATING SYSTEM IN the room I shared with Walter Petrigo ran continuously. There was no thermostat and I would have given anything to open the window. Unfortunately, snow packed against the building made that impossible.

Petrigo grumbled about the early hour we would have to rise. "This is like boot camp, an endurance test." To cheer him up, I told him that Hodgson had arranged for the Air Marshal to bunk with Syd Thompson.

My skin felt dry and scaly in the heat. Static electricity jumped from the hairs on my legs to the sheet, a virtual lightning storm. There was no way to get any rest, let alone sleep. Walter threw the covers off his bunk. I rolled from side to side, utterly incapable of being comfortable . . . "Damn it!" I said in frustration, jumping out of bed and turning on the light. Somehow, I was going deal with that window.

"That snowdrift goes right to the roof," said Walter.

I snarled, stomped to the closet, dressed and snapped off the light. Outside,

I grabbed a snow shovel, trudged around the building and attacked the drift blocking the window. It was bitterly cold but shovelling kept me warm. An hour later I finished and trudged back inside.

"Where the hell have you been?" Petrigo said.

"Where the hell do you think?" I pulled back the curtain. The snowdrift was still there.

11

HE'S A WORKHORSE

MARCH 8, 1969

AT SEVEN A.M. OUR PARTY straggled out of the searing heat of the Department of Transport complex into the ripping, tearing cold, shielding our faces from the wind. Pat Carney had discarded her leather pantsuit and, like the rest of us, was now swaddled in wind pants, a parka, fur hat, mitts and thick boots. I was dog-tired from lack of sleep and my lips were starting to crack, the consequence of repeatedly licking them during my midnight foray.

Inside the Twin Otter I stomped my feet and wriggled in my seat to get warm. No one spoke until the engines sang to life and warm air filtered through the cabin. Then I heard Syd Thompson's voice boom from three seats behind me. "Some silly bugger shovelled snow outside our window last night. I was going to get up and tell him to bugger off until I realized we'd be able to get some air. Me and the Air Cadet slept like newborn babies!"

The Air Marshal, seated with me in the front row, didn't say anything about his demotion. Petrigo, across the aisle, chuckled. I gritted my teeth, muttering, "Walter, you say anything, I'll kill you."

Daryl Brown and Bill Monaghan taxied the Twin Otter onto the runway, gave the engines full throttle and pulled us up into the dark sky. Pat Carney crossed her fingers for luck.

Daryl had his parka hood pulled over his head and was sucking on a tube connected to the instrument panel labelled 'oxygen.' He had yet to say anything. When I leaned forward and tapped him on the shoulder his hood slipped down, revealing a head as bald and as smooth as a bowling ball.

My laughter caught the attention of the others who promptly joined in. "What the hell happened?"

"We were pissed as snakes, all these other pilots and me. They bet me fifty bucks I wouldn't get my hair shaved off. Seemed like a good idea at the time."

Hodgson was taking a nap in the rear. His wool hat, like a crown with appliqués on the outer band, was pulled askew over his head. I looked at his baggy eyelids and full jowls and noticed the first sprinkle of grey in his moustache. Just how long could his blissful, infectious enthusiasm possibly last?

As the darkness softened, we watched weak slivers of light create shadows on the jagged ice and rock below. I turned to Air Marshal Campbell and, over the drone of the engines, acknowledged that I had never dreamed places like Grise Fiord existed. "People live utterly isolated from the rest of the world."

He nodded, losing some of his formal military bearing. It seemed to be one of the hallmarks of northern life that people thrown into common adversity relaxed social and other barriers.

"I'm surprised by all these ordinary problems, like hauling heating oil to their homes in forty-five-gallon drums. These people have never had someone to help them with their simplest needs. How frustrating it must be to have no store and no airstrip."

"Stu is dishing out what these people need and want, but he's also teaching them about how to take their destiny into their own hands," said Campbell. "I know he's right when he says that in a few years they will be able to take control of their own communities."

The Air Marshal caught me staring at Fournier who sat with his face turned to the window, his head smothered in his hood. "He's not very old," I said.

"Neither is his boss. Chrétien is only thirty-five, and already a parliamentary veteran. Rumour has it that when he was appointed to Northern Affairs he waded into the middle of departmental chaos and said 'I'm the boss.' He didn't know what he was doing and didn't have a plan for the North, but he was the boss.

"Chrétien's a lot like Stu. While Stu spent his early years in a union that had to fight for everything it got, Chrétien comes from a province that feels it's been deprived. Stu invited Fournier so he can forge a relationship with Chrétien, build his power base. It's a good strategy."

Campbell's words made me realize the power base I was lucky enough to have in Hodgson. The Air Marshal was both wise and practical. No wonder Hodgson had such high regard for his advice.

Pat Carney walked towards the cockpit and leaned inside. Half a minute later she yelled, "You asshole!" and turned back into the passenger cabin, red-faced and hopping mad.

I leaned into the cockpit, and asked Brown what he had said to annoy her. He chuckled. "She asked about our location. I said I didn't know and I meant it. Then she wants to see the map, and I tell her I don't have one. She didn't believe me, so I pulled out this old National Geographic world map."

"So how do you know where we are?"

"It's not an exact science. We're too close to the magnetic pole for the compass to work." Brown tapped the instrument panel. "The needle tips towards it, then starts spinning. The gyrocompass processes at fifteen degrees an hour, see. Well, you might forget the time you left whatever community you were in, so you take a rough guess. That way you get a feel whether you're too far east or too far west, or you have a sense that there ought to be a river or a bunch of streams below. You can go for hours and not know just exactly where you are, but you have an idea of what time each landmark should pass by."

The furrows on my brow told him I was confused.

"The best way to navigate up here is . . . look, suppose you're leaving Yellowknife, you follow a line on the map, you get the gyro and the solar compass set, you get the wind drift calculated and then when you hit the Barrens you know you're on the right track. So you just go straight out from the treeline until you hit your target. Up here we have no radar, no control towers and no navigational aids."

"So how do you fly at night, when you can't see landmarks?"

"Well, you have the stars and moon to go by. You have to be inventive. It may be -30 and the cockpit windows are frosted over, so you just sit there and scrape the glass a little every once in a while and take a peek at the sky."

"And on that theory you are flying us all over the Arctic in the dead of winter?"

Daryl feigned indignation. "I always get my passengers to their destination. I only crashed once. I was flying an old Buffalo freighter down to Edmonton for an overhaul, and the engines just wouldn't run right. She quit on me just north of the city, so down I go. I couldn't see anything! When she stopped rolling I cracked open the hatch and discovered I'd ploughed through a slough and the whole plane was covered with green shit. I fell out into a great big puddle of the stuff and then walked to a farmhouse to use the phone. The farmer took one look at me in my goggles and flying helmet, all covered in green shit, and thought for sure the Martians had landed!"

I laughed and moved to the back to take a seat beside Syd Thompson. He growled, "So I saw you talking with the Air Cadet a while ago. What did he tell you? Heh! Heh!" His deep, rumbling voice was audible to everyone on the plane, but he didn't care.

"Wants to know what you're doing on this trip."

"I don't know much about the Arctic. Certainly knew it was damned cold!"

"He wants to pick your brain," I said, pointing at Hodgson. "He thinks you can cut through the crap and see what's at the heart of our problems."

Ed Cowan turned from the seat ahead and joined our conversation, notebook in hand. "You probably know him better than anyone here."

"Stu and I go way back together. We've survived a hell of a lot. The thing I remember most is going to his house in Vancouver. There was always a phone hanging out his ear, always working and bullshitting with someone. I mean it never ceased. And he's the kind that can get into all kinds of mental skullduggery too—how to do this and how to do that. It's the way his mind operates."

Cowan said, "I've asked about his time in the union, but I don't know if he's spinning me a line or what."

"Well, I wasn't there right in the beginning, not in Vancouver," Syd continued. "But I heard enough about him. Stu was in the navy during the war. After that he wound up at the MacMillan Bloedel plywood mill, the biggest in the world at that time. It employed 1,100 people and was a real good base for the labour movement, accounting for a fifth of the membership. That's where Stu became active in the union. Anyway, about a year later he was elected to the publicity committee of Local 217 of the IWA. He's always been real keen on publicity. You boys have likely noticed that. Heh! Heh! Then he quit the union."

That was news to me.

"There was a strike so he took his car with three friends to picket a meeting of the boss loggers at the Banff Springs Hotel in the Rockies. They went via Washington State, where a drunk pulled out of an intersection and smashed into Stu's car. The cops threw the Canadians in jail for the night and let the drunk go! The next day, Stu and his gang patched up the car with union placards and headed for Banff. When they got there, the Mounties gave them thirty seconds to get out of town, and when they got back to Vancouver the union refused to pay for the repairs to Stu's car. So he quit."

Cowan scribbled in his notebook.

"Stu was a popular guy, though. Heh! Heh! He was sitting in a bar in Vancouver one day when the union fellows came to plead with him to come back to help take the union back from the communists. By early '48, he'd beaten a bunch of other workers in the election for plant chairman."

"Communists?" asked a perplexed Cowan.

"Yeah. The communists were real active among the unemployed before the war. The unions grew by leaps and bounds during the war, and communism was a fairly popular movement, with Russia being an ally. But after the war the whole climate changed, and people realized communists were in a position of leadership that was way out of proportion with their numbers. The international union wanted to clear 'em out and 1948 was the year of revolution. But the communists had taken over at district level— they moved the bank account to another bank and changed the union's name. Moved out lock, stock and barrel. The only thing they forgot to take was the membership. They marched without an army!"

"So what did the union members do about it?" I asked.

"They waited to be persuaded to support their union and not take off with the communists. That's where Stu came into his own, meeting men on the shop floor, in the lunchrooms, by the factory gates, making speeches and haranguing them so they'd know which side they were fighting on. He was a master. Still is. No fancy words, just plain talk that everyone understood, straight from the heart. It wasn't all talk, mind you. There were some fistfights."

"What happened?" I asked.

"Well, in early '49 Stu was elected financial secretary of Local 217, which got him off the shop floor and into his first full-time paid union position. Oddly, things got tougher for him after that. He had this natural ability, but he wasn't experienced or educated, if you know what I mean. He was suddenly a union official who knew less than the veterans around him, and there was lots of feuding and fighting going on. He couldn't even write a letter. Had to get Pearl to train him how to do it.

"Anyway, I came on the scene in '54. I got work at the Weldwood mill and stepped into the shoes of the outgoing plant chairman right away. By '57 I was third vice-president of the local and that's when I got to know Stu. Before you know it, there were conflicts between me and Whalen, the local president. He was getting terrible wage settlements for us. We had inflation back then too, you know, and some years we got no pay increase at all. I decided I'd run for first vice-president and become business agent, see if I could get us some better settlements. Whalen didn't agree with me doing that and started playing politics to make life difficult."

Syd stretched back, enjoying himself. Cowan was lapping it up along with Carney and Vaydik who were now also listening.

"It became a really vicious fight. When I ran for first vice, I was slaughtered. The writing was on the wall. I had to take these guys on or my days were numbered. I sweated it out for a while and then decided I'd run for president at the next election and take Whalen's job. One day, Stu came to my house. He said he was expected to back Whalen, but Whalen might lose and that wouldn't do his own plans any good. I spent an hour and a half with him and realized I needed him on my side. He said he would support me, but not publicly. It was the key to success, let me tell you."

"How do you mean?" Kay Vaydik asked.

"Well, for instance, Stu called me up one night. He told me that Whalen breaks out in cold sores whenever he's in trouble, and right now he's covered in 'em!" Syd nodded his head. "I became local president and Stu became one of the most capable operators in the union. He knew how to work with people, how far he could push them. He's got that sixth sense you've got to have in politics. He can smell how things are going to go. It's really important. Otherwise, you're always on the wrong side. Good politicians have that sixth sense. Some never get it.

"Once I won, Stu and I became close friends. He was the kind of man I could work with. I left the financial side to him. All I did was sign the cheques. And we started to turn the local around. Stu organized a union newspaper and helped design our new offices. We got involved in the British Columbia Federation of Labour and the Canadian Labour Congress conventions. We sent Stu to other parts of the country where workers were trying to organize.

"Stu was a hard worker. Spent more time in the mills and in the lunchrooms than any other union official I ever saw. Most people don't go to union meetings, so we used to speak in the lunchrooms to keep them in touch. Mohammed going to the mountain. In the mills, each shift had two main breaks of twenty minutes each, and that's when Stu would speak. He'd speak twice each shift, and there were three shifts a day. He'd be talking at four in the morning sometimes.

"He's a very persuasive speaker. But the best I ever heard was when he went to a meeting of the BC Lions Football Club. He was one of the people who'd paid $20 to help start the team in 1954. Anyway, the Lions were losing badly in '61 and Stu wanted an investigation into what was going wrong. He was able to force the investigation by a vote of 514 to 485.

"There was a *Vancouver Sun* columnist named Denny Boyd who said that when Hodgson got up to speak, it was like Heifetz getting up to play the violin. Called Hodgson one of the five greatest speakers of history—the others being Matthew, Mark, Luke and John. Boyd wrote a column that said Hodgson was rolling his eyes, pounding the rostrum and calling down hell-fire and damnation on all members of the Lions' executive when a guy in the audience was so overcome he jumped up, threw back his head and shouted 'Hallelujah, brother, Hallelujah!'"[6]

"Does he have any social life?" asked Cowan.

"Well, he never was much of a drinker really. I like a drink, too much sometimes, but we'd go for lunch and spend afternoons at the beer parlour and Stu would just talk. I don't know what makes him tick. You don't see any specific ambition driving him. He just works. His dad was like that, had a real dirty job in MacMillan Bloedel's shingle mill. It's a hell of an existence, even now. It's an industry that hasn't changed over the years. It's hard bull work, with sawyers and packers paid piecework, just for what they produce. The place is constantly full of cedar dust. I couldn't think of a worse place to work in the whole industry than a shingle mill.

"Stu's a workhorse, that's how I'd describe him. It's as if working is the greatest satisfaction he could have. When he turns on to something, he just works. If you have a one-track mind and devote all your energy to one specific thing, you're bound to be successful, and that's Stu. He's absolutely one-track." Syd paused and looked around the plane. Hodgson had moved well forward of us to chat with Fournier.

"I would say Stu didn't do his union work. He lived it. When you went for a drink, he was talking shop. When he goes to bed, he probably talks shop.

---

[6] Gorde Sinclair, "Hodgson Narrowly Escaped Newfoundland Lynch Mob," *Edmonton Journal,* July 13, 1974

But you don't associate it with ambition somehow. It's more of a drive that seems to give him real pleasure."

"The union must have been sorry to lose him," I said.

"We were sorry all right. Everybody valued Stu, and if he'd stayed with the union there would have been a place for him. No doubt about it. He wasn't destined to stay financial secretary, either. He was meant for bigger things, maybe as a national or international officer. The labour movement is desperate for people with his kind of ability."

"So you didn't put anything in his way when you heard the government wanted him to serve on the Territorial Council?" Cowan asked.

"Hell no, I encouraged him to go. He was earning $10,000 a year as financial secretary, maybe $5,000 less than the Deputy Commissioner's job was worth when he finally took it. When he was first invited to sit as a member of the Council, members weren't paid. Only the wealthier people got the appointments, I guess. He came to me with his problem over money and I told him the local would pay his wages for a while. The union also paid all his expenses when he travelled between Vancouver and Ottawa. First time the labour movement subsidized the government of Canada, and for a whole month!

"Stu was the first labour man on Council. Got appointed through Don Lanscale, who was legal counsel for Forest Industrial Relations, the employers' bargaining agency. These were the people we negotiated with, sometimes every week. Lanscale recognized Stu's abilities and was also a very powerful backroom Liberal. I think it was through him that Stu got to know Art Laing. They met with Stu at the IWA convention in Vancouver in May of '64, and by June the same year Stu attended his first Council meeting in Ottawa.

"It was all above board, of course. Stu belonged to the New Democratic Party. Him and me went to the founding convention of the NDP and were early supporters of Tommy Douglas. But Stu can get along with all sorts of people. At one stage of my life, I wondered about that. I used to be a pretty bigoted individual, believing boss was boss and union was union and never the two shall meet. Since then I've come to the conclusion that a little honey will draw one hell of a lot more flies than vinegar. You have to get results, with a minimum amount of trouble for the people you represent.

Stu is good at that, he understands people, and he can work with people like Lanscale and Laing far better than I could, or ninety percent of other union people could."

"My God, you people are noisy," said Hodgson as he came up to our little circle. "Your voice would wake the dead, Syd."

"I was just explaining your bad points to *The New York Times*. I'll tell you this—I'm seeing problems you and me tackled ten years ago in the union. People up here have to catch their own food and make their own clothes. There's no phones, no doctors, no safe way to travel, no jobs and no entertainment." He paused to let the thoughts sink in for the rest of us. "Ten years ago we had to take woodland workers who were treated like dirt and teach them how to fight for their rights. We showed them the way to a decent and dignified life, and you've got to do exactly the same thing here."

Hodgson nodded. "I've seen a lot. Terrible conditions in logging camps, on the waterfront. From a union point of view, it always starts with one thing, the need for recognition. The people of the North have no unity and no collective power. Things have to change up here, but they never will unless someone starts to make a fuss."

"Heh! Heh! You're the man who can make plenty of fuss," Syd said with a chuckle. "I figure you're in your element up here, Stu. It's virgin territory. Get everyone on your side and raise hell with those civil servants in Ottawa."

"The federal civil servants don't bother me. I'm not afraid of anyone when I stand on my feet. I don't mean to say I didn't get beat a few times. I got licked lots of times. But at least I have the guts to stay and fight. And it can't be any more hazardous than that time in Newfoundland."

"Tell these fellows, and gals, about Newfoundland."

"Just a minute, I've got to get something to sit on," Hodgson said. He went to the back of the aircraft, came back with a suitcase and set it in the aisle between us. "Just about ten years ago to the day," he began, "the pulp workers of Newfoundland, the guys cutting logs out in the bush, were trying to organize a union. They only earned a dollar an hour, working ten hours a day and living in the worst conditions you could ever imagine. Filthy, frozen tents out in the bush, no fresh food, no clean water. Some lived in tarpaper shacks hardly fit for henhouses, with rats everywhere and two-tiered bunks and one worn out, dirty blanket. You'd have as many as twenty-five men all in one small place, with an oil drum wood stove called a bogey in the centre and everyone sleeping feet to the middle to keep warm. They'd lay their clothes over the bogey to dry them out. In the mornings you couldn't get a drink till you'd cracked the ice off the rain barrel."

Everyone was spellbound. "Joey Smallwood, the premier of Newfoundland, was doing his damnedest to make sure the effort to organize a union failed, even though a government panel had approved the workers' membership in the IWA. Well, the Vancouver office sent me over there as an observer, to help out any way I could. It was pretty bad. Smallwood had already whipped everyone into a frenzy, going on the radio to tell all of Newfoundland the IWA was the greatest danger to ever threaten the province. Said it wasn't a strike, but a civil war. The townspeople of Grand Falls were forming vigilante groups against the loggers. Soon the place was like an armed camp. One morning I could sense something was going to happen. The town was full of striking loggers and sure enough, a police constable was killed. Had his skull cracked open by someone with a three-foot chunk of birch when the cops routed a bunch of loggers, with their wives and kids, who were blocking a street. Seventy cops cornered them between two snowbanks at the end of a street and started swinging their clubs.

"Right away Smallwood was on the radio, whipping everyone into a fever. He said in four and a half centuries Newfoundland never saw anything like it, that the real criminals were not arrested, and that all Newfoundland knew who they were. He said there wasn't enough room in Newfoundland for the IWA and his government, so one or the other would have to go. He ordered a state funeral for the dead policeman and that night a crowd of townspeople carried the coffin in a big procession through the streets and down to the railway station, past our union office. We knew they were out for revenge."

Hodgson paused for a moment, gathering his thoughts. "They'd picked up rocks and sticks along the way. All of a sudden, a big chunk of ice came through the window. I turned around and here was one of our guys from Toronto with a rifle in his hands. I said, 'What are you going to do with that?' and he said, 'I'm going to shoot the first bastard that comes through that door.' And I said, 'What are you going to do with the second one?' And he said, 'I'm going to shoot him too.' 'Well,' I said, 'I hope you've got lots of ammunition because there's a thousand guys standing outside that door.' I told them, 'Look, I'm no hero, we can't stand up to this, and we'd better get out of here.' Then I grabbed the rifle and threw it out the back window. And we all went out after it and dispersed in the dark streets.

"I found my hotel and went upstairs and here was the manager with tears running down his face saying, 'It's taken me twenty-five years to get this little inn, and now those people are coming to burn it down to the ground and hang me. I don't know what to do. I've done nothing wrong except give you a room. You've got to go.'

"I said, 'Gee, I can't go, I don't know where to go. My clothes aren't packed.' He said, 'Oh, that's all right, I threw them out in the back alley.'

"So I ran out into the street, picked up my clothes, and shoved them into my suitcase. Just then, a fellow came running by and said, 'Hey, the mob's coming and they're going to hang a guy that's staying in this hotel.'

"Well, I wasn't really sure about that but in any event, as luck would have it, just as the mob started to come down the street a cab came by. I hailed it, jumped in, told the driver I was a shoe salesman from the west coast and I wanted to get to the next town because sales were so lousy.

"Before long though he made the connection with the union and the west coast and kicked me out in the middle of nowhere. I walked up the road for a little while and came to a railroad station. Didn't know what to do but by golly if a train didn't come along. I didn't wait for nothing. I jumped on that train and I thought, boy, am I ever glad to be out of here. We hadn't gone more than three hundred yards though when the conductor came around and shouted, 'Grand Falls, next stop.'"

Hodgson waited patiently while we finished laughing. "I'll tell you, I went over the side just like I went over the side during the war, only this time I was scared stiff, I don't mind telling you. Me and some other guys ended up hiding out at the Gander airport, trying to get home. The local ticket agent wasn't interested in helping us out but Pan-Am let us on a flight that was refuelling. Had no idea where we were going and didn't care. Turned out to be New York, so I ended up going through there to get back to Toronto. Next morning, I got up in the hotel, looked in the mirror, and thought I must have aged at least thirty or forty years because my hair was all white! Turns out I'd put toothpaste in my hair and brushed my teeth with Brylcreem!"

We roared with laughter.

"But in the end the boys in Newfoundland did get their union!"

Fascinating stuff. It helped us all see a man who could do things for the North.

The drone of the plane's engines changed pitch as we banked into a gentle descent. We'd flown south of Resolute, down Barrow Strait and Lancaster Sound, around the enormous Brodeur Peninsula of northern Baffin Island, and inside Admiralty Inlet to reach our destination. Barely discernible in the early morning light was the picturesque settlement of Arctic Bay, nestled between frozen shore and mountains, clinging to the northwest shore of Borden Peninsula, a craggy limb of the world's fifth largest island. After two hours of cramped flight, the beauty of this settlement was a welcome, cleansing sight.

We flew in between the inlet's sheer, towering walls and dropped quickly to the short rocky beach. It was a difficult location for an approach and landing, and one wingtip came perilously close to the rock face. Then we hit the ground, snow flying and wheels squealing, as Daryl forced the aircraft to stop before the end of the makeshift runway. It was time to meet the inhabitants of Arctic Bay.

ARCTIC BAY'S COMMUNITY HALL, A similar structure to that in Grise Fiord, was jammed with people. Among the interplay of adults talking in the measured Eskimo language, the hall was bombarded by the hubbub of babies crying, toddlers thundering up and down the plywood floor, mothers soothing their young and the door opening and slamming shut as another late arrival entered. Each time the door opened a blast of cold air and fog billowed into the room. I kept my parka done up tight and my mitts on. My nostrils swam in the distinctive smells of sealskin and fur, a strong and oily combination that was definitely peculiar but not unpleasant.

At the entrance, a mother with a particularly unhappy baby in the back of her parka calmed the child by crooning softly and doing a distinctive type of jig. She placed one foot well ahead of the other and began a step in which her feet shuffled back and forth and her body weight was transferred slowly to and fro.

Tacked on the wall were numerous bulletins. One handmade poster announced: Ice Thickness: 24 Ft. 9 Ins.

Another, from the Atmospheric Environment Service at Resolute, read:

The sun never rises from Nov 7 to Feb 4, inclusive.

The sun never sets from April 30 to August 13, inclusive.

Maximum Temperature Today: -25°F.

Minimum Temperature Today: -52°F.

Wind: 15 MPH.

Wind Chill Factor: -90°F.

Hodgson, Simonie Michael and Bill Kempt, the local schoolteacher who, like Cloughley in Grise Fiord, doubled as area administrator, seated themselves at a plywood table at the front. As we waited for the stragglers to get settled, I studied the landscape through the little window by my shoulder. The hall looked out over a bay named for a whaling ship called *Arctic* that anchored there in 1872. Ninety people lived in Arctic Bay, and another two hundred hunted for a living in nomadic camps scattered around the region. Hunting seal, polar bear and white fox was the main occupation and means of sustenance. The settlement had a little store operated by the Hudson's Bay Company, a one-room school, an Anglican mission and a series of small houses. All of the white residents of Arctic Bay were in the audience: the Hudson's Bay clerk, the Hudson's Bay manager, the power plant operator and Bill Kempt.

I asked the Hudson's Bay Company clerk, seated next to me, if there was a community leader. He explained that most Eskimo communities had no clearly labelled leaders. If anyone received special designation, it was because of his or her proven skills as a hunter or a healer or a prophet. No one exercised political dominion over others. Indian communities had been the same until the white man's treaty parties went to each band and demanded someone be named leader, just so he could mark his X on an unintelligible piece of paper. But of course no treaty parties ever visited the Eskimos because no one had coveted their land.

An Eskimo in rough pants and a long, checked jacket moved into the empty space in front of the seats, carrying a large hoop with a handle fastened on the side. It was a drum, flat and somewhat larger than a barrel hoop, with a skin stretched over the outer rim. The man twirled the hoop back and forth, giving the side a whack with the thick, short stick held in his other hand. Then he twirled the hoop in the other direction and gave it another whack. Boom. Boom. The sound reverberated through the small building. He repeated the twirling and beating motions faster and faster until the room filled with a firm, steady rhythm. He squatted down and began a hopping shuffle, keeping time with his drum. Boom. Boom. Then he began to chant. "Ayee. Ayee." Several women rose and spilled into the open space, joining the drummer in his song. The drummer's torso was almost doubled over and his legs bent as he moved to the powerful rhythm. With his eyes closed, he gave the appearance of being totally absorbed and transported by his art. The women swayed back and forth, echoing the drummer's guttural chant.

He was singing and telling the history of the community, the power of the land, the strength of the spirits, said the Bay man.

When finished, another drummer performed a new song and dance, followed by several more. Both men and women took turns, each performing a unique song. The hall was animated, excited. Everyone watched and smiled appreciatively. When the drummers finished, two women stepped forward and, with their faces four or five inches apart, started breathing hard, in and out, each into the other's mouth. A haunting sound erupted and built to a crescendo. It was a stirring performance.

"Throat singing. Passed on from generation to generation," explained the Bay clerk. "Very difficult to do."

Bill Kempt thanked the performers, announced that he was putting on his area administrator's hat, and introduced Hodgson. As in Grise Fiord, Hodgson called for someone to act as translator. Some minutes passed before a young man stood up, came forward, and took a seat beside the Commissioner.

With the young man's help, Hodgson talked about how the group was stronger than the individual and how several could overcome a polar bear when one hunter alone might be killed. There was a lot of whispering and knowing smiles when he talked about the way muskoxen work together to protect the weak when danger approaches. Some of the people looked covertly at Hodgson and spoke a few words to each other in Eskimo. He paused and looked puzzled.

The translator said, "Muskox! Umingmak! Looks like you!"

Hodgson grinned, then seized on the fact he had the audience's attention. He turned to the blackboard and with a stubby piece of chalk graphed out a pyramid to show the relationship between the big government in Ottawa, the government in Yellowknife, and the myriad of communities like Arctic Bay. Soon he had squiggles, lines, arrows and circles to show that some power was now handed down from Ottawa to Yellowknife, and that members of the Council of the Northwest Territories, like Simonie Michael, represented and spoke on behalf of Arctic Bay and other Baffin Island communities.

Hodgson was well aware these people knew absolutely nothing about the functioning of government, about European democratic traditions, about protocol or politics. He wanted to give them an elementary primer, using explanations like his snowmobile analogy that were simple but not conde- scending. Speaking in English, he made an effort to adopt the unhurried cadence of the Eskimo language—a slow, measured delivery with lots of pauses that helped build rapport with his audience.

It was a lot like watching a one-man play, in which the actor entrances, mystifies and then enlightens his audience. I admired Hodgson's skill, his natural ability to engage an audience, even this one, which was more uncom- prehending than he'd ever met in his union days. The pitch of his voice, his posture, eye contact, facial expressions, hand gestures and the way he walked in front of the crowd to involve everyone was masterful.

An hour after the meeting started the back door opened and, along with a rush of ice fog, in shuffled a plump, short woman with a wide, toothless smile and tattoos on her face. The crowd fell silent.

"Atuat," whispered the Bay clerk. "Eighty-one years old! Hadn't encoun- tered white people before she was forty or more. They call her Grandmother. Hunted until she was well into her seventies, and once killed a polar bear using nothing but a spear. People treat her like The Queen."

With the help of a cane, the grand old lady walked past the audience to the open space where the drum dancers had performed. I stared at the vivid blue tattoos on her face. There were parallel lines from her mouth down to the middle of her chin; more swept across her cheekbones and descended from her hairline to the bridge of her nose. She was maybe four feet ten inches tall and hunched over from age. Her skin was wrinkled but her hair was still dark and her eyes clear. Born in the late 1800s, she had fully experienced all the harshness of a nomadic Arctic existence.

Atuat plonked herself down on the floor in the open space before the seats and stared up at Hodgson, giving him a big gap-toothed smile. Hodgson walked from behind the table and extended his hand. She took it for a brief moment and said something in Eskimo before she let Hodgson return to his place.

Hodgson threw the meeting open to questions, and there were plenty. As with Grise Fiord, they were about ways to solve the privations and isolation of the residents, not about how Hodgson's new government could have any bearing on the realities of their lives. Hodgson patiently answered them, throwing out instant solutions in some cases, offering to come back with answers to others, skilfully keeping the audience involved. When three men started discussing a point privately, he spoke to one of them and flashed a smile to encourage open discussion. If an old lady looked doubtful, he'd stop and give her time to ask a question. The meeting continued for another hour. Then, after about two minutes of silence, he asked, "Are there any more questions before we close this meeting?"

Atuat motioned and someone darted forward to help her to her feet. She leaned on her stick and looked at Hodgson as she spoke. She spoke slowly, thoughtfully, melodiously. Sometimes, when I thought she was finished, she was just considering her next words. Hodgson listened as if he planned to spend the next two weeks in Arctic Bay.

The translator spoke, "Ten years ago I lived in a snow house in winter and a tent in summer. It was the old way, but it was a difficult way to live. Now we have houses and we enjoy living in them much more. We are warm and dry all the time."

There were nods and murmurs of agreement around the audience.

"You promise to do many good things for our community. For that we are grateful. We are grateful that you want to help."

Hodgson nodded, waiting for her to speak again.

"I have one request. Could you build a community bathhouse for us in Arctic Bay? I had a bath once, and I'd be happy if I could have one more before I die."

I was stunned, suddenly aware of how much we take for granted in our southern lives. Hodgson looked at her with a smile. "I will arrange to have the materials shipped up on the summer sealift and the people in the community will build the bathhouse this fall. And when it's built, I want you to be the first one to use it! Next year, when I come back, I also want to use it."

Smiles of appreciation filled the room. Atuat beamed and walked to the

Top: A born orator, a young Stuart Hodgson exhorts his colleagues in the labour movement

Above: The new territorial government stops to refuel in Churchill, Manitoba, September 18, 1967

Left: Open for business – John Parker hangs the sign announcing the arrival of the territorial government, September 19, 1967

Above: Jake Ootes whips up a dog team

Left: Tlicho hereditary Chief Jimmy Bruneau at Rae, with Barbara Lynch (Ootes)

Below: Travelling by komatik, circa 1970

Above and left: Outpost camp near Igloolik, 1972

Bottom left: Peter Irniq (left) on a komatik with John Ningark, Pelly Bay, 1972

Below: Note taking at Resolute, 1972, using syllabics, the writing system introduced by missionaries

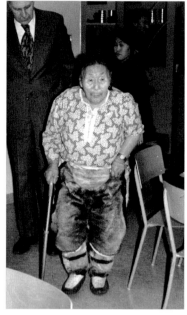

Above left and right: Meeting with Atuat, the matriarch of Arctic Bay who once killed a polar bear with a spear, March 8, 1969

Left: South Camp, Sanikiluak (Belcher Islands), 1969

Below: The whole community turns out to greet the Commissioner

Above: Residents pay close attention at a community meeting

Below left: Pilot Daryl Brown praying before take-off, March 18, 1969

Right right: Digging a runway on the sea ice at North Camp, Sanikiluaq (Belcher Islands), March 18, 1969

Above: Stuart Hodgson with Yvonne Adderley, Prime Minister Pierre Elliot Trudeau and Bob Ward at the first Arctic Winter Games, Yellowknife, 1970

Above: HRH The Prince of Wales' first solo trip was to the Northwest Territories in 1975; (left to right) Jean Chrétien, Pearl Hodgson, Prince Charles, Lynne Hodgson, Eugene Hodgson and Commissioner Stuart Hodgson

Above: Tea Dance, Rae, June 30, 1971

Left: James Wah-Shee with Julian Yendo, the last living signatory to Treaty 11, and Supreme Court Justice William Morrow

Below: The first assembly of the Indian Brotherhood of the Northwest Territories, July 1, 1971

Above: Mountie carrying the Territorial mace; the page boy on the right is Peter Irniq

Top right: Simonie Michael, the first elected Inuk legislator in Canada

Right: Abe Okpik, appointed member of the Northwest Territories Council responsible for Project Surname

Above: Members of the first Executive Council of the Legislative Assembly of the Northwest Territories, 1977 – (left to right) Peter Irniq, Minister of Economic Development and Tourism; Arnold McCallum, Minister of Local Government; Gary Mullins, Assistant Commissioner; Stuart Hodgson, Commissioner; John Parker, Deputy Commissioner

table where she extended her hand to Hodgson. Hodgson bent down and hugged her, to the delight of the others. They behaved like lifelong friends.

The meeting had come to a close and Bill Kempt announced it was time for lunch, a welcome respite. My eyes were raw from the tobacco smoke, which rolled through the room like sea fog.

Lunch was at the tiny schoolhouse overlooking the frozen bay. As we walked outside I became aware of the variety of sounds my boots made on the hard-packed snow: squeals, squawks, growls and, at times, a hollow, resonating boom. I began to appreciate how hard and dense the snow can become during the long cold winter. The wind had whipped up sloping drifts which, in some cases, reached as high as the roof line of the houses.

With the rest of the community residents we squeezed inside the one-room school and sat in the small desks, or perched on the floor with our backs to the wall, wolfing down sandwiches served by the young girls of the community. Glossy pictures of trees, horses and chickens adorned the walls, pictures of flora and animals these Eskimos would never see in person. I wondered how a new teacher who spoke no Eskimo taught students who spoke no English.

"Been a long time since I sat in one of these!" I said, perched on a diminutive chair. "How about you?" I asked Daryl Brown. "Ever sat in one of these?"

He passed a hand over his bald head and told us how he used to fly kids from the camps and settlements along the Mackenzie River and Arctic coast to Yellowknife and Inuvik. Kids had to go to the large residential schools run by Catholic and Anglican missionaries in the bigger centres like Inuvik, Chesterfield Inlet and Yellowknife.

"Rae Parker, the social worker out of Yellowknife, would fly with me to find kids to take to Yellowknife or Inuvik. She'd sit beside me, like a spotter. Every time we saw a camp, we'd set the plane down and pick up the kids. One time we saw some tents between Wrigley and Norman Wells. We already had a dozen kids in the back. We put down near the beach and saw five or six kids running off into the bush. We opened up the hatch and an old man came over in his canoe. We asked if there were any kids to go to school. He said, 'No.' Rae said, 'But we saw some when we flew in.' He just said something incomprehensible and paddled back to the beach. He was sensible. Most parents didn't know what to do. They figured they had no choice. Rae used to tell them they didn't have to do it, although she wasn't supposed to say that.

113

"There was always lots of weeping and wailing when you took the kids from their families, little six-year-olds and up. The government would give me a list of how many to pick up at each camp."

Daryl looked down and focused on his coffee, stirring it in a distracted fashion. Hodgson had quit eating and was listening with an expression somewhere between fascination and outrage.

"It was really cruel," Daryl continued, stroking his beard. "They'd come on board with a little moosehide bag with some little toy inside like a stuffed squirrel or something, and that's all they had in the whole world. One spring, when we were taking kids home for the summer, we dropped a couple of kids, maybe seven or eight years old, at Cape Parry on the Arctic coast. When we picked them up in the fall, we found out that wasn't their home! So they didn't see their parents for two whole years! It was barbaric. God, we'd have two in a seat in the C-46, and that's bigger than a DC-6. It was tragic."

"The kids lost their love and respect for their parents and the old way of life after being separated from them for so long. They took up the white man's way of living and found it really hard going back to the hunting and trapping and fishing way of life."

Daryl looked up from his coffee and stared at Hodgson, but the Commissioner just shook his head.

12
OLD MEETS NEW

THE FROZEN WASTELAND THAT PRESSED in on the bay spawned a demonic wind that slashed and spat at us. The fifteen-miles-per-hour wind and -40°F temperature cut through my clothing like razor blades. I was glad to climb inside our aircraft, comforted by the sound of the engines and the heat in the cabin.

Once airborne, we flew east along the northern shoulders of Baffin Island, across mountainous Borden Peninsula and icebound Eclipse Sound. In the crystal clear air we could see forever. The way to Pond Inlet, our next stop, was mile after barren mile of ice-encrusted granite and rock, with awe-inspiring glaciers calving enormous icebergs. The Baffin Island coastline is the spawning ground for the many icebergs that float down Davis Strait and into the North Atlantic. I wondered if the iceberg that sank the *Titanic* originated here. There was no sign of life—not a tree, bush or any visible refuge for a living thing.

At Pond Inlet, fifty or so Eskimos and a handful of southern émigrés swarmed around the steps of the aircraft to greet us. The area administrator was Bob Pilot, who I knew from the Northern University program. He had years of Arctic experience, as a former RCMP member who had served in Grise Fiord before joining Northern Affairs.

While we milled about taking care of luggage with the help of locals, Daryl Brown and Air Marshal Campbell chatted about the airstrip with Pilot. The Air Marshal, himself a former pilot, complimented the superbly smooth runway, complete with lights. Bob Pilot acknowledged the work of the community mechanic, Ron Hilton, who had spent most of the summer levelling the area. He said that, aside from Resolute and Frobisher Bay, Pond Inlet was the first community in the High Arctic to have runway lights, an essential requirement not only for the day-to-day purposes of transportation but in case of a medical emergency. Weldy Phipps from Resolute had located the lights at an abandoned DEW Line site and had transported them along with the transformer and a windsock. While Bob Pilot gave the credit to others, I knew full well that his ingenuity, resourcefulness and network had helped solve his community's problems.

A smooth road led to the edge of the plateau then continued down a sharp drop to the beach where several dozen houses, a sharp-spired Catholic Church, a Hudson's Bay Company post and an RCMP detachment backed the terrace, their fronts facing the frozen sea. Once we were over the crest, the wind dropped dramatically and it was almost pleasant at beach level. I turned and gazed at the mountains of Bylot Island directly to the north. Across the inlet a mountainous iceberg was trapped and would remain frozen in place until August. It was a thing of beauty, an ancient ship created eons ago and launched by one of the nearby glaciers. I snapped two photographs before my camera became so cold it was inoperable.

Pilot pointed to the iceberg and said that it was the community water supply. I wasn't sure whether to take his comment seriously. He explained that, when the ocean thaws, residents of the community tow an iceberg into the bay for the winter water supply, while in the summer they take water from the streams at each end of the community.

On the beach, several Eskimos in traditional caribou and sealskin clothing were finishing the construction of an igloo. They were accompanied by a dog team hitched to a komatik similar to the one at Grise Fiord. The dogs lunged in the fan hitch and an Eskimo cracked his long whip, controlling it with incredible skill and accuracy.

Hodgson was invited to go for a ride. He agreed to a short trip, explaining that he was anxious to start the community meeting. On his return he urged me to go on a longer ride to the iceberg. I knew Bob Pilot had the local schedule and accommodation arrangements under control, so I accepted the offer, knowing that missing it would be a permanent regret.

The driver held out a caribou outfit with a welcoming grin. I slipped into a raw caribou hide parka and trousers, each of two layers. The outer layer had fur facing outwards, while the inner layer had the fur facing inwards. I felt almost too bulky to walk, but wonderfully warm. Caribou skin clothing is the warmest in the world; no synthetic material has ever been able to match its insulation value.

On the sled the driver piled furs around me and then, bulging in all his caribou skin clothing, whipped his dogs into a frenzy. He stomped behind the sled, whistled imperiously and gave his whip a crack. With a lurch and a crash we were on our way, squealing and hissing away from the shore onto the sea ice, where we crossed a battlefield of ice mounds that had been ripped, slashed and heaved by relentless easterly winds and tides ranging from three to seven feet.

Soon we'd cleared chasms and crevasses near the shore and were onto a smoother ice surface. The driver cracked his whip and we rode like the wind—the same wind that bit my nostrils and chilled my face. My cheeks were burning and the light from the ice and snow seared my eyes.

The iceberg loomed ahead, its massive profile making a mockery of the little church on the beach. Shafts of light glinting green and silver bounced off its crystal facets. It seemed to glow from within. My sense of awe, of being utterly dwarfed, reminded me of past trips to great cathedrals and remote mountains. Suddenly my driver yelled at the dogs and brought them to a halt. "*Nanuq!*" he shouted, stomping forward and pulling a .303 rifle from under the covers of the sled. I searched the white horizon and spotted the polar bear in the distance, between us and the iceberg. We had encroached directly into its range.

The dogs barked and strained; the hair rose on my head. Polar bears, with huge claws and teeth, can weigh as much as 1,200 pounds, and stand up to twelve feet when upright. They have legendary powers of strength, cunning, persistence and speed, and the distinction of being the only carnivore known to attack humans without provocation. At this distance, the bear was little more than a fuzzy blob, slightly yellow, like pissed-on snow. If it weren't for its distinctively humped rear ends, hunched shoulders and little black snout, I would have sworn it was just a puff of Arctic mist.

Polar bears are capable of frightening bursts of speed, but this one wasn't in the mood to race today. He shook himself and receded with a shambling, heavy walk.

"Dangerous," my driver said with a wide grin. It was the first time I'd realized he could speak English. "Eating seal. Won't bother us." He slung the rifle over his shoulder.

"Lots of bears here?"

"Ayee," he said. "Our water!" He pointed at the iceberg. "Once a week we come with a wagon pulled by a cat tractor. Haul chunks of ice back to the houses."

"Why is this place called Pond Inlet?"

He laughed. "You *kabloona* [white men] call it Pond Inlet after an English fellow called John Pond. We call it Mittimatalik, after one of our people who is buried here." Throughout the Arctic, place names for landmarks and communities were imposed by explorers, traders, missionaries and government officials with little regard for local tradition. Inhabitants were ignored when it came to searching out and applying local names.

"Good hunting?" I asked.

"Ayee. Seal, walrus, narwhal."

"And lots of polar bears!"

He yelled and swished at the dogs lunging and yapping in eager anticipation of more action. These husky dogs could pull more weight than an animal twice their size and had traditionally carried packs, sniffed out seal holes, provided warmth for people out on the land and, in an emergency, even saved people from starvation. The increased use of snowmobiles meant that dogs were now on the way out.

We moved ahead, gliding over the now smooth plates of ice, and circumnavigated the iceberg. Inside the haven of my fur blankets, I closed my eyes in order to imprint this experience into my memory. I was at 75 degrees north, four hundred miles north of the Arctic Circle, in -40°F weather, on a stone-age conveyance driven by a person who lived in a different world. The contrast between this lifestyle—the privations, the warmth of these people, their boundless hospitality and instant friendliness—with my own left me awestruck.

The sound of the driver's yells and the swish of the sled persuaded me this was really happening. I looked out and saw we were close to the beach again. The driver pointed ahead. "We built an igloo to show you the old skills are still important. Inuit live in houses here now, but we still live in tents and snow houses when we are out on the land, away from the community."

"Why do people want to live here in Pond Inlet instead of out on the land?"

"Easier life, especially for the older ones. If you get sick there's a nurse. There's a store and a school." He hesitated. "But they've only recently come."

He brought the dog team to a halt. "Put these skins inside," he said, pulling the furs off the sled. "They'll make a fine bed for tonight. Then you can say you have slept in an igloo!" I searched frantically for an excuse but all I could muster was a blank stare. And before I knew it, he had disappeared down the tunnel of the snow house. On hands and knees I crawled through a very low opening, down a slight incline and into the first compartment. Directly ahead was another tiny opening covered by a skin flap. Still on hands and knees I raised the flap and gazed into the second room, the floor of which was elevated about twenty inches. From my kneeling position it was possible to see little more than the feet and legs of my guide. I crawled through and stood up in a circular domed compartment about ten feet in diameter. A clear ice window set high in the dome admitted a stream of daylight. About one-third of the floor space was a snow platform for sleeping, sitting and working. That is where the guide placed the caribou hides. My traditional outfit seemed entirely appropriate here.

"The dome stops warm air from sitting up near the roof, as happens in your kind of house."

I smiled, enjoying his critique of southern engineering skills. "Tell me about the igloo."

He rose onto his knees and, with a multitude of hand gestures, explained the floor area was where the cooking was done, over a seal-oil lamp called a *kudlik*. The raised snow bench was where the family slept. The platform was raised because cold air would settle in the cavity below. Home for these nomads of the northern desert was a simple, temporary thing.

"And what about you?" I asked. "You don't live in a snow house anymore."

"Not today." he said. "But I was born in a hunting camp and lived in a tent during the summer. My parents moved with the seasons, just like the people in the camps around Mittimatalik still do today. When I was six, a plane came and took me to school at Chesterfield Inlet. That's seven hundred miles away."

"There's a school in Pond Inlet today."

"Yeah, that's good. Now kids don't have to go through that nightmare. But we didn't get a school here until a while ago." He paused and stared at the snow floor. "I came back from school one summer and my parents were gone. I didn't know why. My parents got tuberculosis and were taken by the *C.D. Howe* medical ship to a hospital in the south, but I was never told where they were taken. I still don't know. All I know is that many who went south for treatment are buried in the south. My parents never came back."

I didn't know how to respond.

"That's how I came to live in the community here. I was taken in by an uncle who taught me to hunt. Now, everything has changed. Many of us live in houses. We eat food that is not as good for us as natural meat. We use snowmobiles instead of dogs, heating oil and electricity instead of our old kudliks. We use big motorboats instead of kayaks. Some change is good, some is bad. I suppose it is unavoidable. Still, it makes me sad that some youngsters here say it's a waste of time to learn the old skills.

"Look at what has happened since my grandfather was a boy. Back then my family lived a nomadic life, moving about on the land wherever there was game to hunt. A hundred years ago, Scottish whalers picked this as a spot to make contact with Inuit hunters and the Hudson's Bay Company came to trade goods. Soon, a larger than normal number of families were living in this one spot because they knew they could pick up a cooking pot, or a knife or something like that from the traders. Then the European churchmen moved in, because wherever there's a crowd there's an opportunity to save souls. More Inuit started living closer to this place. Then the government noticed what was going on and decided to send police here and build a school and an administrative office. Even more reason for people to come and live nearby, especially when the government started sending in nice wood houses with stoves for cooking and supply ships full of things."

He was silent for a moment. "Inuit were nomadic because the game is spread very thin over this land. When a lot of people settle in one spot, there's no way they can all make a living off the land, even with snowmobiles that take us further than dogsleds could. That's why, even though things should be much better for us today, in some ways they are worse. In some ways we have less than before, because we can't go back to the igloo when our heating oil runs out, and we can't eat a snowmobile engine when we're lost out on the sea ice."

As we left the igloo to check on the meeting, I thanked this man who lived in two cultures. I had enjoyed his company.

"We smile while talking to strangers because this will ward off any evil spirits that might be tempted to jump from the visitor to us," he said. "We believe in honesty, too. If we find a rifle and some fishing gear stashed on the edge of the seashore, nobody will touch the stuff, even if it lies there for years. We figure that one day the man who owns them will pick them up."

TWENTY OR MORE SNOWMOBILES WERE parked outside the school. Inside residents, young and old, chattered, coughed and smoked up a storm. The meeting was just over. Hodgson was thoroughly relaxed, stretched back in his chair at the head table with his hair wild and his trouser legs billowing out of his kamiks. He was the picture of happiness, radiating contentment and a sense of accomplishment. I joined Bob Pilot in conversation with two young white women, the nurses of the community, who were young, pretty and remarkably vivacious. Pilot told me Walter Petrigo and I were supposed to have dinner with them.

I asked them where they were from.

"I'm from Yorkshire, luv. My friend is from London. Most of the nurses 'ere in the North are from England or Australia. We're the only ones batty enough to come up 'ere, I suppose."

"That ain't it," her Cockney friend scolded. "It's because we were trained in midwifery and it comes in real 'andy 'ere. We rely on our assessments and perform emergency services without a doctor, unless we can get through on the radio telephone. We treat everything from toothaches to 'arpoon wounds. Not much of a social life though, so we're glad to 'ave you for supper. The cupboard is getting bare except for some tinned veggies. There's a dance 'ere first. Then we'll go for supper."

Hodgson joined us. Bob Pilot complimented Hodgson on the meeting and his commitment to solve some of the community's problems. He said it would be great if they were the only problems. "The list is endless."

"I'm sure," Hodgson acknowledged.

"We need more houses. There are no jobs, no future for the kids and no proper care for the elderly. There's no decent mail service, and very poor radio telephone reception."

Hodgson nodded. "Same in every community." Hodgson started to speak with the nurses and Pilot tugged on my sleeve, indicating he wanted to talk to me privately. He said it was time for him to move on and he'd certainly like to work for Hodgson in some way. I felt a flush of importance and pride over the effect my boss had.

The crowd stilled as a soft, rhythmic sound punctuated the air. A woman with a squeezebox, an ancient concertina, moved into the open area. Spontaneously, several men and women formed a wide circle around her.

"'The Whaler's Jig,'" said Pilot, as the musician began to squeeze an old sea shanty from the instrument. It was a simple, repetitive droning that animated the dancers to a fast jig step. They moved in a large circle and twirled themselves about like Jack Tars on the foredecks of old. Shivers ran up my spine as I realized I was peeking in on a way of life that died out years ago everywhere else.

"The first Europeans the Eskimos had contact with were whalers," Pilot said, explaining that the discovery of whales in Hudson Bay and along the Baffin coast had opened the Arctic to droves of whaling ships, ending centuries of isolation for the Eskimos, for better or worse. Over the years, traders came for fur, ivory and blubber. The whalers introduced Eskimos to steel needles, knives and rifles. "That's why you can't just walk in here today and tell them to forget their modern troubles and go back to the old way of life," he explained. The law arrived when Eskimos killed a deceitful Newfoundland trader in 1920, and the Hudson's Bay Company built a store soon after. When the school opened in 1961 many families moved in from outlying hunting camps. "Hunting, fishing and trapping are still important, but they can't support the whole settlement. We need to create jobs for Eskimos to earn money. We need something more than driving the honey wagon or sweeping floors at the administrator's office." I nodded agreement as the dancers shuffled and kicked their sealskin kamiks.

Now everyone, Hodgson included, clapped to the music. The dancers worked themselves into frenzy; a set could last for up to half an hour. I was mesmerized by the rhythms and movements, filled with energy and enthusiasm and a real affection for these northern people. We were all transported to another realm, another time, leaving behind for a few hours the privations and the fears for the future of life in Canada's Arctic.

MY BREATH CREATED STREAMS OF vapour in the freezing igloo. I thought of my companions, snug in the transient centre, a three-bedroom house with four bunk beds per room. How resilient the Eskimo people were to have survived and adapted to this harsh and inhospitable land, facing starvation, living a nomadic existence with the barest of material possessions, and always building shelter and searching for food. Now these people had to prepare themselves for a new kind of life while at the same time attempting to preserve some of their traditional skills and talents.

I undressed, but even though I lay between the caribou furs the cold crept through. I unfolded my shirt, sweater and pants, which had served as my pillow, and put them back on along with my wind pants and my parka. I had a fitful sleep, dozing in and out of consciousness. The hours dragged by as I repeatedly checked my watch, my only 20th century convenience.

Finally it was 6:00 a.m. Hodgson would be up and anxious to depart in an hour. My joints were stiff from the hard snow bench as I crawled down the tunnel to discover that a wall of snow blocked my exit. After a few frantic stabs, my gloved hand reestablished the opening. A blustery wind was blowing as I stood by the entrance, orienting myself toward the settlement. The last thing I wanted was to wander out onto the sea ice, lost and helpless in the company of those ill-tempered polar bears. I turned my face into my hood and walked directly into the wind, confident I'd soon arrive at the little strip of houses.

Cheers greeted me as I stepped through the door of the transient centre and shook snow from my parka. It was time for great hilarity and much hot coffee. I had performed an admirable feat.

Brown, who stepped in just after me, told us "the weather was out" at Clyde River, our next stop. "Could be a whiteout. Then you can't tell whether you're flying upside down or backwards. But the main problem is wind. I called Frobisher on the air radio and they got through to Clyde. It'll take them an hour to get back to me."

"So what do we do?" Hodgson asked.

"Depends on how much you like this place," said Brown. "A while back I waited in Cambridge Bay for the weather to change and spent a whole week there. Bob Gauchie was there as well. He left in a storm with a load of fish. Look where that got him."

Hodgson eyes roamed the ceiling. "What's the alternative?"

"Broughton Island or the DEW Line site at Cape Dyer. We'd make one of them for sure, but there's no telling what the weather would be like there either."

Hodgson nodded. "Okay. Let's wait an hour for an update."

We drank coffee and waited. Finally, Brown returned and reported the winds were too high at Clyde, and the ceiling had dropped to ground level. "It doesn't look good for the rest of the day."

"In that case, we're here for another day," Hodgson said. "Tomorrow, we'll get back on schedule. Bob, would you let Clyde and the other settlements know we are delayed?"

After three coffees for breakfast, I retired to the bathroom. Disinfectant emanated from the unplumbed toilet, or honey bucket. The bucket was lined with a green plastic garbage bag that, once full, would be tied up and carted outside to freeze. It would be collected by the local garbage detail and then placed on the sea ice to float away or sink with the summer thaw. The sea ice served as the dump in most of these settlements.

Kay Vaydik and Ed Cowan chatted in the kitchen. Petrigo found a cribbage board and some cards. Pat Carney struck up a conversation with Fournier. Syd Thompson and the Air Marshal, in a new spirit of congeniality, were seated at the kitchen table, deep in conversation.

I commandeered a bunk bed and slept most of the day until it was time for supper at Bob Pilot's house. Lois, Bob's raven-haired wife, had prepared an incredible dinner for all of us. It was a virtual feast of sumptuous cuts of caribou, broiled arctic char and our donated turkey, all garnished with canned vegetables and instant mashed potatoes from what I knew was her diminishing supply. We feasted like royalty and I admired her generosity. No doubt the supply of country food was plentiful, but it would be months before the ship would arrive to replenish their southern rations.

The Air Marshal motioned that he and I should go to the kitchen for KP duty. I washed, and the Air Marshal dried, all the while conversing with Lois, asking about life in Pond Inlet, her hopes and desires. I had told him about Bob's wish to join Hodgson's government, so he wanted to seek the views of the spouse, to get to know her better, to pass on his judgment to Hodgson. Her husband had a reputation for being efficient, but Campbell wanted Lois to be able to fulfil her ambitions as well. I admired Lois—she had a warm and engaging personality, a calm demeanour and a charm that would allow her to fit into any situation, from entertaining here in Pond Inlet to engaging in larger social functions. The Air Marshal's experience in personnel matters meant our government was about to get a team of two capable people.

13
HERE BEFORE CHRIST

MARCH 10-12, 1969

THE POWERFUL WIND HAD SUBSIDED but was still biting when we arrived at Clyde River, 250 miles south on the eastern shore of Baffin Island. There were no lengthy greetings on the sea ice. A white fellow bundled in a fur-trimmed parka shook Hodgson's hand and introduced himself as Doug Cressnan, acting area administrator. After quick handshakes with the locals we headed for the community.

Clyde is on the eastern side of Patricia Bay in the dark glare of a brooding promontory standing 1,600 feet above the settlement. The geography helped channel the wind, which burned my cheekbones as we walked.

"This is lunacy," I said to Brown through clenched teeth.

"Don't tell me, tell Stu," he said, pointing at Hodgson towering over the Eskimos, who were stepping quickly to keep up. Hodgson turned to look at the stragglers. His moustache and eyebrows were thickly coated with ice. But he smiled as if he were on a picnic. I blew ice fog into the wind.

The traditional white clapboard walls and red roof of the Hudson's Bay Company store drew closer as we scrambled over the ice ridges. In the Arctic the initials HBC were sometimes referred to as "here before Christ" because the company's arrival in a community often preceded the establishment of a mission. Such was the case in Clyde where the Bay post was established in the early 1920s, when the area was all but uninhabited. As had happened in other areas, the trading company drew in hunters from the region until a settlement was established. Now Clyde River had a population of 120.

"I'm going to the Bay to warm up," said Ed Cowan. Most of the others joined him, but Simonie Michael and I stayed with Hodgson to tour the community.

Scattered about the settlement were an RCMP post, a school and a hodge-podge of miserable, rundown shacks. These weren't the prefabricated houses common in the other communities. These were shacks, hammered together from old lumber salvaged from crates and shipping materials. Snow covered them halfway up the walls. Frost-encrusted plastic sheets covered single pane windows that gazed out over the silent bay.

As our boots crunched on the snow-covered ground, my eyes were drawn to the debris littered around the shacks. Animal carcasses lying on rooftops safe from the dogs; battered snowmobiles, some in a total state of disrepair; old bottles, packing crates and off-cuts of wood poking through the yellowed snow. There was spilled oil, torn plastic bags full of frozen sewage and domestic waste everywhere. Used water was thrown directly onto the ground beside each house, forming massive mounds of dirty ice.

Clyde was built on clay so, in the four-week summer, kitchen effluent gathered in puddles and then dribbled down to the sea. But now, in winter, the drainage system did nothing but build up revolting rinks of ice that spread in ever wider ripples around each house.

Even the dogs looked dejected, their eyes bleary and coats ripped by the wind. Groups of them lay tethered here and there, joined by chains to stakes in the snow. Once proud stalwarts of the Eskimo's travel and survival tradition, they were now redundant pensioners in a landscape dominated by snowmobiles imported from the south.

Naive notions about the Arctic's pristine snow and trackless wilderness were destroyed at Clyde, violated by a savage combination of poverty and despair. As we drew closer, the smile left even Hodgson's face.

"God, how depressing," I said to Hodgson as I caught up with him and Cressnan. His brow furrowed as Cressnan told him that most Clyde residents lived on welfare cheques. "It was once a good hunting area. But fur prices have collapsed and game is now scarce. There's nothing here for people to do, but they can't leave. What would they do? Go back to living in igloos in the middle of nowhere? It's too late for that."

We met a frail woman who Cressnan introduced by her disc number, which sounded like Ahpah E5-251. Through translation she explained she did not receive welfare and wanted to know how she could obtain an old age pension. Hodgson promised to write to her and explain the plan. He told me to ensure his letter would be written in syllabics. It was becoming apparent that we would need a group of people at headquarters to handle the translation of letters and documents and to act as interpreters whenever we needed to communicate with someone who was unilingual.

At one of the shacks Cressnan stopped and introduced Hodgson to the owner who gestured to Hodgson to join him inside. Cressnan put a hand on Hodgson's arm. "People consider it a great honour for visitors to come to their home and drink tea. But then the next man will want you to visit his home too. If you visit one, you have to visit everyone's home."

Hodgson nodded. "I'll try!"

I stayed outside to take photographs. The house was a small square box twelve by twelve feet, flat roofed, built of scraps of packing crate plywood and odd bits of lumber. I unzipped my parka, whipped out my camera, took two quick photos and returned the camera to the warmth of my body. It was a challenge taking photographs in the Arctic. Like my eyeglasses, which I also kept in my parka, the cold camera lens would completely fog over when I stepped from the freezing temperature outside into a warm room.

The low, crude door shut tight behind me as I entered. It was dark until my snow-seared eyes adjusted to the weak glow of a Primus light. The only window was covered with a ragged linen cloth. The atmosphere hung heavy with the stove's warmth and the earthy smells of butchered game.

As my eyes adjusted, I saw a bed with a tubular steel head, like an old hospital bed. There was a bench against a wall, a few homemade plywood shelves here and there, and a water barrel with a plywood cover and a steel bowl on top. In the middle of the room a small oil-fired stove poured out heat, its pipes snaking up a few feet, then across to a corner of the room to vent out of the roof. A big charred pot simmered on the stove. Against the wall was a homemade table and two chairs.

Then I saw something familiar—the walls were plastered with the printed minutes of bygone Northwest Territories Council debates. As the Editor of Debates I had shipped transcripts from Ottawa to the communities around the North. And here they were serving as wallpaper and insulation in this man's home.

The owner shooed his two kids from the table and motioned Hodgson to sit while he took the other seat. Simonie, Cressnan and I sat down on the edge of the bed. The man's wife lifted a steaming pot and poured dark tea into mugs, the steam swirling about us. Silence permeated the room. The man gave Hodgson a tin can which served as a sugar bowl. Hodgson put a big spoonful in his cup, stirred, and then took some sips from the mug. He muttered "mmm," lifted his cup to the wife, smiled and nodded several times. "What's the price of sugar here?" he asked.

Cressnan relayed the question in Eskimo and then the answer, "Very high."

There was silence for another while and then Hodgson spoke again. "How is the hunting this year?" After the answer, another lengthy silence ensued.

We savoured the hot tea. Then Hodgson and Cressnan spoke together. It gave me a chance to whisper to Simonie, "He's not very talkative." I nodded toward the husband.

"That's the way an Inuit conversation is. Older people consider inquisitiveness a discourtesy. We don't feel comfortable asking a guest questions. Answering questions is okay. Besides, we don't believe in talking all the time. We aren't afraid to sit quietly in between bits of conversation." When I heard him say "Inuit," I realized that this is how the people referred to themselves. Eskimo was a term imposed by outsiders.

The man suddenly spoke again to Hodgson. "Fifteen years ago we were travellers. We lived wherever the game took us. Now we have permanent houses, and we like them better than snow houses or sod houses."

I could now confirm that this shack really was a more desirable dwelling than an igloo.

"But hunting is harder," he continued. "Sometimes an Inuk must travel fifteen days from home to get meat. Most people here used to hunt seal and sell fur, but fur is worth very little these days. It barely covers the expense of making a trip on the land."

"Their lives are affected by other people," Cressnan said. "Look what's happened to the price of sealskins. Thanks to a bunch of frenzied activists who haven't a clue what havoc they're causing these people."

"There is nothing else to do here?" Hodgson asked.

"Four men work for the government, one for the Hudson's Bay. A few people make arts and crafts to sell. Otherwise, there's nothing."

"What do you do?" he nodded at our host.

"I hunt to feed my family. I would like to work for wages, but there are no jobs."

Hodgson took advantage of the ensuing silence. He looked at the man and said, "The government hopes to move this settlement to the other side of the bay this summer. There it will sit on gravel, not clay. A new school will be built. When work begins, I'll make sure you are hired, along with anyone else here who wants work."

After the translation the man beamed and nodded enthusiastically. "It's a good idea to move," he said. "It's too juicy here in summer."

Cressnan told us that housing was a big problem in the community. He gave an example of two families totalling ten people living in a prefabricated house of 512 square feet with no electricity. In another case, an Eskimo family lived in a one-room ice house about twelve feet in diameter heated by a Coleman stove. It had been almost four years since the federal government had earmarked $12.5 million over five years to construct new three-bedroom houses for Eskimos—there was no sign of it here.

We rose, shook hands with our hosts and proceeded to the next house. "It's a place in need of housing and without an economy, that's what it is," Hodgson said. "And I have to solve their problems. That's what we are here for."

THE COMFORTS OF YELLOWKNIFE WERE a galaxy away. Ottawa might never have existed at all. I hadn't shaved for several days, nor had a shower since Resolute . Fortunately for us we'd enjoyed the meal provided by Lois Pilot because I knew our forthcoming meals would consist of the occasional community feast of game meat supplemented by sandwiches and stale chocolate bars purchased from the Hudson's Bay store. The lack of fresh and familiar food, the freezing temperatures and long days of moving from overheated halls to cold shacks were wearing on us. Clyde had been our fifth community; we still had nine to go.

The mid-afternoon sky glistened with a thin light as we flew just below the mountaintops down Baffin Island towards Pangnirtung. The spring equinox was approaching but there was no hint of softness in the isolation and bleakness of the landscape below.

Hodgson and I were in the front seats. The hum of the two turboprop engines had lulled me into a doze until the right engine quit. Then it fired up again. And quit once more. My heart skipped a beat. I looked at Hodgson. He looked at me. Carney crossed fingers on both hands and then crossed her arms.

Brown, his right hand on the upper throttle lever, swung his head around and yelled at Hodgson. "These engines are incredible, shut one down and we just keep a-flying with the other!" Monaghan chuckled and Brown lifted his eyebrows, nodding toward Carney.

Hodgson, furious, shouted at Brown to stop his antics.

"Okay!" Brown replied with an unconcerned shrug.

After several minutes of silence Hodgson asked how I was doing with the community survey reports. My expression told him what I didn't want to say—I hadn't followed his instructions in the last two communities. "We have no way of getting this data except on visits like this," he said. He looked straight ahead, chin jutted forward. "Get Mary-Ellen to help you in the remaining communities." With that he got up and went to the back of the aircraft.

I was embarrassed. His had been a simple request and he rightfully scolded me for the omission.

The Air Marshal, who had been sitting behind us, moved into Hodgson's vacated seat. "Stu is finding out what a great undertaking his work is. It's a challenge beyond compare. His nerves and patience will be tested severely. Slip-ups need to be dealt with, and rightly so. Don't brood about it. He needs you to be right back to your old self or you will be of no value to him. Just don't make the same mistake twice," he commanded. I determined never to let Hodgson down again.

The Air Marshal said, "Abraham Lincoln was a failure at everything he tried. Until well past the age of forty, he had no faith in himself. He became a genius when he became confident. You need to believe in yourself. Don't think negatively. Don't get down on yourself. It won't help." He looked at me, wondering if I got the message.

"I understand," I said, and I did.

Campbell looked at me once again. "No one can let Stu down. He is the important one!"

Over Cumberland Sound the aircraft turned inland and entered the Pangnirtung Fjord. We flew between towering walls of rock that dripped glaciers and snow shelves, seven miles of breathtaking scenery.

"The tide rises and falls nineteen feet here," the Air Marshal said.

"What happens if we land when the tide's out?"

"No, no. The ice flexes in the middle of the fjord. Same with any sea ice, it rises and falls twice a day. That's why it's always so broken and rough by the shore."

A small cluster of buildings was squeezed onto a narrow strip of land. Similar to the other communities, Pangnirtung had no airstrip, just a flat, smooth area marked off on the sea ice. Once halted, our wingtips rocked in the vicious wind.

A bright yellow bug-like vehicle scuttled out to meet us, leaving a huge plume of powdered snow in its wake and eventually disgorging two occupants. Hodgson stepped down from the Twin Otter and shook hands with the leader of the delegation. "Who in hell is that?" I asked incredulously.

"The administrator," said Simonie Michael. "Dave Davies. If you want to find out how the federal administration treats us, just watch him."

Standing at attention, his hand out for a crisp, formal handshake, was a man who belonged to another age, another continent, perhaps the British Raj. The small, chubby figure, resplendent in tweed jacket, dress pants and brown oxfords, stood unruffled by the strong Arctic wind, stalwart against the -40°F elements, his round ruddy face topped defiantly with a trim tweed hat.

Beside and somewhat behind stood an Eskimo youth of about eighteen decked out in a Nehru jacket, like a ship's steward. Like Davies, he was extremely underdressed.

We climbed into the Bombardier, an ungainly beetle with an internal combustion engine. Its rounded carapace was mounted on tracks at the rear while its snout was supported by a single ski on one side and a solid rubber wheel on the other, to prevent sideslip. Davies jammed the bug into gear and we crawled forward.

"Mrs. Davies and I would be most honoured if you would all care to join us for a spot of sherry." He had everything organized down to the last detail, all shipshape and Bristol fashion. "Your sleeping accommodations have all been arranged. You will stay at my house, of course, Commissioner. The rest will find beds at the transient centre, and the Eskimo will sleep at the Hudson's Bay house." Hodgson's jaw jutted out, as did mine and no doubt those of the rest of our party. He looked ready to give Davies a piece of his mind but Michael shook his head, anxious to avoid a scene.

Davies explained that whaling had been a major industry until the 1920s, by which time the bowhead whale had been hunted almost to extinction. In 1921 the Hudson's Bay Company set up a post here, followed by the

Anglican mission and the RCMP. It struck me that, other than the policing service, there had been a complete lack of permanent government presence throughout the Arctic. We were the first to undertake community meetings and assess their needs.

We emerged from the Bombardier to be ushered into the Davies home which, as in all the communities, was distinguished by its extra height and breadth, a little piece of southern suburbia transplanted to the North. Davies preceded us up the stairs to the main living area. As soon as he did so, the young Eskimo aide-de-camp flung off his thin jacket with a muttered, "Fuck this, I'm getting my parka," and left the house.

Davies seated us in straight-backed chairs ranged around his living room, handed each of us a cut-crystal sherry glass, and made the rounds with a bottle of Harvey's Bristol Cream. Into each glass he poured an infinitesimal droplet, as if it were the most precious essence on earth.

"Holy cow!" Brown muttered in my ear. "He's going to go all the way around and his bottle won't be any emptier than it was before!"

We watched in awe as Mrs. Davies wheeled a big bowl of English trifle in on a serving trolley. Out came little cut-glass dishes and a dollop of trifle for everyone.

"Your health, everyone," chirped Davies. "I do hope you will all return to dine with us this evening."

"You'll be glad to know," he continued, "We do have water supplies again. It's ironic, you might say, that we're surrounded by water but sometimes don't have a drop to drink."

"Why do you say that?" someone asked.

"State of emergency back in November. The creek we use for water in the summer dries up when winter comes. So we have to cross the fjord to get water from a glacial stream. With a milder than usual fall, the fjord didn't freeze. We rationed water for two weeks and were down to one week's supply. We were set to evacuate three hundred women and children to Frobisher Bay, but by the time conditions were right for flying the fjord froze over."

The marvels of central heating made my eyes droop and my head nod. I was jolted by the ringing of a telephone, a foreign and intrusive sound in this environment.

"My office," Davies declared, "The other phone in the community." He picked up the receiver. "Pangnirtung four-one, Davies speaking," he answered with a fastidiousness that made Brown snicker and Petrigo roll his eyes.

I turned to Hodgson and said, "I'm beat, and I'm coping better than some. How are you?"

"The people of this community deserve as much attention as those in Grise Fiord. Get used to this, young fella'."

14
NO PLACE FOR AMATEUR PILOTS

MARCH 17, 1969

FROM PANGNIRTUNG WE FLEW TO Broughton Island, then Frobisher Bay, where Air Marshal Campbell left us to deal with business matters, followed by Cape Dorset, Port Burwell, Coral Harbour, Igloolik and Hall Beach. We'd left massive Baffin Island and flown south deep into the cavernous Hudson Bay. We were 1,500 miles straight south of Grise Fiord, and headed for the Belcher Islands, just north of James Bay on Québec's Ungava Peninsula.

"You look like shit!" Daryl Brown said, rubbing the fuzz on his head.

"Twelve communities in twelve days. It's killing me." I was seated in the co-pilot's seat. Monaghan was in the passenger cabin, sleeping at this early hour. "No decent food and everyone stinks."

"That you do! But you don't want to shower. Opens your pores. You need all the natural oils you've got. Or better yet, dab on some whale blubber!"

"Seems like whale blubber is all we've eaten. Damned if I'm going to wear the stuff too."

I rested my forehead against the side window and gazed down at sea ice that went on forever. There were no landmarks to relieve the tedium. "Don't you ever get tired of flying these endless miles?" I asked.

"I'd find it harder now to fly out of Montreal, with all the traffic and controllers. Up here I'm on my own. Sometimes it can be tough with no navigation aids or meteorological information. The distances are so huge it can be a lonesome feeling. I've gone on my own four hundred miles into the Barrens to drop off plywood at some lake for people to find in the spring. When it's -40 you don't know if the starter will work or if the battery's going to be dead, so I always leave the engines running. It's an eerie feeling to know you could be stuck there if you don't get that engine started again. It's no place for amateur pilots."

I peered at the expanse of Hudson Bay slipping by.

"I like flying Hodgson around. He's got a good sense of humour and makes sure Monaghan and I are always part of your party. Never had that happen before."

We sat silent for some time and then Brown spoke again. "He has a helluva job to do. Obviously he doesn't go along with the bureaucratic crap and isn't scared of making decisions. Got a good feel for what's needed. He'll make more changes in ten years than the Territories has seen in a hundred." Brown checked his watch and gazed out his side window. "You can help me look for the Belchers.

"Like trying to find a bean in a black cat's ass. Look for a bunch of long, thin islands stretching north to south. At a distance it's hard to spot because everything's covered in snow and the eskers blend in with the sea ice. The homes are likely buried in snow, so we won't see much."

Searching the whiteness strained my eyes.

"You notice when we land somewhere, everyone's just bustin' to get out of the plane to have a piss," Daryl said. "I remember flying the Beechcraft. You could be just busting after a four-hour flight. The Beechcraft has a tube in it with a funnel, and there's a Venturi outside to give it some nice suction. One time in the middle of the night, there was a bright, full moon and a young nurse sitting in the front with me. I just had to go. I figured she's seen one before, so I pulled it out and put it in the tube. Then asked her if she'd like to use it. She said she guessed she would, so she did. You lose all your inhibitions in circumstances like that."

"Up ahead?" I said.

Brown nosed us toward some barely discernible shadows on the vast frozen land beneath us.

Twenty-eight years before, the Belcher Islands had been in the national news as the scene of one of the most horrific murders in Canadian history. Several religious fanatics murdered nine fellow Eskimos in a cult-like frenzy after reading a Bible written in syllabics left behind by a missionary. Looking down, I could easily imagine how physical privation and unfamiliar religion could brew a powerful madness.

THE SOUTH CAMP OF THE Belcher Islands was located on a low, narrow esker that rolled northward like a drab finger of dough, part of several such fingers that lay undiscovered by white men until the whalers arrived in the 19th century. In midwinter the islands boasted no feature that could be called attractive or friendly.

As he had at the other communities, Hodgson smiled and talked with the Eskimos, untouched by my low spirits as he led the parade to the settlement.

"How long has South Camp been here?" I asked the English-speaking youngster walking beside me.

"Actually almost everyone lives at Sanikiluaq, what you people call North Camp. We asked the government for a school but, when the ship came, the captain couldn't find the North Camp so he unloaded the school here."

"You mean he just dumped it off at this point, fifty miles from your community?"

"Yes. People with kids live here, because of the school, or they send their kids to live here with other families."

Some ship's captain had been in a hurry and these people suffered the consequence—as in Clyde River, where well-meaning southerners built the community on mud flats instead of gravel for some unfathomable reason, or Grise Fiord where the people were left to their own devices to survive. It was always the Eskimos who were left behind to cope, adapting to southern stupidity in their patient way. This was a people with great endurance. "Why didn't everyone just move and live down here?" I asked.

"Better hunting at the North Camp."

We reached some low walls of snow blocks that marked the settlement. At first, I thought they were igloos, but they turned out to be windbreaks protecting ramps that led down to the homes beneath—shacks and framed tents buried beneath snowdrifts. Unlike the other settlements, these people had no southern-built homes. Seventeen families lived here, although it was impossible to tell unless you counted the black chimney pipes that poked up like periscopes through the snow. My camera recorded the hallmarks of community life in the Arctic: broken honey bags, frozen in place, and mounds of trash.

I had found Clyde River depressing, but this was ten times worse. I guessed that no other white man with any power had ever stepped on these islands. What do people who live in burrows under the snow care about government? Maybe it was all a big fraud, marching into communities and telling people about progress and improvements. Maybe it would be kinder to leave them alone. But there was no doubt in my mind these people deserved a better lifestyle, and Hodgson had a chance to provide that.

They treated us with great respect and wanted us to visit their homes. The steps leading down to the first were hemmed in by high walls of packed snow. At the bottom of the ramp was a wood frame tent with an interior not unlike the houses we had visited in Clyde River—a raised sleeping platform, a kudlik to provide light, and a woman boiling some sort of game in a pot over a fire.

"Don't you ever get trapped by snow filling the entranceway?" Hodgson asked.

After the translation the homeowner showed how the door opened inward, not outward so that it could always be opened, and any snow filling the ramp or tunnel could be dug away.

We were escorted to several more homes before arriving at one of only two buildings visible in the community, the transient centre, a small house normally used as a hostel for students attending the adjacent one-room school. During the school break, the transient centre served as our accommodation as well as the community bathhouse.

"I want a shower!" said Ed Cowan, stepping into the bathroom, eager to get in before anyone else. Soon we heard a pained obscenity; he emerged a short time later.

"That was quick!" Brown said.

"There's a hole in the wall! Snow was blowing over me and the water is just about frozen!"

"Yeah. Better smelly than sick."

That night there was a feast at the school before the community meeting. The line started at the cloakroom and snaked around a corner. Syd Thompson, ahead of me, said, "I hate to admit this. Heh! Heh! I miss the old Air Cadet. Didn't figure he was my sort at first, but he grew on me. Just before we parted company at Frobisher Bay, him and me sat up all night shooting the breeze. He's an interesting type. I can see why Stu gets along so well with him."

Like the rest of our party, I was hungry. "Seal meat, cooked or raw. Your choice," said Brown. Seal meat has all the fats, proteins and nutrients necessary for survival in this frozen desert and helped ensure Eskimos rarely got sick. But I wanted some familiar food and loaded up instead with pink Arctic char and bannock. No doubt I was as stupid as the explorers of old, who died because they refused to eat local food.

While we ate, the Eskimos brought in soapstone carvings and set them on the windowsills. They were beautiful pieces of stonework, a testament to Eskimo patience and skills honed in arctic isolation. Splinters of bone and thongs of hide added to the complexity of many items, each piece a gem, painstakingly made and artistically brought to life. The beauty and delicacy of the carvings stood in stark contrast to the desperate poverty and harsh environment that marked South Camp. They were quickly spoken for. The best, one weighing about five pounds, depicted a hunter on a polar bear's back. Priced at only $12, it was now mine.

Near 8:00 p.m. the room had been rearranged for the community meeting. By now Hodgson had a smooth and well-orchestrated format, a pattern of introducing himself and his travelling companions, of outlining his vision of government, then throwing the meeting open to questions, all the while doing his best to let the people, not a white administrator (there was no administrator at South Camp), drive the discussion. It worked well. Slow and shy questions developed into lively interest.

An hour later the air was thick with tobacco smoke, and the pleasant monotone of the Eskimo language continued its dance with the voices of the translator and of Hodgson. To stay alert, I studied the people. The women wore big shawls and head scarves, not the perky parkas worn in the High Arctic. Everyone sat stolidly in the plain tube-frame schoolroom chairs, their features and clothing reinforcing my impression of this little community— they looked poor.

At 11:00 p.m. the talk was still about the problems we started out with, the same we'd heard in every community: send in vehicles to haul water and pick up garbage; we haven't seen a nurse in six months; we haven't had an airplane in four months.

By midnight everyone in our party, except for Hodgson, Mary-Ellen Davies and me, had fled. My heavy eyelids and querulous stomach made following the discussion difficult. There was always one more person waiting with a question, always one more answer for Hodgson to give. Mary-Ellen dropped her pen, no doubt from exhaustion. "Go to bed," I told her, taking her notepad to record the proceedings.

An hour later I scribbled a note to ask Hodgson if it was okay for me to leave. He gave a nod to indicate he could manage just fine without me.

It was past one in the morning, but not pitch-black outside. The clear sky, stars, and moon provided enough light to see clearly for some distance. I felt as if I were on a ghost ship trapped forever in a frozen inland sea. I thought of the vast distance in time and space between the Belcher Islands and the world of my upbringing.

The packed snow boomed and squealed under my boots so I stopped to listen, unnerved by the unbidden silence, the absence of the daytime cacophony of dogs, children and laughter. Hairs prickled on the back of my neck as a tingling, a sensation bordering on sound, embraced my senses. A whooshing presence, soft as rabbit hair in the breeze, powerful as the sparks of a storm, left me staring, transfixed, at the sky.

The Northern Lights, the *aurora borealis*, shone as I'd never seen them shine before, dancing and crackling in the clear night air, weaving crimson and green veils that shimmered in waving falls and folds of incandescent beauty. It was an electrical magic show, with some unseen hand moving a magnet beneath the night's black velvet, making coloured iron dust specks dance and flow and regroup in ever-changing hues and forms.

I watched as the veils of light moved across the sky and then dissolved, a parody of the veils of bureaucratic ignorance and neglect that Hodgson was trying so desperately to tear from the face of the North. I saw them fade to nothingness and wished his obstacles would move aside with such ease and grace. Against the timeless majesty of the Arctic and the isolation of the Belchers, what hope was there for these people and for Hodgson with his heroic ideals?

15

DIGGING OUT

MARCH 18, 1969

THE NEXT MORNING WAS BRIGHT, clear and cold for the short hop to the North Camp, our last stop. The prospect of returning home was uppermost on everyone's mind.

Hodgson and I were seated up front, near the cockpit door. "What time did the meeting end?" I asked.

Three in the morning. When there was a long silence, I stood up and said if we'd covered everything perhaps we could end the meeting. One of the men wanted me to know this had been the first meeting they'd ever had and it was a lot of fun. They'd really like to do it again some time."

Within fifteen minutes we were over the North Camp. Brown banked the plane over a cluster of homes, pulled the throttles back and descended toward the sea ice. He banked left and right, and then cursed loudly.

"What's the problem?" Hodgson shouted.

"Looks iffy down there."

"What do you mean?"

"No landing spot marked off. Looks like there's a crust on the snow, but I don't know how deep it is to the hard ice."

"Try a different area?"

"Talked to the community manager on the radio phone last night. He told me it was safe to land in front of the community."

"I want to land if possible," Hodgson said.

"Sure."

The plane descended and Brown let the wheels touch the surface. Plumes of powder spurted into the air as the wheels rolled along the snow. Instead of closing the throttles and letting the full weight of the plane bear down, Brown revved the engines and lifted the plane skyward again, a demonstration of superb skill.

140

"Guess it's as good as we'll get," he said. We came around again and settled into an approach marked by the Twin Otter's tracks.

Carney crossed her fingers and held her arms high in the air. We all waited silently. The wheels touched, rolled for a hundred feet, broke through the crust and jerked to a bone-jarring halt, throwing everyone forward. No one spoke. Brown turned his head into the cabin and yelled, "Hang on!" He rammed the throttles forward, racing the engines in an attempt to pull the plane forward to shallower snow. If anything, the movement pulled us deeper. He shut the engines down and turned off the circuits. In the distance, residents of the community headed out to meet us.

No one said a word as we clambered out of the aircraft. I stood with Brown and Hodgson surveying our situation. I had hellish visions of our imminent return to Yellowknife being postponed indefinitely. "We're stuck," Brown said firmly, as though letting us in on a great revelation.

"Then we're going to have to shovel a runway," Hodgson said, as if that was nothing unusual. "How deep is it?"

Brown dropped to his knees and scraped away snow to show where the wheels sat on the ice. "At least eighteen inches."

"Can we take off if we clear a runway?"

"It's complicated. The manual calls for 1,200 feet of runway, seventy-five feet wide. That's a lot of digging and we don't have much time."

"Why?"

"Look out there." Brown pointed to dark clouds on the horizon. "If the wind shifts that will come rolling in like a blanket and we could be stuck for days."

By now the people had reached us and began shaking hands. We recognized some of them from the meeting last night.

"We left South Camp on our snowmobiles last night," said one. "We enjoyed the meeting so much we decided we'd like another one."

"Well," chortled Hodgson, realizing the enthusiasm of these people. "We've got a problem and we need your help. I'm afraid we can't have a meeting, but I'll make sure I come and see you again soon. In the meantime, we have to dig a runway, and finish it today. If every man here will help, I'll pay $200 to your co-op. Can you bring shovels?"

The Eskimos glanced at each other, then left to find shovels. Hodgson greeted the administrator, who introduced himself as Ernie Sieber. He and his wife Patricia had moved to the Belchers in 1968 after administering the settlements of Arctic Québec on the east coast of Hudson Bay. He was responsible for the Belcher Islands' two camps, and for the development of the new Sanikiluaq Co-op, known for its superb soapstone carvings. Sieber mentioned he would prepare coffee and lunch for our party. He struck up a conversation with Fournier then invited him, Carney, Vaydik and Mary-Ellen to his house.

The shovels arrived and we all bent to the task while Brown began marking out a runway. The day was gorgeous, cold but sunny with hardly a breath of wind. The black clouds remained in the distance and I marvelled at the Arctic's equal capacity for great beauty and great danger. Heaving snow to the side of the runway soon had me sweating and, after half an hour, we'd advanced only a few feet.

"Jake!" Hodgson yelled. "Bring everyone here!" When all were gathered, he said, "We've got to speed this up. At this rate we'll be here ten days." He looked at the Eskimos, challenging them anew. "Instead of paying $200 to your co-op, I'm going to pay $20 to every man here, if you can find a way to get this job finished faster."

There were animated gestures, muttering, and conversation in Eskimo, and then they headed back to the settlement. Petrigo leaned thoughtfully on his shovel. Cowan let his drop to the ground. Hodgson turned his back and started heaving snow away from the aircraft. "He's insulted them," I murmured to myself.

After a few minutes the Eskimos returned, cheerfully brandishing big broad knives and carpenter saws. They set to work. "You should have told us to get saws in the first place." said one. "We thought it was odd when we were told to bring shovels."

They ripped into the packed snow with the knives and saws, outlining big blocks and lugging them to the edge of the strip. We all joined in, this time letting the Eskimos lead the way. While we heaved and strained and sweated, and worked furiously, they worked at a measured, practiced pace. "Work slower, be patient and you can work all day," one of them advised. "Work fast like you do, you'll be tired in no time."

After two hours the runway grew noticeably, the sides piled high with blocks of snow, creating a gully.

Hodgson yelled at Brown and me from his work area. "We'll eat in shifts. You guys go first."

It was easy to find the administrator's house, which sat up on high ground, clear of drifts. A large living room window looked down on us, and behind it was Jean Fournier, in conversation with Sieber.

Brown's breath steamed in anger in the cold air. "Fornicator. I wondered where he got to. Remind me to leave without him." I was concerned that Brown would say something to Fournier so I explained that his report to Chrétien would have a significant impact on our future. The time he spent with Sieber was valuable.

Inside the kitchen Carney stirred a ladle in a huge pot. "Where's the food?" Brown demanded as he sat down at the dining room table, glaring at Fournier. Carney ladled out a dollop.

"Where'd you learn to cook? Corn, porridge, beans, soup, fish, everything is in here."

"Eat it or leave it," Carney said with exaggerated sweetness.

"Daryl. Cut it out." I was becoming fed up with his sarcasm and belligerence.

He muttered something, dug in and finished by swiping his plate with a slice of bread. "Hey," he yelled into the kitchen, "that was good." Carney brought more.

Back at the airstrip the Eskimos were now several hundred feet ahead of the aircraft. Brown was energized and picked up a shovel. Hodgson walked about with a wide shovel, scraping off any leftover clumps of snow.

Ed Cowan yelled at Hodgson, "You don't do so bad for an old fellow."

"How old do you think I am?" Hodgson yelled back.

"Oh, fifty maybe."

"I'm younger than you are, pal. I'm forty-five."

Every once in a while one of our party would straighten his back, wipe his forehead with a sleeve, and stare at the grey clouds that crept across the distant sky. Then he'd get back to work with a look of determination. We worked for what seemed like hours more, lifting blocks to the side and shovelling loose snow behind the Eskimo party of snow carvers.

"Jake, come with us!" Hodgson commanded as he came by with Syd Thompson. When we were out of earshot of the others he said, "We're going to the co-op craft shop. These guys do better without us anyway."

Soapstone carvings big and small, all beautifully finished, filled the little frame building from floor to ceiling. They were realistic in style, a contrast to

the more primitive carvings produced in some other northern communities,
featuring feathers on a bird, tusks for walrus, an ulu for a woman and a harpoon for a man. I coveted more than I could buy. There were also pails full
of miniature carvings for $100 per bucket. Hodgson took two, saying they'd
make great promotional gifts.

As we staggered back to the plane with our booty, Brown demanded,
"What have you got there?"

I shoved a big box in the doorway. Hodgson added his two buckets of finger-
sized trinkets. "Just helping the co-op, that's all. Why don't the rest of you
take a break and go have a look? We'll carry on."

When they returned, tension started to rise, fuelled by a determination
not to be trapped. Everyone wanted to have that runway finished before the
light died.

By late afternoon we were ready to load the aircraft and prepare for takeoff.
We'd collected at least another three hundred pounds since the start of the
trip, including my beloved narwhal tusk from Grise Fiord. I feared our latest
acquisitions would be the straw to break the camel's back.

Hodgson dusted the snow off his mitts. "What do you say, Daryl? It's four
o'clock and we don't have much daylight left."

I was grateful we had as much daylight as we did. Brown contemplated
the two feet of clearance beside each propeller. "Five hundred feet, about
a third of what we're supposed to have. We'll have to get up to speed fast. I
can't steer until we reach forty miles an hour and that will be a problem with
these sidewalls. We have to hit sixty-four miles an hour, that's the minimum
for takeoff. But there's no wind right now to give us lift. Tell you what—if we
build a ramp at the end, so it sets the tail down when we hit it, it will help us
get airborne."

We stowed the boxes of carvings in the rear compartment and jammed the
other luggage and sleeping bags in front of them. We tied the luggage down
with rope, weaving it back and forth through the handles to form a net.

Ed Cowan headed back to Siebers' place to get Fournier and the women.

When they arrived, Syd Thompson nodded towards Fournier and said to
me, "Heh! Heh! Useful contact for Stu." He looked at me and said, "Save me
a seat beside you?"

My cheekbones felt the loss of the sun's cheer. The horizon billowed blacker than before, while the sky above us was drained of all colour by the onset of dusk. "Come on Daryl," I muttered, stamping my feet back and forth, anxious to begin our escape. Cold sweat ran under my armpits. I noticed the others were anxious as well. Hodgson stood with the Eskimos who had gathered to witness our departure.

"Okay, let's go," barked Brown as he returned. He was about to climb aboard when he halted. "Whoops, nearly forgot!" He walked to the front of the aircraft and reverently dropped to his knees in front of the nose wheel. He raised his eyes and hands in prayer, his bald head, full-blown beard and wolf-skin parka making him look like some possessed monk. We were annoyed by his mockery but it was a great photo, so I grabbed my camera. There he was on his knees in front of the aircraft, his eyes closed with his fingers clenched around each other, shaking in concentration as he held them in front of his face. His lips were muttering words I couldn't discern. Maybe he was serious? Daryl Brown, whose language was as rough and coarse as a lumberjack, now prayed in front of the plane, in front of his passengers and a community of Eskimo people. Maybe we are in real danger, I thought. Maybe we're not going to make it.

"Let's go, captain!" Hodgson yelled, ushering us to the plane.

Syd Thompson lingered, deep in conversation with Fournier, while the rest of us climbed aboard. Then he got on and joined me near the front, leaving Fournier to take the remaining seat at the very back. "Heh! Heh! Fournier had better hope those soapstone carvings don't come crashing forward."

Brown started the engines and checked the instruments. Out of my window I could see nothing but the white wall of the gully. Clouds of snow swirled about the props as the air whipped at the blocks we'd carved.

Brown revved the engines and reversed the prop blades. He moved us backwards until the tail overhung the downwind end of the runway. Nobody said a word as he jammed his seatbelt on tight and yelled into the back, "Everybody ready?" He opened the throttles as far as they'd go but we didn't move; he had the brakes on tight. The plane bucked and swayed and lurched as the props bit into the darkening air. Carney, seated next to Hodgson, dropped one hand and grasped his large fist, crossed the fingers of her other hand and raised them both to the heavens.

Brown turned to Monaghan and I noticed a bead of sweat on his forehead.

Never, in all the situations we'd been in, had I seen Brown ruffled. Now he was sweating, and Monaghan was as white as a sheet. A voice inside me cried, "This isn't going to work. There's so much to be done, but this is the end of everything."

Syd growled beside me, "I miss the old Air Cadet. Too bad we had to leave him in Frobisher. He'd enjoy this."

No one spoke. We stared straight ahead as Brown released the brakes. We rolled down the gully, swaying from side to side, the propellers hurling great cascades of loose snow as they nicked the walls, the plane bouncing up and down over the uneven ice. Streams of snow hurtled past the windows and we knew that with one tiny mistake, one twist, we'd tip and cartwheel off the side walls.

The Twin Otter accelerated like a bullet down a barrel. We had to be doing fifty miles per hour and were closing in on the end of the runway when the nose wheel hit the ramp. The tail went down and there was a surge of power. We felt a bang and a rumble, and then realized we were airborne.

We exhaled as one, then cheered and clapped in admiration of our two pilots and the plucky aircraft. We were pressed back in the plastic seats as Brown hauled back on the stick, catapulting us almost straight up until we hit eight hundred feet.

Suddenly, with no warning, the engines lost their roar. The plane levelled, and we nosed straight down towards the ice. Our seat belts sliced into our stomachs; I could imagine how the boxes of carvings would be pressing into Fournier's back. When the Eskimos on the ice realized something was wrong they turned and ran in all directions, away from our descent. Three hundred feet above the ground Brown started to laugh. He opened the throttles again and pulled us out of the dive, zooming over the running Eskimos. He dipped the wings from side to side, thanking them for their help.

WE WERE SILENT, LETTING THE stress dissipate. Finally, some of the passengers moved about, chatting and passing the time. Hodgson leaned against the bulkhead with his parka hood pulled up, fidgeting restlessly. He leaned forward to Syd and me, "We take our lives in our hands just travelling from one place to the other."

I looked at him, startled. His determined air of cheery optimism was gone.

"Look at us! It's the 20th century. We're sending a man to the moon, yet we can't leave a place without digging ourselves out. And we're only visitors. This is how the people of the North live every day." Hodgson's energy was sapped. The stress lined his face, and he had dark shadows around his eyes. "We don't have the money to do all the things that have to be done. I can't begin to provide these people with the airstrips, the houses, the fuel storage tanks, fishing boats and nursing stations they need. There's just no way."

Syd Thompson growled, his rasping, gravelly baritone barely kept in check as he waited for a chance to butt in. "That's bull, Stu. You've got what the North needs. You've got the gift of the gab. That's what these people need most, a voice that can be heard by people in power, the people in Ottawa. The money's with the feds, Stu. Heh! Heh! You can't solve all the problems right away, nobody can, but you can go after those with the money. You can rattle the chains of the people with power. I've seen you do it before."

Hodgson didn't respond.

Syd continued. "No one can avoid listening to you. You've proved that a thousand times. I'm watching the way these people listen to you, and I think you can make the people in Ottawa listen to you. If nothing else, these visits of yours raise the morale of the people."

Only Thompson or the Air Marshal could speak to Hodgson in this way, shaking him back to reality.

"Stu, the answer's been staring you in the face all along," Syd rasped. "As you're going around, you've got to organize the people, just like in the unions. Get them stirred up to want to get involved. Extend the whole system of local government, one that will apply to every kind of community, no matter how small. Set up housing committees and welfare committees. Tell all your administrators they're there to work their way out of a job. Let the people start hiring and firing the administrators. That way they'll learn the ropes of government. Before you know it, they'll want to get involved at higher levels. They'll grow and eventually control their own destiny and do a lot better job than us whites have done over the last hundred years."

Hodgson nodded. "Bless you, Syd. You've earned your keep, old friend."

We were silent for a long time. I looked out the window and saw the west coast of Hudson Bay pass below the aircraft. Hodgson broke the silence. "Don't misunderstand me. I have my moments of despair, but that never means I'm ready to quit. As far as I'm concerned, this trip has been a great success. It's taught me enough about the North that I can take on anyone who tries to tell me what needs to be done. And we'll keep doing these trips." Hodgson's voice returned to its exuberant, animated pitch. "I've learned a lot and so have the people I've met. And you're right, Syd, the people need control of their lives. Thanks to you, I think we're closer to solutions to everyone's problems."

"It'll come, give them time," Syd said. "These things have to evolve in their own way. And watch you don't give away your authority to your bureaucrats in Yellowknife. That's your weapon to progress. Turn adversity to your advantage, Stu. The crises are going to be there but that'll give you reason to stay on your toes. Remember that old adage, 'You have to have desire.' It's the starting point of all achievement."

Syd sat silent for a few moments, and then spoke again. "Heh! Heh! Stu, here in the North you're the king. You know what needs to be done. So set yourself a definite goal. Fix it in your mind. You know you don't get something for nothing. When you get back to Yellowknife write out a clear, concise statement of what needs to be done for these people. And set a timeframe. Make it an obsession."

Part Three

EMPEROR OF THE NORTH

16

THE NEXT THING TO GOD

JUNE 1969

IT'S SAID THAT THE NORTH has only two seasons—winter and summer—since fall and spring are so abrupt and short. To mark the seasons, each year a rusty old car was dragged onto Long Lake, close to the airport. Residents would bet on the date the car would fall through the ice, marking the arrival of spring. After the first rain shower, the trees would bud and within days leaves would sprout, marking the beginning of summer.

Summer in Yellowknife is a time of renewal, revival. The sun barely sets beneath the horizon and enough light remains in the sky for almost any outdoor activity to continue twenty-four hours a day, a condition that persists for about eight weeks. At midnight and into the wee hours of the morning, people mow lawns, garden, paint fences, have barbecue parties or picnics, often by one of the many northern lakeshores. Yellowknife's golf course is as busy at midnight as at noon. It's an exhilarating time of year.

The intensity of the summer season helped Barb and me forget the gloom and darkness of winter as we cruised in a small aluminium powerboat on Back Bay. Short-sleeved shirts, shorts and sun hats were a welcome change from heavy duffle coats and fur outfits.

Barb closed her eyes and threw back her head back, relaxed. "I love this!"

"We deserve it. After surviving a Yellowknife winter we damn well ought to stay up all night, every night while summer lasts."

I reflected on the winter trip through the Arctic. "You know, there are more problems up there than you can shake a stick at, and not a solution in sight. I don't know how the Eskimos exist in a land that appears to grow nothing or bear anything. They must be the most resilient people on earth. They seemed appreciative of our visit and of Hodgson's promises but now we have to fulfil his commitments."

I cut the motor to absorb the silence. But soon we were slapping at squadrons of mosquitoes. If Yellowknife has the most glorious summer, it also boasts the biggest and most prolific mosquitoes. These were not the pests I'd experienced in the Ottawa Valley; these were the B-52s of the bug battalion, and there were thousands of them, at times making it impossible to enjoy the outdoors. I slapped on more insect repellent and started the motor again, heading toward Old Town. It was well after midnight and still broad daylight.

The activity around the wharves and supply sheds continued, even at this hour. We studied the brazen little huddle of buildings that grew like hog bristles from The Rock and the Bush Pilot's Monument.

"It's changed just since we've been here," I said.

Not so long ago, hardly anyone in Canada knew of the Northwest Territories and this little mining town. Now, it was becoming known as a vibrant capital with a busy airport, a noisy main street and a list of visiting dignitaries that was growing by the week. The Old Stope Hotel, which had stood on the pinnacle of The Rock in Old Town, had burnt down, and many of the shacks were being replaced by large houses. Up the hill in New Town, there was a development explosion that included new subdivisions, office buildings, the new headquarters of the Canadian Armed Forces Northern Command and the addition of thirty-four rooms to the Yellowknife Hotel. Expansions had been proposed for the Yellowknife public school and Sir John Franklin High School and, as Hodgson had promised Rae Parker, a seniors' home had been built on the old St. Pat's school site. Yellowknife now had a population of 4,500 and was taking on the look and feel of a capital.

The changes were not welcomed by all. Doug Finlayson, the owner of the drugstore, felt that the hundreds of civil servants who had poured into Yellowknife were rank conscious and socially reserved. "These old mining types are easy mixers. The civil servants, they are stick-in-the-muds. I wouldn't say it's not as nice a town to live in," he said and then added pragmatically as a businessman, "but you make more money in it."[7] Next to his drugstore, Finlayson had just built a two-storey office building with a cocktail lounge in the basement. Others, like mining consultant Norm Byrne, pointed to gaps in services, saying the town needed a store that carried engineering supplies, a shoe store, a sporting goods store, and more good bars and restaurants.

"You can't read a national newspaper or magazine without seeing articles

[7] Ed Cowan, New York Times News Service, "Yellowknife's Metamorphosis Leaves 'Folksiness' Behind," *Anchorage Daily News*, April 15, 1969

about the Northwest Territories," said Barb. There had been numerous reports and editorials about Hodgson and his new government. Some portrayed him as a sort of Arctic Superman, out to bring the modern world to the last frontier.

"Explain one thing," Barb said. "Hodgson's got a pretty big ego, so why did he turn down the chance to be on the cover of *Time* magazine?" The magazine's western correspondent, Ed Ogle, who lived in Calgary, had developed a great affinity for the Arctic and had proposed a front cover story on Hodgson for the Canadian edition.

"He was worried about the reaction from the feds and suggested they use Duncan Pryde instead. He's right. A focus on him would rankle the federal minister and the Ottawa mandarins."

"What do you think he's after? For himself, I mean."

"Oh, who knows? He doesn't talk much about himself or his feelings. On the outside he is sensitive about the needs of the communities and the people. Underneath? Anybody's guess. Adulation, approval for what he's doing? Material security for his family?"

"Nothing wrong with that."

I headed the boat toward the wharves and tied up at Wardair's jetty, in front of the Twin Otter that had carried us to the roof of the world. The plane had been converted from winter to summer use and now sported floats in place of balloon tires.

A single-engine Otter floated in from the bay and bumped against the wharf just as a hearse roared into the gravel parking lot, raising a cloud of dust. The town's only hearse doubled as the ambulance and had been owned and operated for the past twenty years by Walton W. Smith, the town's undertaker. As no graves could be dug into the permafrost in winter, he was obliged to prepare plots ahead of time, earning the nickname of "Digger." Digger sometimes also used his hearse as a taxi; the sign on his vehicle read, "Rates— $2.50 Sitting Up, $15 Lying Down."

Digger, in poor health and on the brink of retirement, eased himself from the dilapidated vehicle and picked his way toward the float plane as the side door opened and a frail old woman appeared, an intravenous needle in her arm. Behind her, a nurse held aloft the accompanying bottle of clear fluid. The old woman grasped the edge of the doorway and put a foot down onto the float, reaching for the wing strut as she lifted a beaded moccasin toward dry land.

Digger attempted to hold the plane steady but capricious waves made the plane lurch away from the wharf and, as Digger futilely grabbed at the strut, she fell onto the wharf. The poor woman dragged herself up off the ground. "That's how you treat an old sick woman?" she asked. She ripped the tape and needle from her arm and stomped off down the wharf, muttering loudly. Digger took one or two steps after her, then scuttled back to his ambulance and fired up the engine. The nurse jumped in beside him and they took off after the patient while Barb and I, and all the mechanics who'd gathered, shook our heads.

"Jake!" someone called. David Searle stepped onto the wharf from another float plane, smoking a cigar that gave off a pungent cloud of smoke. Searle took the cigar out of his mouth and stabbed the air. "Keeps the mosquitoes at bay."

I nodded.

"Our Council session will prove to be interesting. We need to make changes."

I raised an eyebrow. "How so?"

"Well, we're just there to rubber-stamp Stu's budget and legislation. The Commissioner does what he wants and has the Council nod in agreement. Stu is the next thing to God of the Northwest Territories, and he knows it." He took a puff of his cigar, before continuing. "He makes the laws. He writes the budgets. The Commissioner has everything the Council wants—power, resources, dollars, influence with the Minister and the ear of the Prime Minister. You can't have that kind of imbalance forever, not with a Council as rambunctious as this one. They want some of that power for themselves."

I nodded without speaking. I knew Hodgson thought the Council would have to wait.

"Council members are tired of being an obedient little advisory body. I think we're going to see a real tug-of-war." Searle smiled and was gone, harrumphing up the wharf trailing cigar smoke.

"WE COULD DO WITHOUT THE jackets," I said to Bernard Gillie, the Director of Education.

"He still has trouble with women in pantsuits. Doesn't think it's proper office wear," said Gillie. "I don't dare take off my jacket."

The past year had seen Hodgson complete his roster of departmental directors: Education, Public Works, Territorial Secretary, Industry and Development, Treasury, Local Government, Legal Services, Social Development, Personnel and Information Services. Directors had the administrative responsibilities of a deputy minister and the quasi-political responsibilities of a cabinet minister. They were required to appear before the Territorial Council to present briefs, ordinances, financial proposals and to answer questions pertaining to their departments. With the exception of the Director of Information, who answered to Hodgson, they were accountable to either John Parker or Clarence Gilchrist. As the Commissioner's executive assistant, I was included in these meetings.

We were waiting for Hodgson in the boardroom of the Arthur Laing Building, the government's new four-storey headquarters, due to be officially opened by the man himself on June 14, nine days from today. The room was modest, sparsely furnished with six fold-up tables pushed together to form a rectangle and steel tube chairs with vinyl seats.

Hodgson joined John Parker and Clarence Gilchrist at the head table, opening the meeting. "Gentlemen, we've got a big job ahead of us. I trust each of you has reviewed the report of my tour of the High Arctic you received from Jake." He held up the seventy-page report. "Ottawa has been trying to bring the North into the mainstream since 1953 but they never got very far. Now it's our responsibility, but it's the people who will ultimately decide whether or not the North properly finds itself in this century."

The directors nodded as Hodgson continued. "Of course, we all realize that one of the most pressing problems in the North today is how to transform a hunting and trapping population into a modern society. There's no simple answer.

"The North is fraught with problems, especially staggering distances and inadequate communication. The Eastern Arctic seems so far removed from the West it should be another country. Right now transportation lines in the Territories run only on a north–south axis. There's an urgent need for a lateral route linking Yellowknife with the Central and Eastern Arctic regions. Most of these communities don't have airstrips, telephone service, or radio reception. Even garbage disposal is a problem. They have nothing and it is our job to put those services in place."

He turned to Gilchrist. "Clarence, contact the airlines. We need scheduled airline service to more communities, more routes. And the same goes for CNT [Canadian National Telecommunications] and Bell Telephone. Tell them we need telephone service into the communities."

He paused and motioned towards Bill Morgan, the Public Works Director, who'd started tapping his pen. "Yes, Bill?"

"We should remember, Commissioner, many of these problems are still out of our hands. For example, the feds are responsible for building airstrips."

"Right," Hodgson agreed. "But the feds aren't going to build the airstrips anytime soon. If we sit back and say it's their responsibility, airstrips might never get built. In the meantime we can ship in a bulldozer and let the local people build their own strip. But you have a point, Bill. We've got to hit the federal government with detailed reports on what's needed, where, and at what cost. Any time we need something, whether houses, airstrips or water delivery trucks, we have to prepare detailed reports so that at budget time we hit the feds between the eyes with substantiation.

"It's no good saying we need ten new schools this year. We have to say for what communities, how many students and why this is urgent. We need statistics and comparisons to argue our case. State that the incidence of gonorrhea is twenty times higher than the rest of Canada. The average life expectancy for Eskimos is thirty-eight years. A fifth of all deaths result from injuries, violence and accidents. Our unemployment rate is fifty percent. We've got to knock Ottawa dead with this kind of detail. That's going to have to come from your departments. I want to see results!"

Hodgson rattled demands off the top of his head, a stark contrast to the patient listening of the community meetings. "The North is changing. You don't see many igloos anymore. Most of the Eskimos I met prefer southern-style houses. Nobody wants to paddle a kayak when he can go out in a motorboat, nobody wants to use a dog team when he can have a Skidoo. These are all material things that people want. They also want schools, jobs, health services, water delivery to their homes. If we can give them that, it's a start."

Hodgson paused for a drink of water then turned to Bernard Gillie. "Bernard, I want each community to have a school that teaches up to Grade 8, not just Grade 4. I don't want these young kids flown to Frobisher Bay, Inuvik or Churchill. We need more regional high schools so kids don't have to travel so far.

"And while I think of it, you should all know I've assigned Abe Okpik to get rid of those awful Eskimo disc numbers. I'm calling it Project Surname. Abe's going to go down in history as the man who gave the Eskimos back their names."

Abe, as he was known by everyone, had started with the name Auktalik, "man with a mole." Then he got his number, W3-445, which he later dropped in favour of Abraham Okpik. A former appointed member of the Council who now worked for the Territorial Secretariat, he would have to speak to about ten thousand of his people about the need for proper surnames and given names and help each individual choose. Selections would be processed under the Name Change Ordinance, approved by a territorial judge and recorded on a citizenship card. His travels would fulfil his grandmother's prophesy when, tying his umbilical cord with the sinew of a ptarmigan, she had predicted that "one day he will fly like a bird all over the world."

Hodgson continued, "Our success will depend on what we accomplish at the grass roots level." He motioned to Sid Hancock. "Sid, update us on what you are doing."

Hancock was an admired and respected veteran of the North, a one-time schoolteacher turned administrator. "We're concentrating on extending the community council system everywhere, but we'll have different levels. Our concept is similar to the village, town, and city level used elsewhere in Canada except we have two levels below that of village—settlement and hamlet. A very small settlement can start with an appointed council that's advisory to the area administrator. Next level is an elected council. For those communities that can administer their own affairs, we have hamlet status.

"Right now we have two towns and three villages with their own administrations, but over forty are still run by the area administrator. We'll start by creating advisory bodies for housing, welfare and the like. Eventually those with elected councils can hire their own staff and run their own show."

Hodgson explained that the role of the white administrator would change from colonial boss to administrative tutor until he worked himself out of a job. "As far as I'm concerned, development of local government, the empowerment of people is the cornerstone of building the future of our territory. This is where our success or failure will lie.

"Pine Point and Fort Simpson are good places to start down the road to organized and empowered communities. I'll travel to each next month to raise the flag once their elections have taken place.

"Next spring, the federal government will hand us administrative control of the Eastern Arctic except for federal programs like health services, policing, the courts and natural resources. That means we'll be responsible for the entire Northwest Territories.

"You gentlemen, you're going to have to burn the midnight oil, do the bull work and prepare budgets and proposals. Give me the backup numbers. And remember, I'm going to continue to travel around the Territories to make sure you guys are doing your jobs. From here on in, everything we do has to improve things for our people."

With sudden intensity Hodgson said, "All right! We all know what has to be done. Let's do it and make sure it's done first class! At the next Council session let's show them we've done our homework."

JUNE 16, 1969 WAS THE opening date of the summer session of the Council of the Northwest Territories. Several women were once again seated in the front row in the Elks Hall, clacking away with their knitting needles, eyes glued on their work, their ears alert for juicy statements. Politics and its personalities continued to be the most popular entertainment in Yellowknife.

Hodgson was in full spate with his opening address, one hand gripping the lectern, the other stabbing the air. His eyes alternately checked his notes and ranged above the crowd, his brows adding dramatic impact. He cut a powerful figure at the podium—his voice resonant, his demeanour comfortable, his message clear despite his unsophisticated grammar.

He spoke of increased responsibilities and a record budget of more than $40 million, projected to increase to $65 million next year to support a population that had increased to 32,000.

"I am confident this administration is ready to accept whatever responsibilities it may be asked to take on. The proof in any pudding is in the eating. People of the Northwest Territories expect a great deal of their government and we do not intend to let them down."

He reminded councillors that the territorial government had taken control of the Keewatin District on April 1, 1969, and would take control of the Eastern Arctic on April 1, 1970. He then spoke about his plans to celebrate the Northwest Territories' centennial and to create the first ever Arctic Winter Games.

THE NEXT THING TO GOD

Hodgson made no reference to the establishment of an executive council. Disappointment on the faces of councillors said it all. Like everyone else, they were aware of recent newspaper headlines proclaiming that the Territories were moving toward provincial status; rumours were circulating that the Minister, Jean Chrétien, would be making speeches in Yellowknife and Whitehorse soon. They wanted more authority, but Hodgson was determined to remain in control.

His next task was to introduce a special guest, James Smith, Commissioner of the Yukon who, unlike Hodgson, reported to an elected council chaired by a speaker chosen from amongst the members. Smith was the chief executive officer and head of the public service. While he had the power to veto bills, he did not take part in the deliberations. Hodgson had been forewarned that Smith would speak in favour of an elected executive council.

"It's certainly a privilege not often accorded to two members of the most exclusive club in North America, to sit on the same platform together," said Smith reflectively.

"The Northwest Territories is a tremendous size. They have a tremendous-sized Commissioner. We in the Yukon being a peanut compared to you, we have a peanut-size Commissioner." Smith's self-deprecation brought gales of laughter.

"Probably the greatest single impediment that we who live in the North face is the lack of understanding as to what this part of Canada is all about. I think one of the biggest single contributions we could make to Canada as a nation is to stand up and let the rest of Canada know that we're about to become self-sustaining and tremendous contributors to Canada's economy, instead of being a drag on the national income.

"You have some members who are elected, and on my side of the Mackenzie Mountains the Council is totally elected. They say that the Commissioner of the Yukon forms Her Majesty's loyal opposition, and whether he likes it or not he has to publicly defend the actions of his government, and be prepared to withstand the onslaught of seven of the most loquacious people ever to come north of the 60th parallel.

"I think you know some of my councillors and I'm sure that they know some of you, and no doubt behind the scenes, Mr. Commissioner, these people are plotting against the two of us to try to eliminate us as quickly as

159

possible from the political scene. I may say that from where I sit, I'm quite interested in having my position eliminated from the public scene. I don't think there's any question at all as to the ability of people in my part of Canada to take a far greater part in their day-to-day government. They have been able to elect people since about 1900 and by now, they should be able to take on a lot of the administrative responsibilities that are inherent in this type of process."

As the applause died down, Hodgson called for replies to his opening address. "Mr. Searle?" he intoned.

Searle waved a copy of the Carrothers report in the air. "There's a recommendation in the Carrothers Commission report which hasn't been implemented so far. It is essential, and I hope when the Minister of Indian Affairs and Northern Development, the Honourable Jean Chrétien, makes his long-awaited announcement on the future evolution of government in the North, he will incorporate it in any changes he proposes to make. Should this recommendation be excluded, then all other changes, whether they be more council members, a lower voting age, or a name change from Territorial Council to Legislative Assembly, will be window dressing."

I had expected a vitriolic attack, but the lawyer maintained his poise, his words precise and emphatic. "The recommendation to which I refer, Mr. Commissioner, calls for a real executive council. That goes to the very heart of what we are doing here. This is the step in the evolution from colonial to ultimately, in time, provincial status. The bringing into the executive arm of government of, hopefully, some of the elected people is a must . . . a must if we are to cease to be, in my colleague Mr. Trimble's words, 'Strangers in our own land.'"

Council members shouted "Hear, hear," and applauded wildly.

"Look what I've got." The CBC reporter sitting next to me showed me a note from Hodgson advising the press members to stop sending notes to council members. "The practice is common in all Canadian legislatures, including the House of Commons," said the irate reporter.

During a break I broached the subject with Hodgson. "The notes help the reporters clarify a member's stand."

"They have to stop prompting councillors," he replied, clearly in a testy mood.

I told him he would annoy the councillors as well as the press if he persisted.

"Fine. And by the way, tell that CBC reporter from the south he has to dress in a shirt and tie while covering the council session."

Next up was Councillor Don Stewart, former mayor of Hay River. He shot directly at Hodgson. "Just by the nature of this Territorial Council, you and your executive carry a great deal of responsibility. Indeed, this type of government is unique in Canada. The elected people really have very little control of the operations of this particular government. On CBC Radio, I heard this Council referred to as a 'rubber-stamp council.' I don't think that's what we are. However, there are times when certain things do happen where people might get this impression."

The audience overflowing the gallery watched Hodgson closely. He was unmoved.

Hodgson called on the next speaker. "Mr. Trimble?"

Trimble fixed Hodgson with his stare. "What we need, Mr. Commissioner, is a full implementation of the Carrothers Commission recommendations." Trimble reminded the listeners of a letter from Hodgson's predecessor, Bent Sivertz, warning Council of the federal government's intentions regarding the North. 'Delay unto death,' he had written. Trimble acknowledged the thunderous applause that followed with a deep bow to his fellow councillors.

Next to weigh in was Air Marshal Campbell, the prime initiator of the Carrothers Commission. "Here we are, Mr. Commissioner, following the practices of British and Canadian parliaments, and yet we have no parliament. We in the North have no cabinet or government in the accepted parliamentary sense. The electorate should not be led to believe that we have a parliamentary type of government.

"The British and Commonwealth parliaments have a cabinet that is responsible to that legislature for its actions; it is a responsible type of government. I outline this background to enable me to make a reference to an omission of action on one of the most relevant, if not the most important, recommendation of the Carrothers report—that there should be an executive council in order that we might enjoy some semblance of the British democratic parliamentary system.

"An executive council composed of elected members would coordinate finance programs, prepare the budget, legislation, et cetera. In my opinion the need for an executive council is clear; it is the next stage past the colonial type of government that we now have."

Replies to the Commissioner's address were wrapped up by Councillor Chief John Charlie Tetlichi, whose Grade 3 education belied his wisdom and experience. After a self-deprecating comment that he was the least educated man present, he emphasized the importance of the people, their livelihood and their culture. "One must go along patiently and bring his points of interest to the public and explain them. We Indian, Eskimo and Métis must deal and bring our problems to our Council and we must meet together and talk it over and put them to understanding. We have to know one another, Mr. Commissioner, and not fight amongst ourselves. Our old way of life is in danger because the game and wild resources of the North are limited. And our population grows. Perhaps we have only one path to follow. That's ensuring, with your help and the help of governments, that our children come into the 21st century prepared to take their place as a distinct part of the people of Canada."

He said that schools in the Territories should concentrate on teaching native children in their own language and that, instead of providing French as a second language, schools should offer Indian and Eskimo languages. He spoke about the employment situation in the Territories and urged, "the local Indian person should have the first opportunity rather than us having to bring people from the south."

AT THE CONCLUSION OF EACH council session, the Hodgsons hosted a reception for the councillors. Barb and I were invited to help out on those evenings so, on the evening of June 27, we walked the block from our home, meeting up along the way with David Searle and his wife, Dodie. Dodie, a slim, attractive woman with brunette hair, was in a cheerful mood, but Searle grumbled over the events of the afternoon. "Hodgson's a wonderful fellow, but why is he so intractable on this idea of sharing power with the real representatives of the people? He's become a dictator, a god, besotted with his own power."

"Relax!" Dodie said. "We're just about there."

"Oh, sure," Searle responded. "You've been to Hodgson's parties before. He never relaxes. He uses them as extensions of the council session, one more chance to influence and coerce us. All in a very charming way, of course, but it's plain what's going on. He uses all of these cocktail parties and private dinners to make sure he knows exactly where we stand before he lays out his game plan.

"He's our premier, prime minister, lieutenant governor, speaker, monarch—everything but God Almighty. Where else does someone who prepares the government's legislation, programs, spending estimates and agenda also chair debates of the governing council? That's power!"

"But he's doing this for the good of the North," Barb said.

"I'm not attacking Stu personally. None of us doubt he is working for the good of the Territories to establish a competent, responsive administration. It's not just a personal power trip for him. He's filling a power vacuum while doing the job handed to him by Ottawa. And by God, he does his job superbly, there's no denying that. But he regards the Council as an interesting hurdle to work around to reach his objective."

Pearl greeted us at the front door, regal as ever in a formal dress. Tall, slender, soft-spoken and close to her husband in age, her blonde hair and open face gave her a trim, no-nonsense but attractive appearance. She wasn't close to many people, but she was a wonderful hostess who always welcomed people into her home with charm and grace. She was great at her role as the wife of the Commissioner, providing firm support for the home and family, raising their children, Eugene and Lynne.

Pearl was involved in a number of Yellowknife activities including the Imperial Order of the Daughters of the Empire (IODE) Nahanni Chapter that, with the help of Nora Michener, wife of the Canada's Governor General, was raising one million dollars to purchase incubators for the settlements in the Arctic. She was also an accomplished potter who, with a determination much like her husband's, had recently spearheaded the rebuilding of the Yellowknife Crafts Centre.

We were ushered into the house, a good-sized one by Yellowknife standards. The furnishings were sedate and of good quality, not pretentious but appropriate for the couple's rank. A highly lacquered and polished coffee table made from a large slab of tree trunk, presented to Hodgson by Syd Thompson and his union associates in Vancouver, formed the centrepiece in the living room. A fieldstone fireplace dominated the wall at the far end of the room.

"So where's the Commissioner?" I asked Pearl.

"Just follow the noise," she smiled and gestured toward the basement stairway. The basement consisted of a bedroom, an office lined with books, most of them catering to Hodgson's passion for history, and a rumpus room decorated with a number of Eskimo carvings and Eskimo prints. Surprisingly, a display case was crammed with miniature liquor bottles.

Hodgson motioned from behind the bar. "Give me a hand, will you?" He dropped his voice to a rasping whisper I feared was loud enough to be overheard. "I've never seen such a solemn crowd." The crowd, as he called it, consisted of all of the council members and their spouses.

"They're unhappy about your intransigence."

"I'm not here to make people happy. I'm here to get things organized."

"Here, take this tray over to the Air Marshal and Bobby Williamson."

I manoeuvred myself and the tray through the crowd. After handing the Air Marshal and Williamson their drinks, I turned to find myself face to face with Georgina Blondin, the Indian Princess I'd met in Ottawa. It had been two years since I had photographed her on Sparks Street. Since then, there had been lots of news and gossip about her upcoming marriage to Duncan Pryde. They now lived in Yellowknife, with Duncan making regular visits to his constituency in the Central Arctic and Georgina continuing her work as a secretary in a Yellowknife law firm.

"Hi," she said, as beautiful as ever.

"Nice to see you," I replied.

She flashed a stunning smile as Duncan joined us. We moved to the bar where Georgina asked Hodgson, "So, now that Council is over, what is the Commissioner up to this week?"

Hodgson laughed, pleased to be able to control the conversation. "Let's see. My big program is local government, to establish community councils."

"You don't think the Indian band councils are good enough?" Georgina said, more a taunt than a question.

"They're the best at what they do, but band councils govern the Indians and they don't include all the other people in the community."

Duncan moved away from the bar and Dodie Searle stepped into his spot. "I never saw anyone with so many new ideas. You're flying faster than fireworks. I can't imagine you running a government when it is well established and there are no more challenges left for you to tackle."

Hodgson grinned. "I won't be bored for a few years," he responded. "Next year is the Centennial and Yellowknife will gain city status. We'll kick off the celebrations with fireworks on New Year's Eve and invite Minister Gene Cretain." Hodgson continued to mangle the minister's first and last names. "He will be our guest of honour. We'll have the biggest Commissioner's Ball the North has ever seen, followed in March by the first-ever Arctic Winter Games, bringing in athletes from all over the Arctic, along with visits by the Prime Minister, the Governor General and then The Queen."

Dodie, impressed, pursed her lips and tilted her head in admiration. "Sounds wonderful, but what is this going to cost?"

"All taken care of. Several months ago we had a planning conference here in Yellowknife. I hired Jim Whelly as head of the whole thing. One hundred delegates were flown in from all over the Territories—Indians, Eskimos, Métis and whites working through interpreters to hammer out the details. Jim and I went to Ottawa and applied for a special appropriation, a million dollars, or something like that. And we got it."

Georgina gave him a sceptical look. "Why is 1970 significant? One hundred years isn't much when we've been here for thousands of years."

Hodgson was again unflappable. "You have a point." He hesitated, then explained. "It's significant for a number of reasons. It's a hundred years since the British fur traders, the Hudson's Bay Company, gave up governing Rupert's Land. It's also the year when all the federal programs will have been transferred to us and the year the North makes its debut as an entity to be taken seriously by the rest of the country. We'll have unprecedented national attention focused on us. As the theme for Centennial is unity, we'll bring Indians, Eskimos, Métis and whites together and unite the North."

Hodgson repeated his plans to any who would listen, all the while pouring drinks I served. By 11:00 p.m. only the Air Marshal, Barb and I remained.

"Stu, you have to realize these councillors are going to breathe down your neck. I do not disagree with their desires. But I understand your position, in case you wondered."

Hodgson smiled. "I never doubted it." He placed his hand on the Air Marshal's arm. "I hope no one is really holding their breath for me to hand over any power. Not yet."

Campbell raised an eyebrow. Hodgson continued, "You've got to remember what Bent Sivertz said about Ottawa's policy of divide and conquer and delay unto death. They conquer us in the North by giving us scraps of administrative power and withholding all economic power. To build up the administrative power, I have to be in the driver's seat for a while." The Air Marshal nodded.

"And Ottawa adds insult to injury by refusing to tell us what their long-term plan is for the North. They promised a policy statement last October. Now it's delayed until the beginning of next year. Who knows when we'll see it?" He shook his head and finished his glass of ginger ale. "I never expected it to be easy. But things changed when Pearson and Laing dropped out of the picture. Trudeau and Cretain are an unknown kettle of fish. I haven't been able to get a handle on their vision of the future."

"You've developed a good relationship with Fournier," I said.

"It's just tough to get this new minister and his staff to understand the problems of the North, that's what I'm saying. They're new when it comes to northern problems and concerns. In the old days, the Air Marshal here could go to his friend and neighbour, Lester Pearson, and get him to see reality. Or I could talk to Art. We don't have that kind of pipeline now."

"Do what you do best," the Air Marshal said. "Persuade Trudeau and Chré-tien to spend time up here, and you'll get them educated soon enough."

"You're right." Hodgson admitted. "And the Centennial will be a good time to start."

17

LIGHTENING ROD

AUGUST 5, 1969

HODGSON PACED AND GAZED OUT of the window, his mind on Rae. "If Rae votes in favour today, we're away to the races," he said. "The other Indian communities will follow." He looked at his wristwatch. "The polling station's been open three hours. Wonder how it's going."

Erma interrupted from the doorway. "Commissioner, Chief Bruneau and a delegation are here to see you."

Hodgson looked as if he'd been hit by lightning.

Erma ushered in the Chief, dignified and resplendent in his uniform and bowler, along with several elders and the young translator we'd met in Rae. In the tense silence that filled the room, I became aware of the smell of their moosehide jackets.

Hodgson, eyes fixed on Bruneau, invited the delegation to sit at the conference table. "I hope you bring me good news."

Bruneau took a pipe out of his mouth and sat erect, returning Hodgson's gaze. He began his monotone chant, with frequent pauses to allow for translation. The translator spoke in the same monotone, but with a slightly challenging tone. "The Chief has come to ask you to stop the election," he said, his face serious behind his spindly Fu Manchu moustache and heavy-rimmed spectacles. "This election is not what we had expected."

Hodgson sat rigid. "This is a surprise to me," he said. "I understood that your band council wanted the election and had in fact pressed Mr. Leishman to hold it earlier than planned." Hodgson spoke in a controlled fashion, careful to show respect to Bruneau.

There was stony silence for some time, and then the Chief talked again, followed by the translation, "We thought this election would be different to others we've had, the ones that elect only white people. We always vote for our own man in territorial elections, but it's always a white man who's elected.

The Chief does not understand this and does not want this kind of election for our community."

"But the people in Rae can elect whoever they want."

Hodgson's words were translated and he waited for a reply. Again there was that stony silence, those remote, stern faces, perhaps the result of years of contact and disappointment with white society.

"We thought this election would be good for the community if it gave us power to control how money is spent on the things we need," said the young man. "Our band council drew up a list of fourteen names of band members we thought should run for the community council. We submitted these names to Mr. Leishman so he could put them on the ballot. And today, when we came to vote, we found two white names had been added to the list. So I told all my people not to vote."

Hodgson nodded, trying to find the right words. "But that's the whole idea of an election. Anyone can put their name forward if they feel they can serve their community well. It doesn't matter what race they are. As I understand it, a trader and a contractor added their names to the ballot."

"They did," was the reply. "The Chief says you must understand we do not trust an election like this. In our experience, the white guy is always elected. We have the Minister of Northern Affairs committing genocide with his White Paper ending our special relationship with the Crown, and now your government is trying to take over power inside our very community. The Chief cannot support this election."

The young man fell silent and the Chief leaned back, finished. Hodgson looked puzzled. He finally broke the silence, "If you tell your people not to vote, the white men on the ballot will be sure to win the election."

"It makes no difference. The Chief rejects your election and your community council."

Hodgson just stared at Bruneau, this ancient, frail man who obviously had absolute power over his community.

It dawned on me how much we'd taken for granted, how alien our way of thinking was to these people. We hadn't the faintest idea how they viewed the world. I was angry at Harry Leishman, the community administrator, for allowing this screw-up, for leaving Hodgson to get egg all over his face, for not forewarning us of this possibility.

"Very well," Hodgson said. "Thank you for coming." Hodgson stood, indicating the meeting was over. Bruneau rose to his feet and led his group out of the office. Hodgson saw them to the door. When they had gone, he exploded. "This is outrageous!" He glared at me. "What has Leishman been doing there for a year?" He was now practically shouting. "The whole thing's down the toilet!" He threw his arms up and paced around his office.

For the first time in two years he'd lost a round. I realized how sensitive he was to the possibility of failure, and to the criticism that would come with it. He wasn't in control and that bothered him. He couldn't dominate the Indians at Rae, not the way he controlled everyone else. This revelation shocked me as much as Bruneau's actions infuriated Hodgson. I'd thought Hodgson was invincible, but here was a quiet and gentle Indian chief bringing us both back to reality.

"I don't get it," Hodgson said, looking for me to absorb his anger. "Something's going on that I don't understand. Maybe Bruneau's not the only one pulling the strings here. Maybe that young man is something more than a faithful translator. Go out to Rae, right now," he instructed. "Scout around, get a hold of Leishman, and come back with some answers. This is a disaster!"

As I left his office he said, "I'll tell John Parker to nullify the election."

AT THE RAE COMMUNITY HALL, the voting station, all was quiet. The only noise came from a group of kids playing on the grassy pathways outside. Leishman looked small and beaten. "So much for the election," he said, as much to himself as to me.

"Chief Bruneau and a delegation visited the Commissioner this morning, to have the election stopped. What's going on?"

"I don't know," he said, eyeing me with suspicion. He didn't seem concerned that the Chief and his councillors had met with Hodgson. "Last year I came to Rae to do a slow sell on the idea of an elected community council, and before I knew it they're supporting the idea. Then today they turn around and tell me to bury it."

Leishman was not the sort to engender much sympathy. His hair was untidy, his pants baggy and dirty. "Well, this is a boondoggle. I didn't want to push too fast, too soon," he said. "I spent time learning names, identifying the different factions, without seeming to pry. I visited a lot and drank many cups of tea." He gave a dispirited shrug and paced in front of the table with its voter list and ballot box.

"When the federal government gave the people here some houses to live in, everyone figured the electric power came free too, so they didn't pay their bills. Then they objected when the power commission came in and cut off their power."

"What's that got to do with the election?"

"I told them that if they had a community council, it could look after problems like that. It would be a link with the government. By June they were all for the idea. Then the Chief demanded immediate elections and gave me a list of fourteen names nominated by the band council. So of course, I decided to go ahead."

I wandered around the hall, impatient with Leishman's mood. "Well, this is a disaster. How come you didn't know about the possibility of a boycott?"

Leishman shrugged his shoulders. I didn't expect much more from him. "What have the people told you?"

"Sweet tweet. I opened the hall first thing this morning and a few whites voted, then some Métis people drifted in, but no one else. Of eight hundred people, we had maybe thirty-five votes cast—none by treaty Indians. I figured it was odd, so about ten o'clock I found a kid and told him to go find the Chief. The kid came back and said Bruneau had gone to Yellowknife to have the election stopped."

"Who are the shit disturbers, the ones who work behind the scenes?"

"Probably the guys in the CYC." In 1966 the federal government had created the Company of Young Canadians, a Crown corporation that trained volunteers to help marginalized groups better engage with the political process. In an era of protests and activism, it had frequently fostered young, romantic radicals.

"Are they close to the Chief?"

"Yeah, they think the band council should be strengthened, not replaced by a community council."

"And who's in the CYC?"

"James Washie, Louis Rabesca, Caroline Pickles. She was sent here by Adult Education. I hear she's marrying Washie soon."

"Where can I find Washie or Pickles?" He gave me directions to Caroline

Pickles' place. I might find myself in a hornet's nest, but I needed to confront the people Leishman mentioned.

Caroline Pickles was from Toronto and had been among the first CYC members trained in community development. I found her home, a tidy one-room log cabin, introduced myself and asked if we could have a chat about the election. She said nothing but motioned me inside. James Washie stepped from behind a curtain, his face serious.

I explained to them that I needed a better understanding of what was happening.

"The chickens are coming home to roost!" Caroline said quite merrily. "The Indian people have had all they're going to take."

"Of what?"

"Your government's ugly form of racism. I've only been here two months, but I saw enough in my first hour in the North to know I'll spend the rest of my life fighting the kind of system that's working here."

I didn't understand, and she read the frown on my forehead.

"Two white guys from Yellowknife," she said. "They drove me out when I first signed on with the housing education project. They dumped me off with nothing but a sleeping bag and the promise I'd either be crazy or pregnant before this summer was over. One of them asked the other what he thought of Rae. He said it was easy to handle if you took the Chief's wife some crockery or a scarf every once in a while. Kept the Chief quiet, he said. I made up my mind then that no matter how unfortunate, how unfriendly the people of Rae might be, they couldn't be any worse than that pair."

I was taken aback but accepted that she was right. I nodded. "You're the one on the ground. There's no reason for me not to believe you. But the Commissioner ordered me to find out what's gone wrong regarding the election. The Chief had a meeting with Hodgson this morning to have the election annulled. I talked to Harry Leishman over at the community hall and he tells me you guys are with the CYC and likely talking with the Chief and band council."

Washie joined our conversation, his voice controlled, gentle. "I was introduced to your system when I went to school. I was taken away from Rae when I was eight and packed off to St. Joseph's Mission at Fort Resolution, on the opposite side of Great Slave Lake—the other end of the world to me at the time.

"First thing I remember is the nuns saying 'savage, savage' over and over and making me kneel down on my knees all the time and pray to a god I didn't understand. I didn't get out of residential school until I was seventeen."

He fell silent. I waited for him to continue. "And now we've got the federal and territorial governments doing the same thing, telling us what to do, always working behind closed doors, behind the scenes, with all sorts of experts deciding what should be changed in our communities."

He spoke in a quiet, methodical way, taking time to put his thoughts into words. "Treaty Indians don't have direct access to the minister in Ottawa any more, and that's what we need most. Chrétien is supposed to be responsible for treaty Indians, but we're governed instead by a colonial government and a dictator called Stuart Hodgson."

"Hodgson's intentions are entirely honourable," I said. "Eventually he wants Northerners to run the government. He's working towards that, very hard."

"Hodgson doesn't even want to hear about our plans for community development, because they might jeopardize his settlement councils," Washie said. "They might upset the boat for the almighty Commissioner and his territorial government."

There was silence for a few moments. "Hodgson is here to build a government for all Northerners," I replied.

Washie said the community council program was in direct conflict with the band councils. He expressed concern that Chrétien had turned over responsibility for Indian people to the territorial government and that the federal government hadn't lived up to promises made when Treaty 11 was signed.

Since 1967, when Indians first read Treaties 8 and 11 in their own languages, they had maintained that Ottawa had not honoured its commitments—land which was to be allocated to them had not been, or land allocations had been misinterpreted. Their opposition was growing as resource development increasingly threatened their way of life and they realized that the federal government maintained that they had ceded some 370,000 square miles of territory. Native people had begun to organize, first on a community level (the Thebacha Association in Fort Smith, the Deninoo Association in Fort Resolution, Sunrise in Hay River and the Tree of Peace in Yellowknife) and later on a regional basis.

"The federal government came up with this version of Treaty 8 and Treaty

11 and said we ceded all our land and all our rights and they were giving us a payment of $5 a year and that was it! We agreed to a friendship treaty—their version is totally untrue. They even have signatures of the various Chiefs that took treaty, but the written version differed from the oral version that we heard time and time again."

He was calm and articulate. "Once it wipes its hands of us it will never live up to the promises made. We agreed to share this land, not give it away, and until that's accepted by Ottawa, we can't let them slough off their responsibility. Every day we see some new government person coming into our community wanting to make decisions for us."

There wasn't anything I could say. My job was to find out what was going on, and that was becoming clear.

"There's only one way we, as Indians, can have an effect on the federal government's actions," Washie continued. "We can't forget our heritage."

"What's the message?"

"That we've been shafted, that treaty obligations haven't been met, and it's time they were. We have claims to the use and enjoyment of the land, and those claims haven't been honoured."

"But that's a concern you have with the federal government. Hodgson's mandate, handed to him by the Prime Minister, is to build a functioning government, following the Canadian model and tradition."

Washie didn't acknowledge my comments. "The Chiefs used to get together a couple of times a year with the Indian Agent. He told them how things were going to be and they always just sat there and listened and went home. There was another of these meetings some time ago in Fort Smith. I went with Chief Bruneau. For the first time everyone was upset about the same thing—the treaty obligations that haven't been met. We told the government people to leave the room while we formulated some questions. The government people came back in and we got them to admit that Ottawa is determined to hand responsibility for us over to the territorial government. So after that meeting, we got together in a motel room and decided to form an organization that would give us a voice, some power to influence. The Secretary of State Department has cash to fund ethnic groups like ours. We'll get some of that money. This is our land, and we intend to control what goes on in it."

WHEN I GOT BACK TO Yellowknife, I drove down Franklin Avenue to Old Town, across the causeway onto Latham Island and then to Rainbow Valley. I wanted to speak with René Fumoleau, a missionary revered by the Indian people throughout the Mackenzie Valley. Born in France, Father Fumoleau, a Catholic priest, had spent many years in the North and now ministered to the Indians of both N'dilo, commonly called Rainbow Valley, and Dettah, across the bay from Yellowknife. He had earned his place in their hearts by living with them, learning their language and adopting their lifestyle, and now lived in a small house on the edge of the community. If anyone could give me insight, he could.

He welcomed me into his home, remembering me from earlier meetings. He was lean and short, with thinning black hair brushed back from a high forehead and a blue shadow of stubble on his cheeks. He wore a plain plaid shirt with no trace of the cleric's white collar. Fumoleau's smile showed many gold caps and made his compassionate eyes dance.

He was dabbling with something at one side of the room, so I stood politely, breathing in the potpourri smell of woodsmoke, tea, tanned skins and old books. He poured us both cups of tea loaded with sugar. Breathtaking photographs were stacked on the table.

"My hobby," he explained. "I love this land, and its people, and I enjoy taking photographs that preserve their beauty." He retained a distinctive French accent, softened by fifteen years of speaking Indian dialects.

"I'm trying to understand the Indian people better, Father."

"So are we all," he said with a smile. "You'd be surprised how many people still don't understand the Dene." The word Den-nay rolled off his tongue like a drum chant. The people I called Indians called themselves Dene, an Athabascan word for people, the traditional name used long before white explorers ever ventured into their territory.

"The Dene are not of the Western mentality, that's the first thing you have to accept," Fumoleau said. "Their origins are in the Far East, and they think very differently to the way we do.

"I was ordained in 1952 and came north in 1953. When I came to Fort Good Hope, I had the same attitude as everyone else. I was coming to save them, bring them the light. I was raised in the mentality of the French empire. In Africa we tried to change the people who were already there and the Church had just the same attitude. We had no clue about the people here."

"But you continued to be a priest."

"Yes, but soon I could see what was happening. I saw we were not bothering to learn from what was there before us, and I decided to learn. When everyone went out on the land each October, I'd take a dog team and visit their camps. I'd stay a while, then come back to the village, then take off again. They came back to the village for Christmas, some came back for Easter. After Easter they'd go south, for beaver and muskrat. In summer, early June, everybody came back and they went fishing along the river. They lived in their houses, or tents, and we'd visit and talk and drink tea and have picnics. We had a good time."

"I understand you still do."

"Oh yes. But things are changing, and perhaps inevitably so. The days when their greatest concern was finding game to hunt are over."

"Stuart Hodgson was sent north to bring government to the people," I said. "His own desire is to see them embrace the system of governance so that they can solve a lot of their own problems."

Again the priest smiled. "But that's your way of thinking, don't you see? What are the problems? The Dene have been here for ten thousand years. They think the problems of today will be nothing in another ten thousand years' time, so long as they're allowed to live their own lives on their own land.

"There was a Superintendent of Indian Affairs back in the '30s who said the Indian question would sort itself out once all the people were dead from disease. In 1928, six hundred people died of flu, one in every five or six, mostly the older people, with the wisdom and experience, the people holding the structure together. There were 12,000 to 13,000 Dene here before the Europeans came. By then it was down to 3,600."

He spoke in a soft, pleasant voice. "No one asked the Dene if they wanted the territorial government to move north, or if they wanted a western-style government at all. It just came up here without them being asked. Like when the German army invaded western France in 1940. I was fourteen at the time. We didn't ask them to come, and they didn't ask our permission either. The coming of the government is a similar experience for the Dene."

"But it seems to me," I said, as my thoughts came into focus, "that the

Indians—sorry, the Dene—don't have a structure of government at the moment. How can they resist our idea if they don't have anything better?"

"Let me tell you about the Indian way of government," he said with a smile. "Whoever told you their decision-making process is inferior to yours? Suppose there's a decision to be made, the people get together and discuss it. It might be someone not behaving properly, or a hunting matter. An agreement is reached by consensus, after everyone has talked it over. Things are understood, rather than imposed.

"For instance, someone might announce a feast will be held Sunday. No one is told what to bring or what to cook, but when you get to the feast everything is there. Their political system is the same. They sense what people want, and influences are balanced. Power in the village is always geared so that no one person or clan will be in a position to impose something on anyone else. That's why you seldom see a good trapper as chief—it would be too dangerous. Economic power has to be divided, or someone could be a dictator. Now do you start to understand why your system seems so alien and inappropriate to them, Jake?"

"But they say they're forming an organization of their own now. I spoke to James Washie at Rae and there's no doubt it's going to be a political organization, with leaders and policies and rules. It would exclude the other people who share this land, like the Métis and the whites. Doesn't that go against the Dene tradition?"

"Perhaps," the priest replied. "But now, for the first time, they see they will be crushed unless they do something quickly. They made treaties allowing white people to travel in their land, in return for some token handouts, and now they're told the treaties don't mean what they thought they did. Furthermore, the treaty obligations have been handed over from the federal to the territorial government. They see their community structures threatened by Hodgson's new form of local government. They see whites moving into positions of power at a phenomenal rate. I saw that myself. In 1967, when I was in Fort Franklin, there were five whites in the community, but a year later there were forty-two. You can't blame the Dene for thinking everything's changing on them."

He moved to the kitchen sink and asked if I wanted more tea. "That's why you're seeing the development of so many Indian self-help groups, something unheard of just a year or so ago."

"It's hard to keep up," I said.

Fumoleau smiled at me. "It's the way of the world, Jake. We'd better get used to it."

"Why is all this happening now? It's happening across the country, not just here in the North. What set all this in motion?"

"Who can say?" mused the priest. "To everything there is a season. Again, you have to try to understand the Dene way of thinking. Let me explain." He pulled his chair closer to the little wooden table. "I was in Fort Franklin from 1960 to 1968. The Indian Agent came from Aklavik every three months and had a meeting with the people, told them this or that had been decided by the government and the people said 'Yes, that's okay.' Three months later he came back and said exactly the opposite had been decided, and still the people said 'Yes, that's okay'. I asked them if they cared about anything. I asked if there was anything they'd fight for. I thought it was a lack of interest. But they said they didn't have to care about such things. They could still do what they wanted because the land was still there. It's a strange sense of superiority they have, because the people believe they're still free on the land, they're like kings in their kingdom."

Fumoleau sipped his tea and continued, "After Canada's Centennial in 1967, people from throughout the Mackenzie Valley started meeting with each other and talking together. There was a new spirit, an understanding that the Dene are being crushed and robbed of the land and have to do something about it. I saw little signs everywhere. When the federal government said it wanted to create a national park at Snowdrift by Great Slave Lake, a medicine man came up from northern Alberta and talked to the people. That started a prophetic movement that spread to Fort Franklin. I was there when over forty dog teams came from Lac La Martre and other places to hear a couple of people who were considered prophets."

"Prophets?"

"Leaders of a spiritual movement. Wise people who are able to help others find answers to big questions. They're like psychiatrists for a whole nation, or social analysts. It was like a bomb exploding, the people gaining more consciousness about who they were as Dene. They said, 'What we have is good, we have to live by our own laws, have to go back to the traditions of our elders.' Because of their arrival people started to think of their past and their traditions and they saw their cultural identity was being crushed. It was a revolution, a fervour, an explosion. Everything was new."

"Why are the treaties so important? Do they really care how many fishnets they're given each year?"

Fumoleau smiled at my naiveté. "Two things you should know. There never were any negotiations in the first place, so how can they renegotiate? Secondly, the treaties were all based on two totally false premises: one, that the Dene had leaders with the power to sign away ownership of the land; and two, that those leaders did knowingly sign away that ownership.

"The government parties travelled the North asking Indian leaders to sign treaties that gave up ownership of the land. But there were no leaders, and no Dene believed they owned the land either. The government people picked someone at random to be chief, or had the local Hudson's Bay manager nominate someone, just so they'd be able to get a signature.

"The only reason the whites were able to get the signatures was because they said they just wanted permission to travel on the land. They never said they wanted possession of it. The Dene believe the land owns them, rather than the other way around, so it never occurred to them these strangers wanted possession of it. And of course the whites offered the annual gift of five dollars, a ball of twine, a fishnet for every Dene and a suit of clothes for the chief. That's why we still have Treaty Days each year, when the government gives these gifts out."

"Why did the Canadian government go to so much trouble?" I wondered.

"Resources!" Fumoleau said with a flash of his gold caps. "When the Klondike gold rush started, they said let's get a treaty for the Mackenzie, so we can get in there if more gold is found. That was Treaty 8, made with the people south of Great Slave Lake.

"Between 1900 and 1920 the Norman Wells Dene repeatedly wrote the government asking for medical care and help through lean times. The government said no because there was no treaty. The Dene said give us a treaty, and the government said no because the land wasn't worth anything. Then in 1920 oil was found at Norman Wells and right away they got a treaty.

"It's impossible that any treaty drawn up in those circumstances could be of any benefit to the people. You can't bargain under those conditions. In 1940 there were seventeen schools, little boxes, built in the Mackenzie Valley, more than we could ever have dreamed of—all built because the American army was building the Alaska Highway during Second World War. It wasn't done for the benefit of the Dene; it was done to show that Canada administered the land. It was just a sovereignty question, same as they wanted to establish sovereignty over Norman Wells and in the Klondike.

"Housing, schooling, medical programs are all geared to that." Fumoleau continued. "In 1920 the concern was the Mackenzie Valley. In the '50s it was the Arctic coast, in the '60s it's the Arctic islands where they're hoping to find oil and gas. It's all to do with Canada saying we want this bit of land or that bit of land, and we want whatever resources are under it, so we'll give the occupants whatever scraps we must to show we're the real owners.

"The Dene have good cause for concern. Under the terms of the treaties, they are wards of the Department of Indian Affairs, which must care for them in the name of The Queen of England, with whom the original pact was made. But now, under Chrétien's new White Paper, he proposes that responsibility for the treaties pass from the federal government to the provincial and territorial governments. That's why Chief Bruneau led a boycott of Treaty Days last year.

"The Dene have been exposed to the white man for a hundred years or more. That's what makes them different from Eskimos. Eskimos haven't had the same exposure; they don't have the same suspicions. But that may change too."

Fumoleau glanced up as the door flew open and three young kids rushed in. He reached to a high shelf for a box of cookies. "Just one each now, or your mothers will scold me for ruining your teeth," he chided. The children giggled and found themselves places to sit, perfectly at home with this man who knew more of their history than did most of their parents.

"Thank you Father. You have been more than helpful in explaining this and I appreciate your time. But it's late and this is my birthday. Barb is no doubt worried about my whereabouts."

"Come back any time," he said with a smile. "And remember, a good heart is the solution to many problems."

I ARRIVED HOME AT 6:30. Barb was madder than a hornet and gave me a royal dressing-down for coming home so late. I explained my trip to Rae and visit with Father Fumoleau.

"Forget it!" she said walking upstairs. A half-minute later I heard her lugging something down the stairs. I was afraid it was a suitcase, that I had really screwed up. But it was a full set of golf clubs, bag and cart.

"Happy twenty-seventh birthday," she said, giving me a hug. She told me the clubs had sat for two weeks on the sales floor in Bromley's Hardware with a great big sold tag that read, "Ootes." Everyone in town knew about my present, except me.

"Let's go to the golf course," Barb said. "Try them out."

"What about dinner?"

"We can have dinner later at the Hoist Room."

The golf course is the only one in the world without a blade of grass. The fairways are long stretches of coarse sand and the greens are sand with oil sprayed on the surface. Golfers drag a coconut mat to erase footprints. Ravens frequently steal balls which they presumably take back to their nests; when a ball is carried off by a raven no penalty is assessed. Someone had once tried to fix the raven problem by hanging a dead one conspicuously in a tree. It seemed to work well enough for a time.

I pulled up in front of the clubhouse, a one-room shack dragged there to replace the former quarters, the fuselage of a wrecked DC-3 aircraft hauled over from the adjacent airport. Outside, the nearly toxic fumes of insect repellent prevailed, as golfers fought their way through swarms of mosquitoes and black flies. Several portable barbeques were being tended. As I stepped inside, I was greeted by a host of people chorusing "happy birthday": departmental directors, their spouses, Hodgson and Pearl and many of our friends. To my astonishment, I saw my mother and father standing off to the side. I had not seen them in more than a year.

"We arrived this afternoon," my mother said. "Pap," which she pronounced in her Dutch accent as pup, "retired from the mine last month."

"I'm glad you're doing well, Yake," my father said, his accent dropping the J. "You must be learning a lot from Mr. Hodgson. That was one thing I didn't get until I was older, the upbringing of a man."

My grandfather, my father's father, had left his wife, daughter and two sons when my father was young. They had not had much of a relationship until my father was sixteen, when he went to work for his father. After the war, not seeing many opportunities in Holland, our family emigrated to Canada, my father and mother wanting more for me and my brother.

"I grew up quickly, perhaps as much as your work for your boss is letting you grow and improve yourself."

"I'm happy in what I'm doing, Pap. I have a fantastic job and it's the experience of a lifetime." I could feel my eyes starting to water as I hugged my father.

Hodgson walked over and led me to one side. "What did you find out today, Jacobee?" He put the suffix on my name in the Eskimo fashion, adding "ee" to a biblical name. I might have known he wouldn't let a birthday party get in the way of business. It had been a disappointing day for him.

"The Indians resent the territorial government. They don't like the idea of your community councils. They want the bands to run the communities." I recounted the concerns with the treaties, the effort by the federal government to turn responsibility for native peoples over to the territorial government. "Chrétien's plan to turn over responsibility for Indians to you has given them a rallying point to start their own organization. You'll probably be the lightning rod for their anger."

Hodgson's eyebrows arched upward. He remained silent.

"After I came back from Rae, I went to see Father Fumoleau. He told me a lot of interesting things about the Indian people, the Dene, as he calls them. He talked about their belief in consensus and consultation, along with their reluctance to go along with anything that hasn't been hashed out at great length."

We were interrupted by some people shouting to come play golf. But it was important I brief Hodgson while all this was fresh in my mind. "They are in the process of forming a group to represent the Indians and applying for federal grants."

"Isn't that great," Hodgson snorted. "Ottawa will fund a group who will throw a wrench into everything they sent me north to do." He remained silent for a moment. "My job is to establish a government modelled on the Canadian system with responsibility for all people of the Northwest Territories—Eskimos, whites, Indians, Métis. Natives are in the majority here. Who do they think we're trying to serve? They make up seventy-five percent of the population. If the feds fund individual native groups they'll be funding our opponents. The results could be a calamity.

"In the long run," he continued, "the general idea of our form of government must prevail, otherwise someone, some group of people, will end up the loser. Eventually this government will be theirs, under their control, their direction if they so wish.

"I'm starting to see what my real challenge is, what I really have to do. I have to take umpteen groups of people and convince them it's time to start worrying about unity, government, decision-making and politics."

I reminded him of their scepticism about the system we were introducing.

"I know! I know!" Hodgson said, with some irritation. "And I'm not belittling their tradition. Unity is everything in today's political system. We can't afford to have one system for the Indians, another for the Eskimos and another for the whites. That's the way to stay powerless. The North needs the strength that comes from unity, people working together, a united voice. It doesn't mean eradicating the Eskimo and Indian cultures. Racial groups must learn how to get involved in the one system. That's not being a colonialist. It's the only way of breaking colonialism's chains."

He was collecting his thoughts as much as making pronouncements. "The people have to find their power through the elected Territorial Council. That'll happen in its own good time. They'll learn how the system works and they'll take it over one day. I'm here to develop the system and steer the ship until I can hand more power down the line."

"You're going to be in a tug-of-war between our form of local government and the Indians' desire for power."

"They can keep their band councils, but there's one thing everybody had better get used to. I'm in control, and I'm staying in control until I decide it's time to let go." Hodgson's face was flushed with determination. "I'm not letting anyone else take over a government that isn't complete, or a territory that isn't united and a population that isn't ready. That's the way it is, and that's the way it's going to be!"

18

CANADA'S COLONY

IN NOVEMBER 1969, JEAN CHRÉTIEN finally came north to present his long-awaited policy statement on constitutional changes for the Northwest Territories and Yukon. As Minister of Indian Affairs and Northern Development, he had supreme power over the political and economic development of the North. It was he who recommended to the Prime Minister who should be Commissioner and his department that funded the programs. It was Chrétien who could introduce changes to the Northwest Territories Act to create an executive council or to alter the number of elected and appointed members.

At thirty-four, Chrétien was the youngest federal cabinet minister appointed in the 20th century. His ministry, however, was one of the least coveted portfolios, considered a dead-end job because there was little a politician could do in the short term to alleviate the conditions of the indigenous peoples he represented. The department was strange territory for Chrétien because it had no connection to his Québec constituents, but he believed he was well suited to understanding the challenges of minority groups.

I took a seat in a press gallery greatly expanded to accommodate national media, including television cameras. Predictably, Hodgson's vice-regal imprint was everywhere, a sign that the Commissioner was holding court. Hodgson had determined more room would be needed for Chrétien's visit and appearance before the fall session of the Territorial Council, so this time, instead of the Elks Hall, the gymnasium of the new St. Pat's school had been given the special treatment. The draped flags and the portrait of The Queen set a noble tone in a humble location.

We stood as RCMP Staff Sergeant Dave Friesen commanded "Order!" and marched with the territorial mace held solidly on his shoulder. Behind Friesen was RCMP Inspector Harry Nixon, Hodgson's aide-de-camp, then Hodgson, Binx Remnant and Frank Smith.

Hodgson put on his glasses, read the opening prayer, recognized special guests in the Commissioner's gallery, then announced, "Members of Council, it gives me a great deal of pleasure to introduce the Minister of Indian Affairs and Northern Development, the Honourable Gene Cretain." Members of the press snickered over Hodgson's pronunciation. He just couldn't, or wouldn't, get it right.

Ironically, Chrétien had just as much trouble with English as Hodgson had with French. He emphasized incorrect syllables, pronounced 'the' as 'de,' 'that' as 'dat' and 'North' as 'Nord.' But, like Hodgson, he was not concerned about pronunciation.

Chrétien spoke extemporaneously, gesticulating with his right hand, his left hand in his pocket. "My wife and I are very em . . . bah . . . rassed to be with you pee. . . o . . . neers of de nord." Despite his accent, he engaged the audience with his confidence and charisma. He spoke earnestly and with sincere feeling; there was no question that he deeply believed what he said. "De federal government is firm in its determination to create equal opportunities for residents of de Nord."

He turned to a prepared text, which had already been distributed to members of the press. "Being a Canadian citizen is a rare human privilege in today's world. The advantages to be obtained from this privilege must be available to all Canadians. You people who live north of the 60th parallel have demonstrated an admirable spirit of adventure in keeping with the exciting things that are happening here.

"The most meaningful tribute a government can make to those who serve on its commissions," he said, referring to the Carrothers Commission, "is to give their recommendations immediate consideration with a view to early implementation . . . I propose today to announce the federal government's intention regarding a number of these.

"You are aware, I am sure, that as Minister I have three areas of major concern: the wellbeing of Canada's indigenous peoples; conservation of certain of our natural resources; and the effective development of the Canadian North. All three, of course, are of vital interest to the people of the Northwest Territories . . .

"As recommended by the Carrothers Commission, services now come through the same channels and from the same government agencies for all northern residents, and this is good." This statement reinforced what Hodgson had been preaching all along—that services provided by his government applied to all people in the North.

"As a government, we have two major objectives regarding the North. The first is to protect and further the legitimate interests of the Canadian people in developments in the North . . . particularly resource development and the potentially immense wealth that may result from this.

"The second objective . . . is to accommodate the desire of many in the North for a greater measure of self-government and to do this within Canadian democratic traditions, institutions and values, through municipal, provincial and federal governmental institutions. Canadians generally play a large part in governing themselves and there are very few parts of Canada indeed, where the elected representatives of the people cannot be held fully accountable to the electorate for governmental actions. The Yukon and the Northwest Territories are such areas, however.

"Both of these objectives are of vital importance and must not be thought of as incompatible. If the first objective is to be met, it is clear that as long as the Northwest Territories remains as underpopulated and with as inadequate a tax base as now exists, the federal government must continue to play a strong role in the Territories."

He then spoke of the next steps to be taken with respect to the remaining recommendations of the Carrothers Commission. "I firmly believe that, at this time and for the foreseeable future, the granting of provincial status to either territory is not a realistic alternative.

· "I further believe that the federal government should continue to manage and develop the natural resources of the North for the benefit of both northern residents and all Canadians. At the moment the ownership and management of natural resources in the Territories must remain with the federal government."

Chrétien revealed the steps the federal government was prepared to take to amend the Northwest Territories Act. "These are to increase the number of elected members of the Territorial Council by two; to reduce the voting age in territorial elections; to extend the life of the Territorial Council to four years in place of the present three years; to permit Council to set the indemnity of its members; and to reduce the period for federal disallowance of territorial ordinances from two years to one year.

"The Council has been instrumental in reviewing and recommending a council committee system. The Commissioner and I have considered this recommendation."

There was a stir around the room as people sat up a little straighter and strained to hear better. David Searle leaned forward.

"I am hopeful that between now and the January session, a useful beginning can be made in this direction through the appointment of a standing committee on finance. Through this committee the views of the elected members of the people will be brought to bear on the formation of the budget and councillors will become involved in the actual preparation of the estimates. Such a committee and subsequent developments along such lines will enable council members to take on a more active role in the discussion and planning of territorial programs in close conjunction with the Commissioner and members of his executive committee."

Frustrated exhalations came from council members. Chrétien paused and looked around the room, disappointed perhaps that no one seemed to be falling over themselves with gratitude. Undaunted, he continued. "Reviewing the changes already implemented or proposed above, it is clear that the establishment of an effective territorial public service is one of the major tasks facing the Northwest Territories in the next few years. This is a formidable undertaking, made more so by the proposed addition in 1970 of the Eastern Arctic to the area to be administered from Yellowknife. It is the first time in Canadian history that such a massive transfer of administrative functions from one level of government to another and from a well-established centre of government to a totally new setting has been accomplished in such a short period of time.

"This enormous task has involved the creation of a greatly expanded territorial administration; the phasing out of the whole branch of the federal government . . .

"Prior to the transfer of the seat of government from Ottawa to Yellowknife, the territorial government had a small budget and a staff with limited experience. A territorial budget that was less than $7 million in 1963 is expected to rise to $70 million in 1970–71, and the size of the territorial staff will have expanded from six in 1964 to around 1,700 when the transfer is complete."

Hodgson, seated to the side, nodded approval.

"Some recommendations of the Carrothers Commission remain, and I have examined them carefully.

"One of the early decisions made by the federal government on the Carrothers report was the transfer to the government of the Northwest Territories of responsibilities for the continuing operation of the existing programs of local government. Since then, a new territorial Department of Local Government has been established with special responsibilities for developing and maintaining a structure of local government in communities . . . legislation in the form of a hamlet ordinance was passed this year and already two communities, Fort Simpson and Pine Point, have been incorporated as hamlets.

"The most important area for the growth of self-government in the Territories lies in the local communities. Here government is closest to the people. Here the people of the community, many of whom have no experience with the responsibilities of government, can most easily identify problems and can most easily work out solutions . . . Democracy cannot be imposed from above. It must come from the people. This is why the development of strong local government institutions must be a top priority for the territorial government.

"When the task of establishing the territorial public service is accomplished and when local government will have developed further in the Northwest Territories—and I am hopeful on the basis of the initial progress that this will occur before the passing of too many more years—we should be able to move towards a further extension of territorial self-government and executive responsibility and control. What precise form future constitutional government in the Northwest Territories will take I cannot predict at this time. I am convinced, however, that our approach to matters of constitutional developments must remain flexible and experimental, allowing for adjustments as further experience is gained. . .

"Government in the North, like all things in the North, is going to be tough. There are difficult problems to be overcome. It will take much determination before they are overcome. It takes special people to live and work in the North. Such people can be found working in the territorial government. Such people can be found serving on the Territorial Council, with a great deal of personal commitment and sacrifice.

"Such a person is Stu Hodgson, who has loyally undertaken the task of building a territorial government. This is a great challenge which your Commissioner has accepted with a spirit that has inspired us all. . .

"I know that we are building in the North a society that will be the example to all Canada. Here in the North we have a different segment of the population: we have the Indians; we have the Métis; we have the Eskimos; we have other people; and we have to show to the people of Canada, and we have to show to the world, that in our open society in the North everyone is accepted and looked at because of his human qualities. I know that we can build that kind of society in the North and it is why I am glad I accepted the invitation of the Council to be here today. And next year is going to be a very important year for the Territories because it is going to be their centennial."

Chrétien stepped back from the lectern with a nod. There was perfunctory applause from the audience and Hodgson quickly stepped forward. "Mr. Minister, we extend to you our appreciation for coming here to the capital and making your statement on the future development of government in the Northwest Territories." He glanced at the clock on the wall. "With respect to your address, I would think that members of Council will want to think it over and reflect on the items you have mentioned. I propose at this time therefore to recognize the clock and to call Council tomorrow morning at 10:00 a.m."

Staff Sergeant Friesen picked up the mace and led the procession out of the room. Hodgson signalled for me to bring the car to the entrance. On the way to the airport, Hodgson thanked Chrétien for his statement and for his kind remarks regarding both the Council members and himself.

Chrétien said, "As you've recommended, a standing committee on finance is a good step for now." Hodgson nodded and said other committees could be formed as appropriate, ultimately leading to the creation of an executive committee of Council members, as they gained experience. The finance committee would formulate the budget to be placed before Council in January and would include funding and expenditures for the entire Northwest Territories.

"We will kickstart our centennial celebrations on New Year's Eve with a radio broadcast throughout the North," Hodgson said. "CBC has arranged to have ham radio operators pick up their signal and broadcast to every community. I want to invite you and your wife to be our guests of honour." Chrétien was delighted.

CHRÉTIEN'S MESSAGE WAS CLEAR. THE next morning, the councillors responded. First up was David Searle. Hodgson anticipated he would provide a balanced review, a calm demeanour influencing others to provide productive criticism. But Searle jumped to his feet and, dropping a copy of the Carrothers report and the Minister's statement on the table, immediately got to the meat of the issue. "I will refer to the second paragraph on page one, which begins: 'the most meaningful tribute a government can make to those who serve on its commissions is to give their recommendations immediate consideration.' I would suggest that this has hardly been what one would call immediate consideration of the recommendations of the Carrothers Commission."

"Here, here!" shouted Searle's colleagues, thumping their desks. For the first time I looked beyond the pageantry and noticed just how plain, almost cheap, the Council furnishings were. I'd been in the legislative building of Alberta and the national parliament in Ottawa; in contrast, this Council's surroundings tended to validate the resentment of people like Searle. If Hodgson hadn't put up velvet ropes and a picture of The Queen, this group, responsible for one-third of Canada's land mass, could be mistaken for a parents' group haranguing a school principal.

"The paper refers to the need for the federal government to continue to play a strong role in the Territories for as long as the Territories remain as underpopulated and with as inadequate a tax base as now exists . . . this is the first time it has been clearly spelled out in government policy exactly what these tests are . . . (a) an adequate tax base, and (b) population. There is one slight problem however, with one of those tests. I refer to the test of population, and that is that this will never, of course, be an agrarian area of Canada. We will never have large numbers of people settling large tracts of land, tilling soil, developing their communities. It is obviously a test which the Territories will never meet.

"The minister then refers to my favorite subject, the ownership and management of natural resources. He says natural resources must remain with the federal government, and he looks at this for the present and foreseeable future. The question we asked was whether the federal government would declare itself a trustee . . . our motion was not answered specifically."

Searle then dealt with the granting of provincial status. "I think we have all agreed that, at this time, it is not realistic, but what disturbs me are these words 'for the foreseeable future.' Now, how far do we foresee when we are talking about this, a lifetime, twenty, thirty, forty years? For the first time, we see that the resources will be developed to the benefit of both northern residents and all Canadians. Those words 'northern residents' have never appeared before.

"The paper then goes on to deal specifically with those matters which the Minister plans to undertake. . . Number one: to increase the number of elected members of the Territorial Council by two. The Carrothers Commission, of course, recommended that the elected members be increased from seven to fourteen, and the appointed be reduced from five to four, for a total of eighteen. We have, therefore, had quite a watering down of that recommendation, and a very nominal implementation of it."

Searle did applaud the recommendations extending the life of the Territorial Council and permitting Council to set remuneration for its members. He was also pleased that the federal government could now only veto territorial legislation for one year, reduced from the previous two, even though he maintained this power should not exist at all.

"The next recommendation deals with the creation of an expanding committee on finance. Now this finally, and for the first time, brings the members of the Council to grips with the problem of money, and puts us in the picture in the beginning, rather than in the end . . . But as good as that is, it is a far cry from the recommendations of the Carrothers Commission that there be an executive council. The statement refers to the most important area of growth of self-government in the Territories as lying in the local communities. There is little doubt in my mind that we have extended a greater degree of executive responsibility, and complete representation, to all of our lower levels of government than we in this Council in fact enjoy. It is no accident that the mayor of Yellowknife has, on several occasions, and I might say growing more frequent every day, referred to the town council as the only level of responsible government in the Territories. He's quite right, of course."

The gym exploded with a wave of desk thumping and clapping from the public gallery.

"I wonder whether there is a fear of too strong a provincial or quasi-provincial institution, a fear from what I call the Québec phobia . . . of the particular constitutional crisis that faces Canada today. I wonder if because of pre-occupation with Québec by our Prime Minister, and our Minister of Indian Affairs, both Québec ministers, Québec members of parliament, if we aren't getting the backlash of that phobia, that preoccupation. I suggest we are."

The reporters scribbled fast enough to set their pens on fire. Searle concluded his remarks, bowed towards Hodgson and sat down. A storm of applause thundered through the gymnasium. Several members stepped out of their seats and walked over to shake his hand.

When the commotion died down the Commissioner called on the next speaker, Duncan Pryde, understanding full well that the Scotsman would be in attack mode.

Pryde ignored the drone of comments and conversations as he stood and waved a copy of Chrétien's statement in the air. The atmosphere became tense. "When I heard this policy statement yesterday, I asked myself one question: how did this benefit the Northwest Territories? I can't see any way any person can interpret the statement of Mr. Chrétien yesterday as implying or giving responsible government to the Northwest Territories in any size, shape or form." Pryde levelled his surly gaze squarely on Hodgson.

"We are here, I and 30,000 other people, as shareholders of the Northwest Territories, but the director of this firm is not responsible to the shareholders. Mr. Chrétien said yesterday that democracy cannot be enforced from above; it must come from the people. True enough, but plainly an undemocratic form of government can be, and is being, enforced from above. We here in the Territories and in the Yukon Territory are the only two parts of Canada to have this form of government.

"I am angry, and justifiably so. We are simply trying to take some reasonable steps forward to obtain meaningful and responsible, repeat, responsible government. We are not asking for provincehood today. We are not asking for control of the mineral resources today. We are asking for an evolution toward responsible government, and we still don't have one iota of responsible government at the territorial level, not one iota." The Commissioner's jaw was clenched hard, his face immobile.

"We didn't ask for a loaf of bread, we asked for a slice of bread, and Mr. Chrétien didn't even throw us a crumb . . . Is it to be evolution toward responsible government, or revolution toward responsible government? How long can the Canadian government expect the people of the Northwest Territories to remain so frustrated without starting to take a much stronger course of action? I am quite willing to take a stronger course of action. I have never worried too much about the sheep of Ottawa, and I never will.

"What we have here is a Council, composed of one appointed Commissioner, one appointed Deputy Commissioner and four appointed members of Council, all appointed by the Department of Indian Affairs and Northern Development. I don't intend to imply any personalities about this, because as individuals they are doing a splendid job, but that is beside the point. We hope to evolve towards a democratic government, not a colonial government. I didn't come to Canada to be a colonial. I came to this country to be a Canadian . . . How long can we stay frustrated like this? Saskatchewan isn't run by the Department of Agriculture; Newfoundland isn't run by the Department of Fisheries, but the Northwest Territories is basically run by the Department of Indian Affairs and Northern Development through the Commissioner, who is an employee of that department. Where else in Canada do we have these conditions? What kind of a country are we living in when 101 years after Confederation there are still two colonies within the Dominion of Canada?

"We pressured the Minister to come here and tell us if he would at last grant us this power. And he replied, 'No, you don't get one iota'." Pryde raised his arms, emphasizing his plea for action. Then he sat down, flushed, amid a chorus of approvals and thunderous applause.

Hodgson sat stone-faced and aloof. The time being 11:00 and the date being November 11, Remembrance Day, he saw an opportunity to cool things down and called for two minutes of silence. After the silence, he remarked that it was customary for all the old sweats to get together and have a toddy. "I regret we can't offer you that this morning, but we can, perhaps, give you a ten-minute recess for coffee."

After coffee two other elected councillors warned that, unless basic policy changes were made soon, "there will be trouble." Lyle Trimble, the elected member for Mackenzie Delta, accused the federal government of preaching sermons about a just society but keeping the Canadian North in perpetual colonialism. He said the recent administrative transfers to the territorial government had not included additional powers for its Council. Trimble warned, "We can't wait forever."

Hodgson concluded the day with a statement of his own. Referring to the Carrothers Commission he said, "I have always felt that a tremendous responsibility was placed on the shoulders of the Deputy Commissioner, Mr. Parker, as the only Northerner on the Commission, to travel through some fifty settlements in the Northwest Territories. The Commission wrote the most far-reaching practical constitutional report that has ever been prepared on the Northwest Territories. It is to Mr. Parker's credit that, soon after, he accepted the responsibility of joining the Council and the position of Deputy Commissioner and subsequently became the real head of the territorial public service. You know it is not easy coming in from the role of a civilian into the role of public service, particularly if you come in at the top, because you are supposed to learn the ranks, learn the ropes, as you pass through the lower ranks, and it takes a long time in the lower ranks to put a handle on what you're trying to accomplish, trying to achieve, and I certainly pay great respect to John Parker for the success that he has achieved in these three challenges that he has undertaken."

Several Council members hunkered down in their seats as Hodgson rapped their knuckles for disparaging people appointed to Council.

"I have always believed that if you wish to have responsible people, you must give them responsibilities . . . I believe what has been turned over to us up to this time is with a certain amount of challenge, with a certain amount of feelings on the part of the government to see whether we can rise to this occasion, not only accepting the responsibilities but that we can carry them out.

"These last two and a half years haven't been particularly easy. We have had our problems and had our tough times, and we have made mistakes, but we have never taken our eyes off the objective.

"Now, while commenting on this, perhaps I should say that we expect, in appearing before you that you're going to find out the weaknesses. You're going to suggest that certain changes be made. Most of all, you're going to criticize. There is an old saying that the more criticism you get, the easier it is to take, and that your back gets a little hardened to it, and criticism runs off you like water off a duck's back. Well, having worked for people for twenty-five years, I want to tell you the difference between a duck and a human being is a duck has feathers for the water to run off, and a human being hasn't. As the criticism falls, it hurts, believe me, whether it be from Council or from the general public. But that is your right. That is the right of the news media, and the general public. We are prepared to accept that, and we are prepared to continue to keep our eye on the objective, and that is to put together for the people of the Territories the best possible staff that can be put together.

"In establishing the committee on finance, I'm going to take it upon myself to give a commitment to establish other committees. The great responsibility that lies under the Northwest Territories Act with the Commissioner of the Northwest Territories, having come from the people, having come from this Council, I have chosen to not only work with this Council, but to share more than is required under the Act. I congratulate all of you who, in your remarks today, have put forward your points of view.

"The number of motions that Council has presented, thirty-five or thirty-six of them I believe, and the number of questions, both written and oral, demonstrates both the interest of the Council and your growing awareness of the problems that confront us and the matters you wish further information on.

"I couldn't help but think back to six years ago when Mr. Trimble, Air Marshal Campbell and myself first joined this Council. They can testify that in those days items one, two, three and four on the order paper rushed by and no one ever moved any motions or asked any questions. As a matter of fact, the matter of asking questions was not even in the proceedings of Council. The rules of Council were only two pages long and did not contain much. However in 1967 a new set of rules was developed and I think it marked a turning point in the progress of Council.

"I want you to know that this isn't a one-man show, although many, many times the Commissioner's name is used in the sense that the Commissioner does everything, and this of course is not true. The Commissioner has a certain amount of authority, but as much as possible I try to distribute this authority and responsibility amongst our administration.

"Council wants to play a more meaningful role in the affairs of not only this administration but in the future of the Northwest Territories. We recognize this and although some of the things I am sure that you wanted to achieve, some of the responsibility you hoped to acquire was missing from the Minister's statement, this naturally gave you cause to give some thought to what had happened, where you go from here.

"I suggest to you that the committee system, if properly used, will prove to be one of the greatest achievements in 1970." Hodgson then prorogued the session.

He was silent for a few minutes as I drove him back to the Laing Building. Then he said, "I can't get bogged down with their complaints. We have to tackle constructive projects, like the Centennial." He was back into his positive mode. "We'll kick the year off with a Commissioner's Ball, a ball that will be the talk of the continent! Then it's the visit of the Prime Minister and the kickoff of the Arctic Winter Games, followed by the visit of the Governor General and then The Queen and the Royal Family. That'll get everybody's attention. Planning and detail," he mused. "If we look after the small things, the big things will look after themselves. But let the details slip, and everything falls to pieces."

19
CENTENNIAL CELEBRATIONS

JANUARY 1970

A MASSIVE FIREWORKS DISPLAY HERALDED in 1970 at the stroke of midnight. With a radiant smile and an animated face, Hodgson spoke into a radio microphone. For the first time in history his voice was heard simultaneously in all communities of the North, thanks to the ingenious teamwork of ham radio operators and the Northern Service of the CBC.

Earlier in the evening, Jean Chrétien had joined Hodgson and Yellowknife's mayor, Fred Henne, for a ceremony that included a gigantic bonfire and a torchlight trail ride by snowmobile. Hodgson wore a new three-quarter length red parka, trimmed around the hood, sleeves and hem with wolverine fur.

All across the Arctic people rang in the centennial year with prayers and celebrations, bonfires, fireworks and midnight church services. High above the Arctic Circle, in Fort McPherson, residents celebrated so far into the morning that the Centennial Dog Team Race was an hour late starting. Hay River opened their new B.G. Sivertz Sports Centre to a crowd of over two thousand, so many that some never got inside. Inuvik hosted northern games featuring events that were truly representative of the region—muskrat and seal skinning, blanket tossing, traditional dancing and high-kick competitions.

Hodgson wanted celebrations that would match in scope and imagination the event a hundred years before when, by the mighty stroke of Queen Victoria's pen, Canada grew from a small country huddled along the Great Lakes, the St. Lawrence River and the Atlantic seaboard to the second largest nation in the world, stretching north to the North Pole and west to the Pacific. At the planning conference held the previous February, delegates representing every region and ethnic group in the North unanimously adopted four major objectives: foster unity among all peoples of the Territories, develop an awareness of separate pasts and the shared future, encourage Canadian awareness of a new political reality in the North and promote increased knowledge of the Northwest Territories. The result was a 113-page calendar outlining the events to take place in the various communities. Major events included the first Arctic Winter Games, car and snowmobile rallies, marathon canoe races, a scouting jamboree and the establishment of a permanent committee on historic sites, museums and artifacts.

Hodgson's imprint was all over the process, to the consternation of some. Sid Hancock, the Director of Local Government, had complained to me about Hodgson's persnickety attention to detail on his centennial projects and his apparent total disregard in recent months for the problems of local government.

New Year's Eve celebrations were followed several days later by the Commissioner's Ball, an elaborate and glittering social function with guests from many northern settlements and as far away as Vancouver and Toronto. Three hundred personally drafted gilt-edged invitations had been sent out stipulating two dress options, formal or military.

Barb and I invited several friends over before the event. The ladies were in gowns, the men in tuxedos rented from a local men's wear shop that had flown three dozen suits up from Edmonton.

"We're hearing rumours that the Brotherhood might disrupt the Commissioner's Ball," one of our guests said. The sixteen Indian chiefs of the Mackenzie Valley had formed the Indian Brotherhood of the Northwest Territories the previous October, electing James Washie as President. I had heard the same rumour some weeks before and had alerted Hodgson, who hadn't seemed concerned.

"I suppose they see it as a chance to embarrass Hodgson," I replied. "Indians are holding sit-ins and demonstrations all over the country. But I can't confirm there will be a demonstration tonight."

"There's lots of griping about the spending on the ball," said one guest. "Maybe it'll be a protest by those not invited."

I imitated Hodgson's stern face and growled. "Spending? What spending? I invited the owner of the Calona Winery. He's bringing all the wine, free. I invited Rhys Eyton from Pacific Western Airlines. He's flying up the chefs and silverware from Edmonton, free. Our public works people are doing all the construction. There's no cost!" Our guests chuckled.

We dressed snugly in our parkas, mitts, scarves, and boots to keep the -35 temperature at bay during the trip to the Elks Hall. Outside the hall there was no sign of anything amiss. Either the rumours were untrue or the fledgling Indian Brotherhood had called off its protest.

A blast of warm air and brilliant light greeted us as we stepped into a world of glitter and glamour. This ball had become a real labour of love for Hodgson and had therefore consumed my time. Hodgson would spend hours every day going over minute details such as checking what tunes the band would play, and the design of special coins, decals, pins and flags. Nothing had happened without Hodgson personally checking the details at least three times.

The stalwart Elks Hall had been transformed into a court fit to receive a king. A chandelier of 144 light bulbs fashioned from copper tubing by the carpentry shop of the Public Works Department had been fitted to the ceiling to illuminate every detail on crisply-clothed dining tables set with crystal, flowers and decanters. I thought of my first visit—it seemed a shame that success for Hodgson and the North didn't include the Caribou Queen.

Hodgson looked as if he'd just conquered Mount Everest, smiling under his tidy triangle of a moustache. He carried himself with stately pride and dignity, his naval service medals pinned to his tuxedo. Pearl was dressed in an elegant long-sleeved gown of black lace, embroidered in silver. Her hair was swept up and back from her forehead with a few neat curls softening the sharp, firm set of her face. Hodgson's aide-de-camp, RCMP Inspector Harry Nixon, stood nearby in his ceremonial dress uniform while other uniformed members kept tabs on the arrivals.

As I surveyed the legions of black-suited men and haute-coutured women, I was bothered by the fact that most of the guests were white, except for a few Eskimos and Indians there as guests of Council members, each of whom had been allotted four invitations. Those people meant to benefit from the presence of our northern government were sparsely represented. Hodgson had taken the view that this ball should provide him with an opportunity to publicize the North and curry favour with influential southerners.

Hostesses paraded around the dance floor with trays of domestic champagne shipped north compliments of Herb Capozzi, a well-known British Columbia politician, businessman and owner of Calona Wines. The thirteen-member Princess Patricia Canadian Light Infantry brass band, airlifted to Yellowknife by Hodgson's friends at Eldorado Aviation, made a magnificent sight and played pre-dinner music with sublime professionalism. It seemed Hodgson had tapped every connection he had for this stately affair.

"Evening, Jake!" said Gordon Gibson as he paraded a lady friend through the crowd. Gibson was a Vancouver lumber millionaire whose son was now Prime Minister Trudeau's special assistant. "Let me introduce you to Mrs. Baker." Barb and I shook hands with the woman, who turned out to be the widow of Russ Baker, the Arctic bush pilot who founded Pacific Western Airlines. "It's so nice to be here again!" she said. "Doesn't seem so long since I first came to Yellowknife. It was nothing but a collection of tents thirty years ago."

We were brought to attention by a maitre d' in a tuxedo making his way to the stage to announce the first of three dinner seatings. In the dining area, separated by railings from the rest of the room, we stared in awe at a display of food such as the North had never seen.

"Where did the cutlery, the glasses, the crystal, the ice sculptures—where did it all come from?" Barb asked.

"You know Binx, he's one dedicated super-worker. When Hodgson tells him to do something, he does it. He arranged for the Chateau Lacombe Hotel in Edmonton to bring everything, even the ice sculptures, and they're providing the staff.

"Take a look at the polar bear whisky decanters. Hodgson directed Binx to have them specially made in Japan." They were opaque bottles in the shape of a polar bear standing on a blue block of ice, the stopper forming part of the head. "They'll be collector's items after tonight. But don't drink the whisky, they're filled with really cheap stuff. Crap! Fifty-seven percent alcohol, so Hodgson tells me." Hodgson, who considered himself an expert, had purchased several barrels of the scotch from some farmer's still while vacationing in Scotland.

We threaded our way between the maitre d', the sous-chef, the chef-de-cuisine and the captain-waiter and made our choices among Blue Point oysters, braised haunch of Bathurst Island caribou, tossed tundra salad and Inuvik roast reindeer.

We shared a table with the mayor of Penticton, British Columbia, a man called Stuart whose wife epitomized the glamour of the evening in a black and gold gown shot through with shimmering thread reminiscent of the aurora borealis. She also sported elbow-length black gloves, silver shoes and silver earrings. "Isn't this fabulous?" she gushed. "I met Stasia Evasuk earlier, the *Toronto Star's* social columnist. She's seeing clothes and hairstyles here as fashionable as any in New York." Her eyes scanned the room. "Oh, look at that outfit." We all admired a woman in a chiffon pantsuit. I chuckled, knowing it would irritate Hodgson.

"You're so lucky, living up here." Mrs. Stuart proclaimed. "Everything's so new. And everywhere I go in southern Canada these days, people are talking about the Northwest Territories, about what the Commissioner is doing and the excitement of opening up a whole new frontier. You people live it each day, while I just get to read about it."

"It's exciting all right," I said, thinking that it was not always party time.

She shook her head, the silver earrings catching arrows of light from the chandelier. "I think it's wonderful. You're taking part in Canadian history. There'll never be another time like it."

Dancing began after dinner. At one point, the crowd began ignoring the music to stare at a couple making their way to the dance floor, smiling self-consciously in their traditional Dogrib clothing. It was James Washie and his new wife, Caroline. Is this it? I wondered. Are they going to create a fuss?

I had to admit they looked magnificent. James was dressed in a fringed moosehide jacket decorated with beautiful beaded embroidery on the front and back shoulder pieces. On his feet he wore knee-high moosehide moccasins, embroidered with beadwork and trimmed with wolverine fur. Caroline wore a bleached white caribou skin mini-dress with fringes on the hem and sleeves and moccasins trimmed with white Arctic hare. A beaded headband tucked her blonde hair back and over her shoulders. These were the clothes they'd been married in.

As they moved toward the dance floor, a woman's voice rang out, "What a beautiful dress." Her comment broke the ice. The reporter from the *Toronto Star* reached for her notebook. I searched for Hodgson, afraid he'd object to the Washies' gatecrashing even though it was obvious to me that they weren't here to disrupt, simply to assert their right to participate.

From the far side of the dance floor Hodgson manoeuvred his way through the crowd. I was afraid of what he might do or say. "Glad you could come." he boomed at the young couple, as if he'd invited them personally. He waded into the clearing and clasped Washie's hand, then glanced over at Binx and said, "Next time, make sure we list native dress as an option."

"Darned right, too," Barb said as we watched the pair. "It never seemed quite right, living in a place where most people are native, to make everyone wear European military or formal clothing. I think Hodgson just learned a good lesson."

I admired Caroline and James as they danced with youthful, defiant vigour. When they paused to rest, I took Barb over to introduce them. After some small talk I said, "I hear you're incorporating the Indian Brotherhood next month."

"We are the last across Canada to form our own organization to represent treaty Indians," he acknowledged, but didn't elaborate further. To break the silence, I asked Caroline to dance.

"We sure shocked a lot of people tonight," she said with a chuckle.

"I think you did, and that's not bad."

"The Commissioner has to learn to understand the aspirations of the Dene."

Caroline was extremely astute. She'd probably convinced James to get dressed for the ball, seeing an opportunity to send a political message to Hodgson and the establishment.

"But the Indians also need to know that the territorial government exists and is not going away," I responded.

"You mean the Dene," she corrected me. "I'm not arguing with that. And I think James understands it too. The Dene have been at a disadvantage for too long. You've got all the aces."

"What kind of aces would they like?"

"Talk to James," she said, leading me over to where he stood. After she explained what we talked about he said, "Let me tell you what an elderly Dogrib woman said: 'They could ignore some of us, and beat some of us and steal from some of us, and pat some of us on the head, but they will never be able to do that to us again, because we have our Indian Brotherhood'."

He looked at me and continued in his thoughtful, deliberate way, "Your voice is heard everywhere, even by people who didn't ask to hear it. Our voice is small and doesn't reach all who want to hear it. If we had your money, your communications, our voice would be heard equally."

"We're working to get the CBC to improve radio signals across the North,"

I said. "Your people have access to those signals. You can put on your own programs and shows, if you want. The CBC would welcome your input."

"We don't want to borrow a little corner of your system. We want our own. And we'll start by producing our own newspaper. We're waiting for funding from the Secretary of State."

I was caught off guard. Washie said nothing further, knowing perhaps that this information would come as a surprise to me and to Hodgson. The creation of a communications arm would give the Indian Brotherhood strength to get their message out, bring unity among the Indian communities, and possibly encourage resistance to Hodgson's programs.

20
TOURING PRIME MINISTER TRUDEAU

MARCH 5–8, 1970

PRIME MINISTER PIERRE TRUDEAU WAS scheduled to visit several communities in the Keewatin and Central Arctic before heading to Yellowknife to open the first Arctic Winter Games. Hodgson and I flew to Churchill to meet him. Trudeau's staff and crew deplaned as Hodgson and I boarded the government JetStar. There were no staff, no advisors, just Trudeau, Hodgson and me.

The two men discussed the issues, concerns and needs of the North, as well as the communities to be visited. I sat in silence, awestruck in the presence of the country's charismatic leader. He was a fascinating person to observe, asking probing questions and grasping issues with incredible speed. Trudeau talked about the imminent transfer, only weeks away, of the federal administration of the Central and Eastern Arctic to the territorial government. It meant the addition of about 12,000 residents, ninety percent Eskimo, for a total territorial population of 32,000.

Trudeau said resources would remain a federal responsibility, in trust for the benefit of all Canadians. Resource development in the Canadian Arctic had again become a contentious issue the previous fall when the largest oil find in North America had been made at Prudhoe Bay in northern Alaska. Confidence in finding oil in the Mackenzie Valley and the Beaufort Sea, just to the east of Prudhoe Bay, was high; the Canadian Petroleum Association estimated there was twice as much oil and gas in the Mackenzie Delta and Arctic islands as in the four western provinces combined. And a US oil tanker, the SS *Manhattan,* had successfully traversed the Northwest Passage, proving oil could be shipped to world markets. Revenue from Canadian Arctic finds was anticipated to reach as much as half a billion dollars annually. Nor was oil not the only natural resource of concern. There were more than seventy-five companies operating in the mineral-rich Coppermine area, about six hundred miles north of Yellowknife.

If the Northwest Territories were a province, it would retain much of this revenue. Council members like David Searle asserted that delaying self-government in order to retain resource revenues was a backhanded way of stealing from the North. He continued to accuse the government of perpetuating the colonial administration of the Territories in order to reap the royalties from major oil strikes, maintaining that any move toward self-government had been decelerated since the discovery of oil in Alaska's Prudhoe Bay.

While Trudeau would not give up control of resources, he was committed to preserving the autonomy of the Northwest Territories and the Yukon despite the acquisitiveness of several provinces. British Columbia Premier W.A.C. Bennett had, in recent months, been quietly wooing residents of the Yukon Territory while, in Alberta, statements by provincial cabinet ministers suggested that Premier Peter Lougheed's government was looking with keen interest at the Mackenzie Valley.

Trudeau said his government had a serious agenda with respect to the North. The North was very much to the fore in his thinking and its social, political and economic advancement was certain to accelerate in the years immediately ahead. The Arctic played a large role in Trudeau's sense of national identity, of nation building. He expressed his pleasure that the Northwest Territories centennial celebrations would encompass the first Arctic Winter Games and the first visit to the Arctic by a British sovereign.

Travelling with Trudeau by Twin Otter, we visited the communities of Rankin Inlet, Baker Lake, Repulse Bay, Pelly Bay, Spence Bay and Cambridge Bay. Trudeau wore a pair of sealskin kamiks, an Arctic parka trimmed with wolf fur and a pair of gigantic wolf-fur mitts, gifts from Hodgson.

Our final stop before Yellowknife was at the winter camp of George Hakongak, his wife, Jessie Kungalhak, and their son, Billy. Duncan Pryde had introduced us to them the previous year, explaining in Inuktitut that Hodgson was the Commissioner, the boss of the North. We were again welcomed with great enthusiasm as Hodgson introduced the Prime Minister and members of the party, this time without a translator. George invited us into his tent, insulated on all sides by mounds of snow, for a mug up. Tea was boiled in an open pot on a primus stove and served in tin mugs. The Prime Minister sat silent, thoughtfully absorbing the occasion, very much taken by this experience in this isolated part of the country.

THE CONCEPT OF THE ARCTIC Winter Games had germinated in Hodgson's mind for several years. He had discussed the idea with Walter Hickel, Governor of Alaska, and James Smith, Commissioner of the Yukon Territory and, in the spring of 1969, we had travelled to Whitehorse to firm up their commitment. A number of Yellowknife citizens, public supporters of the games, accompanied us on this trip, including Dario Tomasi, Hodgson's barber. Rumours soon circulated that Hodgson now travelled with his own barber.

After a private meeting with Commissioner Smith, Hodgson and I sat at a telex machine in a local hotel late into the night, him dictating and me typing, to create tickertape to be sent to Walter Hickel in Juneau, Alaska, seeking the firm support of the Governor.

Now his bold vision was realized. Five hundred athletes descended on Yellowknife from throughout the Northwest Territories, Yukon and Alaska to participate in the sporting events of the Arctic Winter Games: drum dances, rope gymnastics, finger pulling, whip cracking, harpoon throwing and muskrat skinning. The Prime Minister was delighted. Hodgson was encouraged, anxious to eventually include Greenland, Arctic Québec and Russia as described in his original communiqué.

JULY 5–10, 1970

AS THE CENTENNIAL YEAR CONTINUED to unfold, the Northwest Territories hosted a number of dignitaries, ambassadors and tourists. Hodgson
metamorphosed more each day into a full-blown potentate. He received visitors not as a bureaucrat servant of far-off mandarins and voters, but as an
unrivalled ruler secure in the mastery of his domain.

Early on, Hodgson had decided a royal visit should be the focal point of the
Centennial, but it wasn't in his power to issue such an invitation directly to
Buckingham Palace, nor even to suggest it directly to the Governor General.
Instead, he should have sent it to Chrétien, who would forward it to the Prime
Minister, who would in turn forward it to the Governor General. Hodgson
knew well enough that such a circuitous route would be too time-consuming
so he shortcut the system, suggesting the idea directly to Governor General
Roland Michener and his Principal Secretary, Esmond Butler, a man who pulled
enough strings to have an official invitation issued. His rationale was that, in
addition to being Commissioner, he was lieutenant governor, premier and chief
executive officer of the North, and therefore entitled to a direct approach.

An unabashed royalist, perhaps due to his mother's English heritage,
Hodgson revered the monarch as a symbol of honour and authority. On
this historic visit by Her Majesty The Queen, Prince Philip, Prince Charles
and Princess Anne, he was determined to make an impression, and the days
following the Arctic Winter Games were filled with endless meetings to
double-check every last item in excruciating detail.

I had been on a planning trip, a dry run, several months before with Briga-
dier-General P.S. Cooper, the Canadian Secretary to The Queen, and coordinator
of the Canadian tour. I was the territorial coordinator responsible for ensuring
our communities and staff organized appropriate and interesting events.

The role gave me a rare inside look at the minutia of planning a royal tour.

A small book was published listing all those who would greet The Queen, the transport to be available, a list of all meals, accommodation in each location and the time, to the minute, of each event, arrival and departure.

The royal support staff, approximately fifteen people, also needed to be accommodated. Hodgson instructed me to provide parkas, mitts and footwear for the staff. His motto was, "If the lady-in-waiting was unhappy, The Queen would be grumpy." He was clear that "everything had to be first class."

The dry run identified few glitches, other than our administrator in Resolute failed to greet us at the airport and had made no arrangements for events. The local RCMP member had filled this role instead. "Tell Sid," Hodgson said, referring to the Director of Local Government. "Get him out of there."

The morning of our departure from Yellowknife for Frobisher Bay, the first stop for the Royal Family, I was late arriving at the airport. "You're lucky you're not left behind!" Hodgson admonished, leading me out to the tarmac. "Isn't she a beauty?" He beamed, pointing to the sleek de Havilland HS125 twin-engine jet chartered for our use. "This thing will fly at 450 miles per hour. We'll be able to travel to the farthest reaches of the North in under three hours. Just think of poor old Jimmy Smith still hopping around the Yukon in his old Beaver." Hodgson loved the game of one-upmanship with his Yukon counterpart.

The small executive jet was a dream. It had a six-passenger cabin, richly appointed with comfortable leather seats, a table to work on and space to stretch out. "This will help us get around the Territories faster. Inuvik in an hour, and Frobisher in three and half. This will trigger a new era in northern transportation."

Packed into the centre aisle was a huge welcoming rug, thirty feet long with polar bear symbols at both ends, rolled into a tube four feet in diameter. "Specially made for The Queen. You will fly ahead to each community and lay the rug for The Queen's arrival." The rest of the cabin was packed to the legal limit with parkas, presents and northern souvenirs for the Royals, as well as flags, banners and bunting.

The engines roared to life and the tarmac rushed by the windows as we raced down the runway. The plane climbed into the clear sky and Yellowknife dwindled beneath us as we flew eastward.

Hodgson was in a good mood, so I broached the subject of the Information Department. "With the Brotherhood now publishing its own newspaper and council members riding you about more control, you need better service from the Information Department." The first department Hodgson established was not carrying its weight. "The government needs a communications plan but it's never materialized. I could do that if I was in charge."

Hodgson nodded. "Let me work on it."

"You know I could be a bigger help to you if I had that operation."

"Leave it with me," he said sternly, obviously wishing to drop the subject.

I persisted anyway. "The North is growing tremendously. The Information Department has a crucial role to play for our government."

"How?"

"The first thing I'd do is establish a printing operation. We could handle all the government printing requirements, improve internal communications with a staff newsletter and print our own publications, especially in native languages. Let the people know what the government is doing. It gives you a chance to explain your vision for local government. We should also establish a group of people who can work as translators to travel with you. It's downright embarrassing for someone to be dragged out of an audience. We don't even know if they are translating correctly."

Hodgson perked up. I continued, "You're the one who told me that a government is nothing without communications. I want to establish community radio stations so people can broadcast their own messages. We can establish a broadcast unit to prepare radio tapes on our government programs."

Hodgson was attentive. "Has a lot of merit. But it's not that simple for me. What do I do with Ted? For the moment I can't do anything."

"For the moment," I responded. "At least you know I'm interested."

FOUR DAYS LATER, ON JULY 5, we rolled out the blue rug and awaited the arrival of the royal aircraft with The Queen, Prince Philip and Princess Anne. Since The Queen and her heir could not travel together, Prince Charles had arrived the day before.

The group on the tarmac included Prince Charles; Governor General Roland Michener and his wife, Nora; Prime Minister Trudeau; Jean Chrétien with his wife, Aline; Hodgson and Pearl; Simonie Michael and a host of local municipal leaders. I stood well behind the receiving line. Hodgson turned, called me over and asked, "Where are the cars?"

"On their way," I assured him confidently. Extra cars had been flown in from the south by Hercules freighter aircraft. There had been endless discussions over who would sit in what car in the cavalcade.

"Are the special licence plates on?"

"You bet." Distinctive northern licence plates in the shape of a polar bear, the North's official tourist symbol, had been made for the royal visit. The Queen's car bore a gold crown, and the car to transport Prince Charles and Princess Anne had a plate with a white crown. Plates numbered one, two and three had been reserved for the Governor General, the Prime Minister and the Minister.

While the rest of Canada debated letting go of Britain's matronly apron strings, the Eskimos couldn't wait to see this monarch they'd heard about for so many generations. There were never any treaties between the Eskimos and the British Crown, but the Eskimo people had developed an understanding of the monarchy from contacts with British whalers, explorers and naval men.

The Queen's aircraft appeared out of the ice crystals that smudged the yellowing sky, causing an excited stir among the crowd. The Governor General, the Prime Minister, the Minister of Indian Affairs and Northern Development and a group of Eskimo Brownies all straightened up. The plane came to a halt where the staircase lined up with the welcoming carpet and the crowd waited in silence for its first glimpse of the monarch. As the door of the aircraft opened there was an exhalation of confusion as a diminutive woman dressed in a blue coat and hat descended the aircraft steps.

"That's The Queen?"

"Where's her crown? And jewels?"

The Queen it was. The Duke of Edinburgh, his arm in a plaster cast and sling, followed, then a mini-skirted Princess Anne.

The crowd's initial confusion turned to excited comments and broad smiles as the Royal Family descended the stairwell. There were shouts of "*Angajuqqaaq! Angajuqqaaq* [the Big Boss]!"

After polite handshakes and introductions along the receiving line, The Queen ignored protocol and began an unscheduled walkabout. The Duke and their children quickly followed suit as the RCMP security detail, ferried to Frobisher from throughout Canada, scrambled to reorganize, even though there was not a huge security concern. The chances of an anti-monarchist reaching The Queen were remote.

Hodgson accompanied The Queen along the line of well-wishers. I saw him cock his head as an Eskimo woman near him complained she'd missed the chance to shake the monarch's hand. He reached in and touched her shoulder. "If my mother was here today, I'd want to introduce her to The Queen," he said with a smile. "Come on, you can be my mother today. I'll introduce you." He eased the excited woman from the crowd and presented her to The Queen.

Governor General Michener, Prime Minister Trudeau, and Minister Chrétien hung back, conceding that this was The Queen's show and Hodgson was the host. It was his day, his royal visit, and they were content to let him enjoy the limelight. A corps of seventy journalists and cameramen from around the world, with the notable exception of the French-speaking division of the CBC, dogged the royal party's every step, travelling in a Hercules aircraft. If Hodgson wanted the Centennial to be an attention-getter, to introduce the North to the world, he'd surely succeed now. While the cameras and notebooks concentrated on The Queen and her family, they couldn't help but also take in the environment of the North and the marvels worked by Hodgson. They picked up on the organizational genius that set him apart. And they picked up on a beaming, rather large man with a trim triangular moustache who looked for all the world as if he'd just been given a knighthood.

A reception was held to introduce The Queen to the media and the organizers. I considered it a great privilege to be included even though, with so many people, it was almost a non-event: a quick handshake, a greeting with the word "Ma'am," and a slight bow, as we had been instructed. But here I was, an immigrant boy from Holland who shook the hand of The Queen of England.

After the festivities in Frobisher Bay, the Governor General and the Prime Minister returned to Ottawa. The tour was Hodgson's show all the way. The next two days were a blur of racing from one community to another, across the Arctic, me and the welcoming rug in our chartered executive jet.

The Royal tour took in Resolute in the High Arctic, Inuvik in the Western Arctic and then Tuktoyaktuk on the Arctic coast. The second day didn't end until after midnight, yet The Queen showed no weariness.

A photo session had been arranged for early the next day on the steps of Inuvik's Stringer Hall, but mechanical problems with the Hercules had stranded the press in Tuktoyaktuk. An RCMP photographer and I were the only ones there. The Royals enjoyed the day with tremendous glee.

Fort Smith, in the southern Mackenzie on the border of northern Alberta, was next on the itinerary and was to feature an old-timers' reunion. In the audience was Stephen Angulalik, an elderly Eskimo from Cambridge Bay who had accidentally deplaned at Fort Smith, mistaking it for Yellowknife. He told organizers he was to be presented to The Queen, so they included him in the old-timers' group, not realizing he was actually part of a Yellowknife event. When Hodgson returned to Yellowknife, it came to light that Stephen Angulalik had not arrived; he was located in Fort Smith and the executive jet was dispatched to pick him up. I imagined the stories he would tell his people in Cambridge Bay: greeting The Queen, travelling all alone in a personal jet specially dispatched for him, and that night again being one of the presenters at a state banquet.

The next day several hundred people greeted The Queen in Fort Providence, located on the banks of the Mackenzie River. Blackflies and mosquitoes swarmed over everyone, including the Royals, who paid no heed, having been sprayed with insect repellent by Hodgson. "Walk into the wind," he told The Queen. A remarkable event saw The Queen, dressed in a brown pantsuit and kerchief, walk the mile to the village with locals all around her. The other Royals also enjoyed the freedom of speaking casually with those walking along.

Prince Philip was to officiate the start of the Centennial canoe race by firing a commemorative Winchester rifle. The staff member responsible for providing the gun was late and the RCMP security detail, already concerned about the crowd around The Queen, was quick to apprehend the frantic young staff person racing down the road with a loaded rifle. Fortunately the situation was resolved in time for the Duke to fire the shot.

That night, being the last of the tour, I hosted the press corps at a reception in the downstairs common room of Akaitcho Hall, former student residence of Sir John Franklin High School in Yellowknife. As the night wore on, tales of being stranded in Tuktoyaktuk blossomed into embellished stories of hardships: sleeping on the hardwood floor of the school gymnasium, lack of food and drink. They were now experienced Northerners, with tales to tell for years to come.

"COULDN'T HAVE GONE BETTER!" HODGSON said, sweeping a hand over the newspaper clippings from around the country. "Look at the publicity." The Queen's visit played well in Ottawa as it both confirmed and demonstrated that the Arctic belonged to Canada. Media coverage had been extensive, adding to Canadians' interest and awareness of the diverse land north of the 60th parallel.

"Some critical coverage too," I said pointedly. I'd heard criticism from people on the street about the extravagance of the royal functions.

He shrugged, "Always some ninnies willing to drag down the positives and successes."

"Some of the media reports pointed out that the banquet was obviously a function for white people," I said. "Sure, you invited a few native people, but the cameras showed the head table with only powerful white people. Even the native performers had to sit out in the hallway, and that made the news."

"What are you getting at?" Hodgson went red beneath the jowls.

I saw an opportunity to address an important shortcoming of our government—the lack of native Northerners in our workforce. "What are we here for?" I asked. Not wanting Hodgson to interrupt, I said, "To set up a government for the people of the North, most of whom are native! And who runs our government? White people. Who's on our Council? Mostly white people. We're not doing all we can to get native people involved."

Hodgson rolled his eyes toward the ceiling, then stared at me and said, "I've insisted on more native studies in schools, using more native teachers. I'm pushing settlement councils. I'm trying to educate people who know nothing about government so that in the end they can take control of their own affairs."

"Yes," I said with a shrug. "But all of your directors are southerners, and a number are retired military colonels more comfortable with rule books than people. They're hiring more and more whites from the south with degrees and qualifications and training no one here can match. In turn, each hires a white assistant. Hell, if you're so hung up on education what about you and me? We're not shining examples of higher education, and we do all right." At that Hodgson chuckled, caught himself and shook his head, saying nothing.

"The territorial government is the biggest industry in the North, the biggest single employer. It wouldn't hurt if some of these assistants were from Rae or

Coppermine. Sure they may not know what they're doing right off the bat, but neither do some of the turkeys our directors hire. If we don't start hiring some native people soon, the day will come when a native doesn't stand a hope of breaking into our system." I paused to think of something to emphasize my point. "The North's population is seventy-five percent native but our government's hiring record of natives here at headquarters is dismal. I don't believe it's more than five percent, if that, and they're probably all game officers."

Hodgson turned away, fidgeting with a file on his credenza. I threw up my hands in despair. "I hear what people are saying. They're condemning you as a colonialist because they see you trying to impose your ways on native people. You're tackling housing, education, health and local government, all in the white way. And what about education? Once educated, what then? Hell, you won't even give the Territorial Council any power."

Hodgson blew out a pent-up breath before responding. "You must have noticed who's advising the Indian Brotherhood now it's obtained funding from the federal government—white know-it-alls from the south. And you say *I* rely too much on white southerners. I've told you before, I'll turn over power as Northerners learn to grasp it. The day will come when the Territorial Council has more power, with a speaker and a cabinet, and the day will come when native people will fill those positions. That's the way it should be, but until they're ready, I have my plan and I'm sticking to it." He looked at me and said, "You're losing sight of all that's been done." He was calm now, controlling the conversation. "Now that Centennial is out of the way, I'll concentrate on the local government problem. Everything's going as it should. If we didn't experience opposition, there'd be something wrong. In the meantime, I'm in charge."

"What if you get a group of radicals running in the upcoming election this December, all like-minded in their pursuit of power? How's that going to play out for you?"

He held up his hands. "I hear you, but let's move on." I waited for him to speak again and, after half a minute of silence, he said, "I've thought over your comments about the Information Department. I'm transferring Ted Horton to Edmonton as a southern liaison officer. You're the new Director of Information."

"What?"

He stood and shook my hand while I stood, flabbergasted. "You'll have control over your own department. Use your power wisely."

AFTER THREE YEARS IN THE Arctic, I had gained broad experience in government administrative processes and an in-depth knowledge of the North. I had progressed from Hodgson's gofer to the head of my own department, the sole director to report directly to Hodgson. I promoted Ross Harvey, who had been with us since the Ottawa days, to Chief of Publications, and I hired Art Sorensen away from the *Edmonton Journal* as Chief of Public Relations.

With Hodgson's support, I had little difficulty in expanding the department. The government's printing bureau was transferred from the Territorial Secretary to Publications. We set up a graphic design section to handle typesetting and layout work so that we were able to print publications, newspapers, magazines and information flyers. We developed external communications initiatives to inform the people of the North about government programs, progress and initiatives. We created a weekly newspaper for government employees, publicizing job vacancies, legislative proposals, dates of Council sessions and personnel news such as promotions and awards. We published a magazine, *Arctic in Colour,* promoting the Arctic across Canada. Most importantly, we hired local people, instituting a training program to hone their skills.

The Queen's visit and the centennial celebrations had shone a spotlight on the Arctic. Hodgson had flown as high as he could, and his showmanship had generated the attention he coveted. Now it was time to focus on the less glamourous challenges of governing, solving problems to improve the lives of Northerners.

Part Four

TURF WARS

22
FRESH FACES

FRESH FACES WITH DIFFERENT ACCENTS and dialects dominated the first session of the newly elected Territorial Council. As Hodgson predicted, Northerners had evolved from community to territorial politics. Four of the eight newly elected members were aboriginal: James Rabesca, a Dogrib from Rae; Willie Adams, an Eskimo from Rankin Inlet; Nick Sibbeston, a Métis from Fort Simpson; and Lena Pedersen, a Greenlandic Eskimo from Coppermine and the first woman elected to Council. The others were white: Tom Butters, a newspaperman and former government administrator from Inuvik; Bryan Pearson, a businessman from Frobisher Bay; Paul Kaeser, former mayor of Fort Smith; and Weldy Phipps, owner of Atlas Aviation from Resolute . David Searle of Yellowknife and Lyle Trimble of Aklavik were the returning members. The appointed members were reduced from five to four. Of those, Air Marshal Campbell and Deputy Commissioner Parker remained.

In his opening address Hodgson, his hand raised in the air, beamed broadly, and bragged, "The Northwest Territories is now the in thing! On the outside, if you can talk about the Territories, tell people you've been there, that puts you in the front row of a conversation—and that's because the Territories is on everybody's lips! It's an exciting place! The curtain of mystery that surrounds it has now been drawn back." There was applause, more or less enthusiastic, depending on which direction it came from.

"I sometimes long for the old days," Hodgson continued, "when I was busy engaged in Vancouver inciting riots and revolutions and holding up the mail like Jesse James, and I think if it hadn't been for the fact that I was a member of this Council I may well be there right now getting stamped along with the rest of them!" Laughter rippled through the audience; all could well imagine Stu Hodgson walking the picket line. Not that he was the same working stiff he used to be. Now he was a recognized and successful public administrator. Before Christmas he'd been awarded the Order of Canada for his work in the North.

"I heard rumours that I will be leaving the Territories soon! This is not so! I have had, I must tell you, some very attractive offers and it only stands to reason once your name and the Territories is as popular as it is now, that people would seek you out and offer you other forms of employment. For my own part I rejected these; I feel that there is still an awful lot that has to be done and the little contribution that I can offer I will continue to make. I have no plans to go anywhere other than back to the office!"

The audience applauded politely.

"It seems to me that now is the time for all of us to rededicate ourselves to the job we originally started out to do—and that is to bring the administration in here and then encourage, develop and educate people so they can run their own affairs. This objective has not changed one iota as far as I am concerned. The key to the development of dignity and democracy in the North is the settlement council, which places power where it should be—in the hands of the people."

He referred to the process of unincorporated settlements being able to advance to hamlet status, moving up the ladder as experience was gained. "This is a new concept, and the road is not always smooth, but we will persist and in years to come the Territories will realize the importance of what we do today.

"The evolution of local government in the Northwest Territories was appropriately marked on the first day of our centennial year," Hodgson reminded the Council. "Yellowknife became the first city, Inuvik became Canada's most northerly town and Tuktoyaktuk was incorporated as the first hamlet north of the Arctic Circle." Hodgson paused with a smile as his audience applauded his words.

Then he touched on the subject of most interest to the elected representatives. "How far away we are from the day when Territorial Council has complete direction of the northern administration is anybody's guess. But I think that if we can make a success of this administration, with the help of Council, over the next four years, we will be ready to move on and say to the rest of Canada that we truly have the capability within the Northwest Territories to have a greater say in running our own affairs.

"The Northwest Territories Council is a most complex body. Although Council does not have complete autonomy, it does have a major input into almost every aspect of life and law that affects us." Council members grimaced, knowing full well they were still under Hodgson's control. "As chairman of Council, I diligently and deliberately give its members a greater say in the affairs of this government than is their lot by law. I have done this because I believe there is no better way of encouraging and accustoming Northerners in the settlements to responsibly handle their own affairs.

"The most important thing to me is the unity of the two native cultures in the North, and this cannot be infringed upon by the kind of chaos and turbulence that exists between different cultures elsewhere in this country. But this could happen here. It could happen when any faction believes that it is more important to be Eskimo than Indian, or Indian than white."

Hodgson spoke for another ten minutes, expounding on the work that needed to be covered. He then called for a recess.

Lyle Trimble was the first to respond to the Commissioner. "The first Council I was elected to in 1964, and several Councils before that one, consisted of four elected members, from the Mackenzie only, and five members appointed by Ottawa. The seat of government for the North was in Ottawa. Policies were developed and the decisions were made in Ottawa, and administered by civil servants employed by and responsible to Ottawa. The Council was considered, and it still is by many today, as a voice crying in the wilderness . . . Appointed members of that time were given the very distinct impression, both from within and without the Council, that their presence on this legislative body was not necessarily required. I expect, and I certainly hope, that after this existing Council fulfils its term of office the seats now occupied by Ottawa appointments will represent the Northwest Territories electorate. However, I must quickly add my very firm conviction, and I mean this very sincerely, that had the appointed members not been present on that Council, or if the succeeding Council had been denied the contribution made by the appointed members who served from 1967 to 1970, we would never have attained the political development which took place the past few years, and which we enjoy today. I believe the appointed members of this present Council will fulfil an equally important role in future northern political, social and economic development."

The next to reply was one of the new members, James Rabesca, from Rae.

He stood with a flourish and brandished a sheaf of papers. "Mr. Commissioner," he said, "I have been telling the people of my constituency that when I got to the chamber of this Council I would prepare my first speech in my Dogrib language. I propose to read it first in Dogrib, and then read it over again in English, sir."

Rabesca held his brief close to his face, reading steadily in the melodic cadences of his native language. After a short while he paused and realized no one could understand a word. We had not been forewarned, but this was a huge oversight by our government. Now that I was fully in charge of the Department of Information, I would discuss the need for translators with the Clerk of Council.

Rabesca continued, "Well, I didn't read them all, so I may as well read them back in straight English . . . I am an Indian and I am proud of it. I know in the next four years there will be many problems coming up that will mean that Indians will be demanding things that the white man has taken away from them. Our people will be coming to the Council table with big questions about why they have not been treated with respect. They will be asking questions about why they are not holding the top jobs in our government. They will be wanting to know why they are dying earlier, why their kids end up in jail more often, why our chiefs and councillors are not organized as the only true Indian way of local government, in our settlements. They will be talking in loud voices and asking why they can't be heard when they want to talk in ordinary voices. They will be refusing the shame of welfare. They will call it receiving rent for the use of the land and everything in it. They will be organizing themselves as Indians.

"I am the only Indian on this Council. I would not like to see anyone trying to say that I speak only for the Indians. Do not ask me to speak about how the Indian people think. They may have elected me, but our people speak only through their chiefs and their voice is heard only through the Indian Brotherhood of the Northwest Territories, and I hope that no matter how many native people come to this Council that no one will say that Indians are represented here. I sit here to see what you are doing. I hope I will be able to do things with you. But it is still your Council and not ours. I will come to speak about the opinions of our people as they voice them in consultation with the Indian Brotherhood Assembly.

"Sometimes you may feel that Indians hurt you as white people, and maybe they will make you mad. Even though we have been hurt and neglected, we are still making sure that our anger is cool so that we can see ahead through the next five years and get what we want, that our Indians are schooled. Yet we need more than your good wishes too. I personally ask for a one hundred percent better working relationship on the part of the government of the Northwest Territories in dealing with the Indians.

"I will push hard for support directly from the government to the people. In the past, the government has been a strange word to many of the native people, and one of my main objectives on the Council will be to bring government to the people—to involve people in running their own affairs. We have been promised that as long as the sun sets in the west and the grass grows and the river flows towards the north that we, the native people, will be allowed to live the way we want to live. But many things make it very hard to live the way we want to live. With all this oil exploration, mining and business enterprises going on, we don't really know what is left of our traditional hunting grounds, our rights to the land we have occupied and considered our own for thousands of generations. This concern is felt by the majority of people in the Northwest Territories. Because this is true. I believe that the Council must make it its first concern to help us settle our aboriginal rights. I think that in order to get anywhere, we have to find out where we stand in the eyes of the Canadian public. By this, I mean that we have to settle the question of aboriginal rights and land rights before we, the native people, can really be considered a member of the Just Society. Thank you."

Rabesca was right about the plight of the Indians and the uncertainty of land ownership. But he was more than an observer; he was now a decision-maker and had a responsibility to communicate with his people. Whether that was directly or through the Indian Brotherhood was up to him.

Lena Pedersen, from Coppermine, spoke of the plight of people in her communities. "Many of our people are just now moving from a rather primitive camp existence into more sophisticated settlements. During my election campaign I visited every settlement in my constituency. I was pleased to see how many of our people lived in houses, but I was dismayed to see how few had either the financial capability or educational background to make those houses into homes for their families.

"My views on cultural and language retention are well known. I will only briefly state here that I want to see everything possible done to teach native languages, native arts and native history to our children. This program must have the government support. Without such support we will soon have a northern people without heritage and without pride. A person without heritage is like a tree without roots. No one would dream of basing a future lumber industry on rootless trees and no more should we expect to be able to build a great people out of a population without heritage and pride.

"Regarding employment, I wish to mention that in southern Canada right now we are seeing demonstrations and protests and great governmental concern over an unemployment ratio approaching seven percent. In my constituency we have an unemployment ratio of ninety percent. If we on this Council acted like the elected legislators in the rest of Canada we would simply refuse to consider any other point of business until the unemployment problem in the NWT could be solved . . . I do insist that the creation of jobs must, and I repeat must, become the primary concern of this government over the next four years. We can no longer be satisfied with the economically slender stopgap measures of a duffle hat production here and another craft project there . . . By themselves they do not constitute meaningful economic and job development . . . In my home settlement alone we must provide a minimum of two hundred jobs over the next ten years. In my entire constituency the figure is a thousand jobs needed within ten years."

She spoke well and with conviction. "Anywhere else in Canada when the average citizen thinks of government, he thinks of parliament. In the Northwest Territories, when the average citizen thinks of government, he thinks of the public service." She looked directly at Hodgson, reinforcing her message that he was the government in Yellowknife, just as his bureaucrats continued to be the government in remote settlements. "This is wrong and unacceptable. The only way we can change this, and we must change it, is to make all public servants spending public funds responsible and accountable for those expenditures to some elected body of the public."

Pedersen paused at the sound of desk-thumping and applause. "As a result of your many trips to the settlements, Mr. Commissioner, the people are starting to realize that their own elected councils have no power, that this Council has no power."

Hodgson glared at her from the podium, clearly angry that she would suggest local councils were a waste of time.

"The only power in this government is the Commissioner of the Northwest Territories. It is really not that I disagree with things you promise or give out during your trips, it is just that I would much rather see these things available as a result of government policies, as directed by elected representatives, than available only by executive order when a settlement is fortunate enough to have a visit from you, Mr. Commissioner.

"This brings me to repeat the old plea—for the establishment of an executive council composed of elected members of this Council, responsible to those who elected them and having the power to decide what will happen in the Northwest Territories.

"We have in Yellowknife a great number of public servants, whose wages and optimum income cost the public a great deal of money. To a lesser degree we have this at regional and area levels too . . .

"Living in the settlements of my constituency, it is therefore almost frightening to realize that all these well-meaning public servants have almost zero impact on the daily or even weekly life of the average citizen. Obviously, most of the policies made at this Council and at the public service headquarters level never quite filter down to the average member of the public. To date, this government has failed to relate itself to the public which it claims to serve. Let us, at this session, attempt to change this so we may provide government which is meaningful to the public. If we accomplish this, then we, in return, will have what every successful government must have, the support and confidence of the public who elected us to serve them. Thank you." She sat down to a perfunctory ripple of applause.

Hodgson glanced at the clock and decided he had time to respond. His jaw was set and he avoided eye contact as he got some licks of his own on the record.

"I have always believed that if you wish to have responsible people, you must give them responsibilities. I honestly believe that the federal government wants to turn over more and more responsibility to the people of the Territories. But as you know, I have only the role of advisor in this.

"I believe that what has been turned over to us up to this time is with a certain amount of challenge; with a certain amount of feelings on the part of the government and others to see whether we can rise to the occasion, not only to accept the responsibilities but to carry them out.

"These last four years haven't been easy for my staff. We've had our problems, and had our tough times, and we have made our mistakes. But we have never taken our eyes off the objective, which is to establish in the Territories an instrument to carry out the programs and policies and the wishes of this Council.

"The administration that we have been putting together is, in a sense, the creation of a force in the North, a force that is based on the needs of the people of the North. This is why the civil servants who come before you to answer your questions are now almost exclusively territorial employees. Very few federal employees retain responsibility for the affairs of the North.

"But more changes are coming. We have already established a committee on finance that allows input from elected representatives into the workings of this government. Now, I am going to take it upon myself to establish other committees. This will make a meaningful contribution into the affairs of the Council and in allowing Council members a greater say, a greater responsibility and a greater input into the programs and the development of these programs than they have had up to now.

"The Northwest Territories Act places a great responsibility upon the Commissioner. But I have chosen to not only work with the Council, but also to share more than is required, because I believe this is a way of demonstrating to the government of Canada and the people of Canada that within the framework of this Council lies the means of developing the expertise that is necessary for the development of the North, and for decision-making in the Northwest Territories."

He looked at several Council members, then at the clock on the wall. "I now recognize the clock and adjourn this meeting of the Council until tomorrow at 10:00 a.m."

HODGSON'S MOOD WAS VILE AS we walked to the Laing Building. He detested the personal attack from Lena Pedersen and had no patience with Rabesca's lack of commitment to the Council. At the best of times Hodgson hated criticism, and this, when his own judgment and institution had been so boldly and publicly denounced, was one of the worst of times.

"That woman could set us back years with one more speech like that." He paused to glare at me. This wasn't the time to point out that Lena Pedersen was just repeating what councillors like David Searle had expressed before.

"And Rabesca!" he said. "I'll bet the Brotherhood wrote every word of his speech and told him to read it. These people come down here full of vinegar, all fired up to change the world with a brave speech or two and they don't realize they're doing more harm than good."

I must have grimaced. "Don't look at me like that!" he said. "I'm the first to want native Northerners on Council, but this just shows that I'm right in trying to educate them from the ground up before they go chasing off on crusades."

23

WE'RE ALL NORTHERNERS

JUNE 21, 1971

IN AN ARTICLE PUBLISHED IN the *Ottawa Journal*, reporter Dennis Bell wrote that, "Official territorial policy, as explained by the government information chief, Jake Ootes, is that there are no Indians, Eskimos, Métis and whites—we call everybody Northerners, treat everybody the same."[8] Despite what Bell had written, we of course recognized there were distinct racial groups in the North. But government programs were not funded according to racial identity, an approach that was challenged by increasingly influential native advocacy groups.

Following the formation of the Indian Brotherhood, the Committee for Original Peoples Entitlements (COPE) was established in January of 1970 to reach a land settlement and royalty sharing agreement on behalf of Eskimos, Indians and Métis in the Mackenzie Delta. Both COPE and the Indian Brotherhood cited the United States government's pending settlement with the native people of Alaska (one billion dollars and ten million acres of land) as a precedent for similar action by the Canadian government.

The Eskimos formed the Inuit Taparisat in February 1971. They too felt shortchanged by Ottawa's interest in the potential of a booming oil industry. At a conference in Coppermine they spoke out against the policies of the Northern Development department and the federal government's intransigence on the question of indigenous rights.

The Coppermine conference heard a long list of grievances. Peter Esau and Peter Sidney represented Sachs Harbour, a community of 127 people on Banks Island and, thanks to a plentiful supply of game and the world's largest annual white fox harvest, one of the very few totally self-sufficient Eskimo communities. Mr. Esau told the conference that a group of oilmen had arrived at Sachs Harbour unexpectedly and told community leaders that

---

[8] Dennis Bell, "COPE Fights for Native Land Rights", *Ottawa Journal*, September 10, 1970

Ottawa had issued permits for a three- to five-year exploration program that would involve bulldozers, seismic crews and dynamite blasts. The oilmen planned to build a big supply depot on the island, in the middle of the trapping grounds.

The Sachs Harbour experience was by no means unique. Territorial Supreme Court Justice William Morrow, speaking at the University of Calgary, had expressed concerns about the challenges facing native people. He said rapid economic development of northern Canada was eroding Indian and Eskimo cultures and could result in an Arctic version of Custer's Last Stand.

"That's a pretty pessimistic view but that's my personal view. The history of our whole continent is based on development. The irresistible forces of business will move in and take over." He said Indian people of the United States were granted certain rights, but "discovery of gold brought people with six shooters and rifles into Indian country . . . And in the end, the US Cavalry ended up protecting these people, not the aboriginal people."

He told the audience a similar situation was developing in Canada, citing the example of the Migratory Birds Act. "One of the original purposes of this legislation was to protect birds for use as food by aboriginal people—but somewhere along the way, we have forgotten this purpose," Judge Morrow said. "If I were a native in the North, the only time I could shoot a duck to eat would be after they've flown south! The season opens September 1, and there aren't too many ducks left up there then. Natives find such restrictions hard to respect, especially when it is permissible for hunters to shoot the same ducks, not for food, but for sport, farther south."

He provided another example of ignoring aboriginal rights. When the country was being settled pioneers were "given squatter's rights. But natives today don't even have squatter's rights, which is rather odd, if you think about it."[9]

In 1971, James Washie, at the vanguard of this movement for indigenous rights, arranged a meeting with representatives of the Secretary of State, the Department of Indian Affairs and Northern Development and the territorial government to identify sources of funding available for Brotherhood programs. As Hodgson later explained to Council, "The Indian Brotherhood wanted to know specifically what type of funds were available for their group or, to say it in another way, what funds were identified that ethnic or cultural

---

[9] Carol Hogg, "Too Rapid Growth Sparks Dim Outlook for North", *Calgary Herald,* January 28, 1970

groups could apply for. The Department of Indian Affairs pointed out that they had funds available in their budget for consultation and for a certain amount of research, and for funding various activities of the Indian Brotherhood. The Secretary of State spoke of funds they have available."

The federal approach put Hodgson in an awkward position. "When it came to the territorial government and our administration particularly, we stated that one hundred percent of the funds that were put before Council and developed by the administration were for the people of the Territories . . . whether they be Indian, Eskimo, Métis, Chinese, Japanese or European. We repeated that all of our programs are aimed at territorial residents. Therefore, they are based on the people who live here, and as the Indians and Eskimos and others are primarily in the majority as far as the population is concerned, this is Council's way and the government of the Northwest Territories' way of responding to requests such as this.

"Now let us keep in mind that the Carrothers Commission stated in 1966 that the Territories should not be devolved along ethnic lines, not along power group lines, not along racial lines but rather along the line of developing at the community level. So we said that we do not have funds available in the same sense that you would have from the federal government. However, as the meeting proceeded, it began to look like there would be a misunderstanding or misrepresentation, and people would say or could infer that the territorial administration and our Council were against a specific race or against a specific culture. I know that this is not true. I know the feelings of the administration and I know well the feelings of the Council . . . Fearing misunderstanding, the administration decided to make available an amount of money and decided that we would recommend to Council $30,000.

"It cleared the air to a large degree with our friends in Ottawa. It cleared the air as far as our group here in Yellowknife is concerned and that we in fact had an interest in the advancement of all races and that we had identified a nominal amount of money which they could look forward to each year to apply for."

Having made this commitment, Hodgson now needed to have it included in the budget even though, in typical fashion, he had already started spending the money. "Now I have to confess right off the bat that I have spent $7,500 of it already and I don't know if that is going to go down too well with you." Hodgson had contributed $5,000 to the Indian–Eskimo education conference held a few weeks prior and had approved an application for $2,500 from the Indian Brotherhood for their newspaper, *Native Press*.

The appropriation required approval of the finance committee, which would prepare a motion to be voted on by all members. The committee, however, refused to endorse Hodgson's decision and instead proposed the following motion: "to provide additional grants and other assistance to support organizations active in the Territories, carry on work and projects of a general nature that assist in the social and educational development of the residents of the Northwest Territories, and further, that the sum of $30,000 be spent on the foregoing basis."

Committee chair David Searle explained to Council that his committee agreed with the addition of $30,000 "but we state that these grants should not be made along ethnic lines." Instead, the grants should be "for organizations and labelled for specific worthwhile community projects and considered on the merits of the project." He encouraged Council to stick to the principle of "doing what we do for the benefit of all people of the North, regardless of ethnic considerations . . . It may well be that COPE or the Indian Brotherhood can show on the merits of the projects that it is a worthwhile thing to do . . . But that is what we thought the test should be, not the ethnic origin of the organization.

"We are not saying that grants should not go to COPE or the Indian Brotherhood, we are saying that they should, if the project is worthwhile, but the ethnic origin of the organization should not be relevant or taken into consideration."

Hodgson appreciated what Searle said, but added, "That is not what the Indian Brotherhood wants. The Indian Brotherhood is quite frank about this." He defended his original wording. "They want to know how much money, in total, is available so that they or other ethnic groups or culture groups in the Territories can bid for it. Now, I am not quarrelling with Mr. Searle, and I'm sure he understands. I'm merely pointing out, the way it is written in here is the way that the Brotherhood wants it. They wanted it written that way so that they know that they can apply for it and it is for them to apply. They do not want it open, so anybody could apply."

Nick Sibbeston, Council member from Fort Simpson and a vociferous advocate for indigenous organizations, supported the Indian Brotherhood's position. "I am a member of the finance committee and I must say I was not in agreement with the rest of the members, but I agree that the wording should have remained as written here because, in as much as we do not want to refer to the racial identification, and I think it is a matter of practicability and necessity, because we have to realize the fact that there are different groups in the North and that Indian and Eskimo people, for instance, just do not have the education and experience and the know-how with respect to getting grants and so on. For instance, as Mr. Commissioner said, this is, I think, the first year that a native group has applied, inasmuch as this fund has been available for a number of years. And so I support the way in which it is put down and then I agree with the principle that a certain amount be earmarked for native groups."

Lyle Trimble jumped into the fray. "I have gone to some lengths over the years in explaining to the people that the territorial government has the responsibility of looking after all people in the Northwest Territories the same as a provincial government does for the people in a province. In fact, the federal MP, Bud Orange, and I made a trip around my constituency a few years ago. Part of our discussion with the people at that time was in explaining where the various responsibilities lay. I have explained to the native people that matters relating directly to Eskimos, and matters relating directly to treaty Indians and the treaties, are matters concerning the federal government, which retains the full responsibility, and that I have no right to involve myself in these matters. Now the territorial administration has turned around and in fact, made me appear as a liar. The territorial administration has taken the administrative responsibility of administering treaty payments etc. which, I might add, the Indian Brotherhood, according to reports I have received, have objected to. And how do I go back to my constituents and say the territorial administration is handling treaty matters but the territorial government has nothing to do with treaties? The white man already has the reputation of talking with a forked tongue, now how are the Indian people going to understand this? And how am I going to explain it?

"Now there is placed in our appropriations a definite fund saying this is for only ethnic groups. I do not care what ethnic group that might be. How do we explain that our responsibility is for all people in the Territories? . . . I realize that the native people in this country—and I use the term native loosely, insofar as I consider the Métis people in the Territories to be native just as much as the Indian and the Eskimo people, they are one people as far as I am concerned, I realize that they, on average, are much poorer than the rest of the people in the Northwest Territories and in the rest of Canada. Now this is a problem and it is inequality that I think we have to face up to, we have to do something about. But I believe that we should attack the problem from the root and not try to divide the people in the Territories. I have been spending the last seven years trying to do the opposite. When I first came to the Territories in 1956, there were very real indications that people were divided, and from the stories I heard I am convinced that in the years preceding that, there was even much more division—division along religious lines. There is division along racial lines and these divisions were perpetrated by the administration and by this Council through the laws that it had established. The federal government, through the Indian Affairs branch of the Department of Citizenship and Immigration, took care of Indian people who were treaty Indians. The Department of Northern Affairs and Natural Resources, a different federal department, took care of Eskimos who were registered. And the territorial government was responsible for everybody else, whether they were non-treaty Indians, non-registered Eskimos or any other race. There were different policies that were followed, different personnel who were administering these policies, and I say this Council was responsible because we had such legislation as the liquor ordinance which gave certain rights to some people and refused those rights to others.

"I am happy to say that most of these divisions amongst the people in the North have been done away with. The liquor ordinance has been changed. The administration of all peoples in the Territories has come under the territorial government, with one policy and one administration. I feel that there has been a great move towards unity among the people of the North. I think we have also been making progress as far as the economic problems of the native people are concerned, but we have not done near enough, and that is the main reason why I have been fighting so long on this Council to get some meaningful industrial development action by this government. But I do not agree that we begin to solve our problem by dividing people again along racial lines, and that is exactly what we are doing. I cannot accept that fact. I agree as Mr. Searle has said, that we should make funds available for the Indian Brotherhood if they have a specific case and a specific purpose for those funds, or for COPE or any other group, but I cannot agree that we justify identifying a certain amount of money in our appropriations and saying this is for certain ethnic groups, because it is fundamentally against my principles and against the way in which the Territories have been going, and I would hope, will continue to grow.

"I consider the people of the Territories to be one people with equal rights, and that is the way this government should operate. Now I realize there are serious questions of aboriginal rights. There are unfulfilled treaties and I feel that the government of Canada must face up to these responsibilities and come to some equitable solution and understanding with the people involved. But I do not agree that this territorial government and this Council, which do not have this responsibility, should get themselves involved in this way. I do not agree that we should be involved in matters of treaties and in the handling of treaty payments, and if the Minister has told the Commissioner to handle these matters, this Council should object and tell the Minister to take care of treaty matters with the Indian people himself, until such time as he has come to a solution in consultation with the Indian people, but not to involve this territorial government. If the Secretary of State feels that his department should give funds to specific ethnic groups, then this is his business and his responsibility, and the federal government has the responsibility concerning aboriginal and treaty rights, but we do not. I do not think we should get involved."

Several more members stated their views. Deputy Commissioner Parker asked that the word cultural be added to "educational and social."

Lyle Trimble said, "I have no argument against including the word 'cultural,' in fact I would recommend that we do so because I personally believe that the cultures of the native people are something which should be developed in the Territories and I'm not thinking merely in terms of the native people. Culture should be developed for people such as me as well. I am talking about native cultures now, do not misunderstand me. There is a great deal in the native cultures which is a lot better than some of the culture I came from." Trimble moved that the word "cultural" be included.

Hodgson jumped in again. "This is like a ship at sea, it is starting to swing around, and the wind is changing now, blowing in the direction that the

Indian Brotherhood recommends. That is what I recommended to you in the first place. What the Indian Brotherhood has asked for, and the soon to be constituted Eskimo Brotherhood will ask for, is they want to know what funds they can specifically bid on or apply for, that are eligible only to those organizations in the Territories. That is what they want to know."

Lyle Trimble wanted to make his position quite clear as well. "As far as I am concerned there are no funds in this appropriation specifically earmarked for the Brotherhood or any other ethnic group, but there is an appropriation . . . which is earmarked for social, cultural and educational development of the residents of the Territories regardless of who they might be."

Air Marshal Campbell, chair of the meeting, called for a vote on the amended motion, which now read "social, cultural and educational development." Six members voted in favour and three against. The Territorial government would continue to serve the interests of all Northerners, regardless of ethnicity.

24

PAGEANTRY AND POLITICS

JUNE 30–JULY 2, 1971

I RECEIVED A SURPRISING INVITATION from James Washie's office to judge the Indian Princess Pageant and attend the Brotherhood's All Chiefs meeting in Rae. I hoped Hodgson would suggest I decline; instead he roared with laughter. "Fantastic," he said, "When?"

"June 30."

"Pick the right girl or you'll be in deep trouble."

When I arrived in Rae, the air was thick with the ubiquitous mosquitoes, woodsmoke; the shriek of kids and the soft thumping of drums. Chiefs, delegates, observers, old folks and youngsters from every community along the Mackenzie River and around Great Slave and Great Bear Lakes milled around tents and tepees. It was a time to see old friends, family and acquaintances. The place had an intoxicating scent and an atmosphere of excitement.

Inside the community hall, with the Indian Brotherhood insignia painted over the entrance, about eighty chiefs and councillors were seated around a huge rectangle of tables. Another seventy or so sat on the periphery, against walls festooned with banners that said, "Our rights, our treaty, our land."

James Washie sat at the head table before a handwritten sign that read "President, Indian Brotherhood." He still looked young but I could see he'd gained confidence and was controlling the meeting. "Tomorrow morning we will start the All Chiefs meeting to discuss the threats to the Indians of the Northwest Territories," he said. My heart sank. I knew I shouldn't have come. "We'll close the meeting for today and prepare the hall for the feast and the Indian Princess Pageant, but first we'll ask Mr. Clarence Gilchrist, the Assistant Commissioner of the NWT government, to say a few words."

Gilchrist had arrived a few minutes after me and had remarked that he wouldn't say much as "the territorial government isn't too popular in Rae." The people, however, were courteous and clapped when he finished his address; the chairman said that they were pleased to see him and appreciated the effort he had made to attend.

I had an hour before the pageant was to start, so I wandered about the community, then sat on a promontory where the wind kept the mosquitoes at bay. I admired the way the evening sun spilled big pools of fire onto the lake and the way clouds of aromatic smoke hung like blue wraiths in the still air over Rae. Sensing footsteps behind me, I turned to find Georgina Blondin, now Georgina Pryde, looking graceful and confident.

"Hi Jake!" she said, flashing a smile. The orange sun glowed on her face. "Did you catch any of this afternoon's session?"

"No, I just arrived. I'm here for the Princess Pageant. I'm one of the judges."

"I know."

She gestured for me to walk with her, steering me toward a pathway running along the lakeshore. "After the pageant there'll be a feast and a tea dance. Are you staying here?"

"I'll stay for the feast and tea dance, but no, I have to go back to Yellowknife and drive out again in the morning."

"I suppose the Commissioner is interested to know what the Brotherhood is up to."

"Yeah. He knows there can be some conflict." She looked at me quizzically. "Over the community council policy." A throng of excited children screamed around the corner of a house, whirled past and disappeared down the pathway.

We were waved into a large tepee to watch Dogrib Hand Games. Several men beat a rhythm on skin drums and cried in two-syllable chants, their heads thrown back, as two teams of four men each stood opposite each other. The players of the active team swayed from the hips up, surreptitiously passing a small token from one to the other until one of the four members hid it in a fist. Then they held out their arms for the other team's guesser to divine its location, using facial expression and signals to try to affect the outcome. The rhythm of the drums added emotion and intensity while the guesser took endless minutes to make his decision. It was all done with a great sense of drama.

The fellow who had waved us in explained that the best two out of three guesses won the match and earned a point. A predetermined number of sticks were used to count points; the team to collect all the sticks won the game. Traditionally the game was played by men. Women were expected to learn how to play but once they reached child-bearing age, for some unexplained reason, were expected to refrain and instead teach their children.

"Opponents have to conduct themselves with the utmost respect. You've got to be honest in life and honest in hand games," said our host.

Georgina and I watched for a while and then moved on along the shore where a CBC film crew was arranging a shot of giggling Indian Princess contestants, self-conscious and excited at the same time. Georgina told me their names: Virginia Football, from Rae; Doris Louyine, from Fort Smith; Florence Harris, from Inuvik; Emelda King, from Roche River; Dolly Cazon from Fort Simpson; and Catherine Kakfwi, from Fort Good Hope. Each wore a beaded headband, traditional moccasins and a moosehide skirt with a modern look, hemmed well above the knee. Their outfits were fringed and embroidered with porcupine quills and moose-hair tufting dyed red, black, yellow and white.

There were shouts from the village and we saw people waving for us to come for the feast, a banquet, to be followed by the pageant.

The hall had been transformed to accommodate some four hundred Rae residents and visitors. Chairs and tables had been removed to leave the floor free for everyone to sit, cross-legged, facing each other in long rows stretching from podium to doorway. Between each row was a strip of floor loaded with pots and plates of food: bannock, boiled caribou, whitefish and potato salad, followed by tea. An elder stood to give thanks and led a prayer, after which we ate. It was a time of generous fellowship and I wished Hodgson were here to experience this with these people.

When all was done, we stood and made way for the floor to be cleared. Several tables and chairs were set up at the front and I and the other judges were summoned to come forward. I shook hands with Roy Sam of the Yukon Native Brotherhood, Omer Peters, Vice President of the National Indian Brotherhood, Jim Koe of Inuvik's COPE, and Dave Reesor, executive assistant to the mayor of Yellowknife.

A young man with long black hair and an almost toothless but infectious grin took the microphone and introduced himself as Antoine Barnaby. He rattled off greetings and jokes to get things rolling, then asked the first contestant to step forward. We waited patiently while Antoine glanced theatrically over his shoulder until beautiful Florence Harris stepped out from a small side room. Antoine wrapped an arm around her shoulder and babbled an introduction. Florence gave a short, prepared speech about the importance of maintaining native traditions and was then asked to go to the judges' tables so we could ask questions. When we finished Antoine called the next contestant. It was a slow and halting process, but everyone was having a marvellous time. Even Antoine's jokes seemed to improve as the night wore on.

I winced a little when one nervous contestant, Dolly Cazon, got up and announced she thought the Brotherhood wasn't really doing a good job for the people by stirring up hatred and resentment. Her father, the Chief of Fort Simpson, was rising when Dolly clarified things, saying she didn't mean that the way it came out. She meant people should follow their dreams, but in a way that doesn't hurt others. The occupants of the hall breathed a sigh of relief and cheered Dolly as she came to our table. I admired her courage, going back to the microphone to clarify her thoughts. She received great marks from me.

We considered our verdict. I was glad of the presence of the other judges, for final decisions were difficult. But there was no doubt that the most engaging and accomplished had been Doris Louyine, the nineteen-year-old Chipewyan contestant from Fort Smith. Her personality, poise and presentation had stolen the attention of everyone in the hall. I was pleased to congratulate Doris and to present her with a cheque for $100 from our government. But who should be runner-up?

After the applause died down, Antoine read out the name of the runner-up, Virginia Football, Rae's very own contestant. A thunderous ovation echoed through the hall. "Virginia is a Grade 1 teacher who also translates for the people of Rae," Antoine intoned. "She has recently completed collecting the legends of the people of Rae and will be making them into a book for use in the school program."

Florence Harris, the eighteen-year-old from Inuvik, was second runner-up. One of the judges commented that she was one of the best public relations people he had seen. There were prizes and enthusiastic applause for all the contestants.

While the hall was cleared for the tea dance, I joined Georgina outside. We watched some men alternately holding their drums over a wood fire and tapping the warmed hide with their fingers.

"They're testing the drums to see if they're ready."

"Indians and drums always seem to go together," I said, more a question than a comment.

"People pray to the Creator through drum songs. They're part of us, part of our lives. They serve our spirituality you might say. It's our spirituality that has sustained us over the generations. Some songs are for fun and dancing, but others are for praying, or healing or seeing into the future.

"In the old days, the Indian people kept moving around, following the game they needed for food. But every summer they stopped somewhere and had a big gathering of all the people. That's when they would have a big tea dance, like the one we're having tonight. The drums play a big part and we are reminded the Creator owns the land and no one, not even the government, can change that.

"You'll see the medicine man sing prayer songs, when people concentrate and ask the Creator for what they need. The medicine man starts walking slowly in a circle as he sings, and the crowd follows him. Everyone sings, and in doing that they are praying too. After the prayer songs, the social part of the tea dance begins, to let everyone have a good time."

On our return, the hall was crowded. At the front stood the medicine man with his drum, just as Georgina had described. He beat his drum, chanting and dancing in a wide circle. Georgina said it was a song of thanksgiving.

After he had circled twice, he began a rhythmic shuffle. Suddenly the medicine man's drumbeat was joined by the drums and the chants of the men we had seen outside. The chanting was loud. The drums beat faster and, one by one, people joined the dance in an ever-widening circle, shuffling independently but in unison. People crowded tightly, shoulder to shoulder, facing into the centre of the circle.

Georgina pulled me onto the floor. The circle moved in syncopated shuffles and before long there were upwards of fifty people chanting and dancing, each foot movement synchronized, setting up a vibration. It was an intoxicating experience, the crowd swaying unconsciously as the circle moved around, the floor of the hall vibrating with the deep-throated drumming. The floor bellied up and down and the light fixtures swayed as if they were as much a part of the ritual as the dancers.

The tempo and repetition of the chant was hypnotic. There was a simplicity, a power and a closeness to naked creation that moved me more deeply than any other experience I'd ever had.

WHEN I ARRIVED AT THE hall the next morning, the All Chiefs meeting was already underway. Feeling conspicuous, I took a seat at the back.

Chief Andrew Stewart of Aklavik was speaking. "When we were governed by the federal government, we were treated far better than we are now. Since the territorial government came down here we have not been treated nice." A flush of embarrassment shot through me. I was too flustered to hear the rest of Chief Stewart's comments but gradually calmed down and was able to concentrate.

Expressions of displeasure continued. Those present were unhappy with the government's policy of what they called 'one people,' and for failure to recognize the special status of the Indian people by right of the treaties. They felt they had lost ground since the territorial government took over treaty payments and special Indian programs.

Chief Tadit Francis of Fort McPherson objected to the territorial government's effort to break the power of the traditional leaders of the Indian people. "The territorial government comes to the settlement, they don't recognize me. Rather they go to the settlement councils which put all the power of running the community into the hands of the whites, and these whites do not care about what the Indian people need or want. I have no authority."

As the morning wore on, the discussion switched to the treaties. I scribbled away on my steno pad.

Louis Norwegian of Fort Norman said he was twelve when the treaty was signed. "I didn't want to take treaty payments because there was something behind it; there was something very wrong. They cheated the people when the white treaty people made the old chief sign."

Alec Charlo, a Rae band councillor, said he was also twelve at the time of the signing of the treaty. He said the white men could change the words around "because they read and wrote English. They have been pushing us around long enough because we are poor and don't know their language, this 'English.' If we could speak their English at the time of the treaty, things would have been different. We would have been the ones to tell them what to do and what has to be done, because this is our land. Now it's the other way around."

Andrew Gon, Chief of Rae Lakes said, "It's been fifty years since treaty, the white people have been taking advantage of our land, our people. All the time they get richer and richer and we get poorer and poorer."

One after another the chiefs and band councillors spoke on the same theme. They said they should work together, just like the white people do, to settle the treaty issue. They acknowledged the signing of the first treaty was a mistake, and claimed they were waking up now with the Brotherhood.

Heads, many clad in baseball caps, nodded vigorously. A murmur of agreement swelled through the hall. Chief Baptiste Cazon of Fort Simpson took the microphone. He said the Indian people should advise the government on how to solve their problems and nodded to James Washie at the head table.

Washie said he disagreed that they should advise the federal or territorial government of their problems. "We have been advising them of our problems for the last fifty years and we are tired of this. The people have lived without the white man a long time. We took care of one another, we hunted and we solved our problems. The chief and the people organized and survived, we do not need the white man's help. The money we are getting is to keep us quiet. We can organize ourselves through the Indian Brotherhood."

The chiefs had blasted the territorial government for their belief in the 'we are all Northerners, we are equal' myth. Washie said, "The territorial government says we are equal. How many of you have jobs, how many of you have contracts, how many of you have good homes? We haven't been given the opportunity to work for ourselves. We can't say we are equal now. We will tell the territorial government when we are equal." Spontaneous applause erupted. After it faded, Washie said Indian people can run their own affairs and they don't need "no cotton-picking white man from Toronto or any other place to come in here and tell us how to run our lives." He explained Indians had lived for tens of thousands of years on this land and got along fine. "We don't need any Commissioner going to Ottawa saying that his Indians are doing fine. We're tired of being patted on the head."

Washie pointed out that Indians in other provinces and the Yukon dealt directly with Ottawa on treaty rights, but not so in the Northwest Territorires. He said the Indians in the Territories wouldn't stand for this any longer. "We're going to get into the fight. Seven thousand Indians are going to be included in this fight."

The steam rising from the head table was aimed directly at Hodgson and the territorial government. Once again I was concerned about being here. But they had invited me and walking out would be disrespectful. I would record the comments and not appear cowed. Better to know what they were saying and deal with the discontent from an informed place.

There was no doubt the treaties were at the root of the frustration. Washie said he had gone to Ottawa to see about the treaties, and was told to see Hodgson, "Who said it was not his responsibility to look after treaty Indians and that the territorial government doesn't recognise treaty Indians."

Ed Bird, Secretary-Treasurer of the Indian Brotherhood and former Chief of the Fort Smith band, stepped forward and handed Washie a document.

"This paper," Washie said above the murmur of the chiefs, "is a position paper entitled *The Threat to the Indian in the Northwest Territories*. I will be presenting this to the National Indian Brotherhood in Regina later this month. Let me tell you some of the things in it."

Washie said the Indian people, through the National Indian Brotherhood, vigorously rejected the White Paper presented by Jean Chrétien in June 1969. While the Prime Minister promised the government would abandon the policy, Washie said the Indian people of the Territories were uniquely threatened, because the White Paper was being implemented and the federal responsibility for Indian affairs was being transferred to the territorial government.

He held out one hand for quiet and skimmed the first page, then said the treaty obligations of the federal government remained unsettled but, notwithstanding this, planning, exploration and development was proceeding without regard to that issue and the prospect of provincial status was drawing closer every day.

"The transfer of jurisdiction from Indian Affairs and the withdrawal of Indian Affairs' personnel commenced in 1967 in the NWT," he said. "With the transfer of jurisdiction and withdrawal of Indian Affairs' personnel, without consultation with the Indian people, Indian status changed drastically. As many Indians have commented, overnight they ceased to be Indians and suddenly became 'Northerners.' Under the centennial theme of unity, the myth of 'northern equality' was propagated and forced upon the native people. Special status was repudiated with the statement 'We are all Northerners—we are all equal'. The Indian people know, of course, that in hard economic terms there is no equality. Statistics on mortality rates, income, housing and education belie the myth. But under the theme of northern equality the territorial government and parties interested in the exploitation of the mineral wealth of the NWT conveniently push aside special status and prepare to open the gates to a flood of southern entrepreneurs and companies who will bury the Indian people in an obscurity that supersedes even the experience of the Indian people of the south."

Washie quit reading and pushed his glasses up his nose as the audience thumped the tables and stomped their feet in support. Off to the side, the Brotherhood's white advisors and lawyers, the southern academics whose prose I knew full well filled his treatise, nodded and clapped approval. Hodgson was right—the Brotherhood could scarcely criticize the territorial government for hiring mostly whites.

"There's another point," said Washie as the crowd stilled. "Both the Commissioner and the Territorial Council, by exploiting the myth of northern equality, are blocking the efforts of the Indian people and the Indian Brotherhood to achieve their goals.

"The Commissioner has expressed his opposition to the formation and the existence of the Indian Brotherhood, and he is uniquely empowered with the means to frustrate the Indian Brotherhood. Funds from the Department of Indian Affairs must go through the office of the Commissioner, and projects proposed by the Brotherhood, such as one for a native health study and another for research into educational requirements for Indian children, are blocked by the attitudes of the Commissioner and the myth of northern equality. Such studies cannot be approved since we are all Northerners, and funds cannot be allocated in discrimination of one group over another.

"The Territorial Council, anticipating the arrival of provincial status and all its benefits, are eager to blind themselves to the reality and blur the truth of the native position behind the screen of northern equality. At its last session, in distributing $30,000 earmarked for ethnic groups, the Council deleted the word ethnic, justifying the allotment of just $3,000 to the Indian Brotherhood, and the rest going to agencies such as the Boy Scouts."

This was met with angry grumblings in a dozen dialects and some suspicious glances around the room.

Washie continued, "The territorial government is of a form similar to that imposed by colonial powers in Africa and Asia in the days preceding the great surge towards independence and the creation of new nations. The Commissioner is federally appointed. He is a bureaucrat with powers that resemble those of a provincial premier and lieutenant governor combined. His role is like that of the colonial governor in Africa. The Territorial Council, like its colonial parallel, is composed of elected and appointed members." Washie flipped some pages. "Settlement councils are another issue," Washie continued, his voice now shrill and penetrating the smoky gloom of the hall. "The traditional means of local government, the chief and band council, is being replaced by a new form called settlement councils, modelled after the municipal governments in the south, and including a government-appointed manager. The settlement council is white-oriented in form and tradition and it is not surprising that with native unfamiliarity with an un-Indian structure, illiteracy or a generally low education level, the settlement councils are dominated by whites.

"The traditional chief and band council have been emasculated by the introduction of the settlement councils. The chiefs are finding their traditional influence being eroded away with the bulk of the funds and effective power in the hands of the settlement councils. They are left without meaningful influence towards either their own people or the government. The side effects are manifold and disastrous.

"The total effect of the foregoing is merely to make it that much easier for the territorial and federal governments to muzzle the voice of the Indian people and facilitate a rapid exploitation of the North without due and just regard for native people and their aspirations. It permits them to attempt the implementation of the White Paper in the NWT.

"The end product would resemble a province as we know it, except one without reserves and one without Indians, only Northerners. The assimilation of the Indian people would be complete, cultural genocide would be realized, and this in a place in Canada where native people form the majority. With the history of broken promises and bad faith on the part of government behind them, the Indian people can only wonder at the intentions behind the introduction of settlement councils.

"Of the population of 34,000 in the NWT, 7,000 are treaty Indians, 13,000 are Eskimos and 5,000 are Métis and non-status Indians. The native people are the majority, a feature found nowhere else in Canada. With solidarity amongst the native people the future of the NWT could be theirs. Such solidarity does not exist because of the great distances that separate native people and because the organization and mobilization of the native people has only begun.

"The Indian Brotherhood of the NWT is very young, and only recently has it recovered from a shaky beginning and acquired the confidence of the Indian community. However, the Indian Brotherhood speaks only for the treaty Indians of the NWT . . . The Métis and non-status Indians appear to have no organization to represent them."

Washie said that without effective organization and mobilization of all the native peoples and in the absence of a unified stand, the native peoples would be at the mercy of the federal and territorial governments and unable to resist the ominous future that lies at the end of movement towards provincial status and the current rate of exploitation of mineral and natural resource wealth. Without organization and unity they would be unable to exploit their numerical advantage and secure a just future for themselves.

"There is an inherent contradiction in the merging of Indian Affairs with Northern Development. Few Indians could ever accept that the priorities of the Indian people can ever be reconciled with the traditional approach of the white man towards 'progress' and 'development' with its ravages of human and material resources and the rape of the environment. The contradiction is manifest in the NWT with oil and seismic crews bulldozing and blasting away and plans for pipelines and parks proceeding with, at best, mere token consultation with the native people, and in flagrant disregard for the concerns of the native people and their demands for a say in what is to be done with their land. The contradiction becomes ridiculous when the Minister for that department displays little understanding of the problems of native people and when his departmental staff has always enjoyed a most intimate relationship with the extractive industries.

"The present pace is hostile to the native interest. Treaties 8 and 11 and claims based on aboriginal rights have not been settled. If the present pace of planning and development continues it will leave the native people without even the bargaining position to settle past grievances, let alone the means to realize their future.

"Planning and development before the boom has rendered little benefit to the native people. Native people were not consulted about the exploitation of the gold at Yellowknife, the oil at Norman Wells or the minerals at Pine Point. Nor has there been meaningful participation by natives in such exploitation. And all this while the land issue remained unresolved.

"The exclusive jurisdiction over and responsibility for Indians and lands reserved for Indians rests with the parliament of Canada . . . " He stopped for breath and whacked the papers down on the table. "There's more." He said the oil would not run away, the minerals would remain in the ground as they have for millions of years. The land that holds that oil and those minerals and across which the proposed pipelines will run is native land, and until the land issue is resolved, the land must be protected for native interests.

Washie said the aboriginal people must unite, speak strongly and with one voice, and demand that the transfer of responsibilities for Indian affairs be rectified immediately. He demanded that the movement towards provincial status be suspended, settlement councils be eliminated and planning and development be halted until the land issues were settled.

He sat back amid a hubbub of translation that led to a thunderous ovation. I tried not to appear perturbed and to remain as inconspicuous as possible. It was my job to transmit to Hodgson not only what had been said, but also the underlying emotion.

"YOU'LL NEVER WIN A POPULARITY contest," I told Hodgson the next morning.

"Let's hear it."

"Tough meeting to sit through. I felt like getting up and leaving but that wouldn't have been wise. I must say though, during the break and lunch they weren't chummy but remained courteous."

I explained the gist of Washie's presentation and told him about the position paper being presented to the National Indian Brotherhood in Regina. "It's a statement of the threats facing the Indian people in the Territories and refers to Treaties 8 and 11 as remaining unsettled. You are mentioned in critical terms. At the root of their anger are the treaties. Washie spoke in vitriolic terms, saying they were being governed by a colonial government, and you're a dictator."

"Well, that's building good relations," Hodgson said sarcastically.

"The Brotherhood wants to get involved in community development, to hire field workers but Washie said they must give you a written proposal for approval before it goes to the federal government. Their proposal was sent to Ottawa last March and it is still sitting there because you don't want to see their plans go through, that it would upset the boat for you and the territorial government. Elsewhere in Canada the Indian organizations deal directly with the federal government, but not here."

Hodgson shook his head.

"The chiefs are united. They want the federal government to return to dealing directly with them again and stop using the territorial administration as a middleman. They are concerned that eventually non-natives will outnumber them and they won't have the majority."

"My job is to provide services to all Northerners on an equal basis," Hodgson interjected. "My marching orders are very specific—set up government services and tackle community growth through the development of local government. Local government! That's my job! When they formed the Brotherhood, it was to be a cultural organization. Because they call themselves cultural, they were able to get about $170,000 per year of funding from the Department of the Secretary of State. Now all of a sudden, they have fifteen staff members, mostly white advisors by the way, publish their own newspaper and have their own lawyer."

"They passed a number of resolutions, all of them unanimous."

"Okay?"

I read the one of most concern. "That the federal government recognize the special constitutional, legal and moral status of the Indian people of the NWT and rectify immediately the unconstitutional, illegal and immoral practice of transferring federal responsibility for the Indian people to the territorial government of the NWT. And that the federal government resume immediately direct dealing with the Indian people of the NWT by appointing, after prior consultation with the Indian people of the NWT, a suitable regional representative of the Indian Affairs branch of the Department of Indian Affairs and Northern Development."

Hodgson reached out his hand and said, "Let's have a look." He read the motion, mused over it, let out a sigh, shook his head and said, "If the federal government continues to meet their demands they'll be developing a parallel system of government to ours. What a mess this could become!"

"They're losing all the control and influence they once had. It's a frustration I can well understand. And they're determined to blame you as much as the feds."

Hodgson replied, "Communities are made up of more than just Indians. There's Métis and there are whites. Under the band council those groups have no rights, no representation. Community councils are the only way everyone will be properly represented."

"I understand, but they don't. What I'm saying is that there were a lot of angry words." We sat for some time without speaking. Finally, I broke the silence. "I think if you were to turn back treaty payments to the feds that would be considered a good gesture. The root issue is the treaties and how the feds haven't met their obligations."

25
FIRST AMONG EQUALS

SEPTEMBER 16, 1971

PRIOR TO THE MOVE TO Yellowknife, the Council of the Northwest Territories often railed against their federal counterparts in what could be described as vitriolic terms. The move to Yellowknife, and the takeover of certain administrative responsibilities, had improved relations, but the Territorial Council continued to decry what it considered inappropriate actions by certain mid-level officials within the Department of Indian Affairs and Northern Development. This jurisdictional squabbling caused a lot of stress for Hodgson, who didn't seem so invulnerable, so implacable, anymore.

Now federal officials seemed willing to fund projects with the Indian Brotherhood, despite the fact that community development had been under the territorial government for several years. "How do I figure him out? I'm sent to do a job, and then Cretain supports the Brotherhood, which is out to destroy my effectiveness." In the morning light, Hogdson's face was lined. His moustache was speckled with grey and his hair was brushed back starkly from a receding hairline.

"I sent Cretain a letter in April stating Council's view that government programs should give equal treatment to all residents, regardless of ethnic origin. And I asked about our role in funding for ethnic groups."

He pressed the buzzer on his phone and asked Erma to bring in Chrétien's reply. [10]

"I received this in mid-August. Cretain talks about the treaties, federal obligations, ethnic differences, blah, blah, blah. Lot of verbiage. I'll read parts of it. He says, 'All of this leads me to the point where I must ask you to pay special attention to the needs of disadvantaged native groups; to give them, in fact, the extra help they need to catch up.'" He looked up for my reaction but continued to read. "'The first essential is that you should recognize

---

[10] Letter from Jean Chrétien, Minister of Indian Affairs and Northern Development, to Stuart M. Hodgson, August 12, 1971

the existence of the various native interest groups and give attention to their demands. I should, of course, hasten to add that I do not expect you to accede automatically to those demands, but that you should look to such interest groups as non-government advisors on the needs of the native peoples.

"In addition to giving closer attention to native demands, I think it would be advisable for you to designate a small group within your administration to deal specifically with their problems and to provide a special channel of communication between the territorial administration and the various native groups. A public position in this regard by the Northwest Territories administration would, I believe, go a long way towards relieving the position taken by some of the native peoples that their special needs are not recognized."

I interrupted, "This letter was written right after Ed Bird was shot." Bird, by then Vice-President of the Indian Brotherhood, had been shot and wounded during a standoff with police responding to a domestic violence call. He had been med-evacuated to Edmonton where he died three weeks later, on August 27. The coroner's jury investigating his death heard testimony from the RCMP constables and from Bird's wife, who testified that her husband had been drinking and, not for the first time, had threatened her with physical violence. "We had the same problem many people have," she said. "He was native, I was white, and the Indian problem bothered him a great deal."[11]

Six days after Bird's death, James Washie had issued a press release stating that he had received two phone calls, one from Chrétien's office and another from an un-named source within the territorial government, announcing that "there was going to be a big change in government policies" regarding the native majority and that "the community development project of the Indian Brotherhood had received favourable consideration." Washie openly wondered whether the timing was coincidental or whether this change of heart was in response to Bird's death.

Hodgson waved his hand, indicating there was more. "Since the Indian people of the Territories have special rights in relation to the federal government under Treaties 8 and 11 and under certain specific provisions of the Indian Act, I propose to accede in part to the Brotherhood request, by establishing in Yellowknife an Indian Affairs representative to handle matters arising from these special rights."

[11] Steve Hume, "Chief Bird's Death: 'Police Shots Justified,'" *Edmonton Journal,* September 11, 1971

"Well," I interrupted, "our government won't have to pay treaty anymore if the feds have an Indian agent here."

Hodgson carried on reading. "I recognize the danger that this action might polarize Indian opposition to territorial programs and runs the risk of splitting other native groups. On the other hand, I believe it is necessary, at least in the short term, to provide a public recognition of these special Indian rights. I hope that your special efforts, already showing great success, in the development of local government and through your community development program, coupled with this public recognition of the special needs of the native peoples involved in the creation of a section or division of your administration, will slow up and reverse this process of polarization."

Hodgson reached for his coffee, took a sip and continued. "I want you to understand that these proposals are not a criticism of you, of the Territorial Council, or of your administration, who, I know, devote a large proportion of your efforts towards meeting the needs of the native people in the Territories. It is rather recognition of the fact that the Territories cannot escape being invaded by southern Canadian attitudes and philosophies and must, therefore, attempt to adapt to this invasion without giving up their own unique policies and programs. I am hopeful that this arrangement will make it possible for the territorial government and the Department to produce a more fruitful relationship with the Indian Brotherhood. You may wish to suggest other measures to meet the needs which I have described and I would be very interested in discussing with you."

Hodgson put down the letter. "There you have it."

We sat in silence, caught up in our thoughts. Through the window behind Hodgson, I could see the four-storey addition to the Yellowknife Inn under construction. The character of Yellowknife was changing at an incredible pace, as was the nature of our work.

Hodgson said, "It's time I told Cretain what effect his actions are having up here."

"What are you going to say?"

"That the Indian and Eskimo organizations are stirring up trouble, undermining the efforts of the Territorial Council. *Native Press* is nothing more than a purveyor of hate. It's Jimmy Washie, and Nellie Cournoyea of COPE, that are stirring things up and doing all the complaining. It's obvious what needs to be done. Get the treaties and land claims settled. That's the root of the problem. And that isn't my responsibility. That's up to Ottawa and the Indians."

"Have you ever talked to Chrétien about this?"

"I've talked to him about turning over funds, by way of grants, to band councils for community projects, studies and the like."

"Scheming to redirect Brotherhood funding to the bands instead?"

Hodgson nodded. "Cretain wants to know by which method this might be accomplished."

"So?"

"I'm going to meet Chief Arrowmaker of Rae and Chief Sangris of Dettah, about general problems in their communities. It gives me the perfect opportunity to pry a little. I hear not all the chiefs are happy with money going direct to the Brotherhood. I'm going to suggest the federal government provide some money direct to the bands, and if they agree I will make a proposal to Cretain. Strike while the iron is hot."

He turned on the phone intercom. "Erma, bring in your steno pad!" He turned to me, "Stay! I want you to hear this."

Erma sat down, placed the steno pad on her lap, pencil in hand.

Hodgson dictated. "This is part of a letter and accompanying documents I want to send to the Honourable Gene Cretain, etc.[12] Subject: Grants to band councils."

Hodgson's head turned to the ceiling and his eyes roamed about as he dictated. Obviously he had thought out his approach and now put the words together. After some preamble he got to the meat of his message. "Chief Arrowmaker's agreement will pave the way for the granting of funds to the Rae Band. In the final analysis, this will cause the Indian Brotherhood to make application to each band council for funds with which to operate. To ensure each band has control of the funds, I suggest you might consider paying each chief $100 per month for the responsibility of funds management. Such payment, inclusive of all bands, should cost no more than $18,000 per annum and will provide the incentive to administer the funds locally.

"If you concur, and wish to proceed this way, depending upon your instructions, I propose to strike while the iron is hot and have an immediate

[12] Letter from Stuart M Hodgson to Jean Chrétien, Minister of Indian Affairs and Northern Development, October 8, 1971

explanation as to the purpose and funds to be made available to Chief Arrow-maker. Following a short trial period with the Rae Band, I am prepared to visit and work out a similar arrangement with the remaining chiefs. I trust you will find this proposal both interesting and practical. Yours sincerely."

I decided to speak up. "You know, other than in my department, we have no native employees here at headquarters. In total we now have more than one thousand employees. Perhaps there is something to be said for Chrétien's . . ."

Hodgson cut me off. His face was flushed. "People can call our government a white man's government but what do they call the Brotherhood? Is their lawyer a native?" Hodgson's tone was stern. "Don't give me that. They're using whites because they need white help either as lawyers, advisors or editors. I don't have to apologise."

"But shouldn't we look at the issue of native employment?" I shot back.

"Don't lecture me!" he commanded. His eyes glared into mine, his mood contrary.

I looked at my watch and diplomatically indicated I should take my leave but, instead of going back to my office, I headed home.

"It seems things aren't getting any easier for you under Hodgson," Barb said as she shut the door on the dishwasher. "He has lots of shortcomings. You ignore that."

"Like what?"

"He's so domineering, has to be in control of everyone and everything. You work well with him because you cater to his needs. But you don't see all the warts. You should still consider going to Ottawa. If Jean Fournier is serious about a job as special assistant to Chrétien, that's what you should do." The job offer—special assistant responsible for northern affairs—had been made the previous month, when I hitched a ride from Yellowknife to Ottawa on Chrétien's plane.

Barb was right about Hodgson, but so far the warts didn't overwhelm me. "I'm not confident I can fit into the Ottawa scene. I'd rather stay here for now. Hodgson is under tremendous pressure and he's just venting."

"You'd better be careful. He's great at making friends but, when they're not of use any longer, he drops them just as fast. Make sure he always needs you!"

26
FUTURE LEADERS OF THE NORTH

OCTOBER 1971

"I'M GOING TO HIRE THE two information officers whose positions were approved in the last budget. And I'm going to hire natives."

Hodgson was fiddling with a small pair of scissors, holding up a hand mirror, clipping his moustache. "Sure," he said. "Lofty goal, but there's not even a dozen native high school graduates. We need people with education."

"Look who's talking," I chided. Hodgson's fingers twitched and clipped a chunk out of his moustache. I laughed.

Hodgson grimaced and gave me a dirty look. I knew I had to placate him but I couldn't hide my amusement. "Sorry," I said, trying to control myself. "But if we don't hire Northerners it will be another reason for the natives to not accept the territorial government as their own."

The under-representation of Northerners continued to be a sensitive issue for the federal government as well. Some years previously, in 1968, Mary Carpenter, an Eskimo girl from Sachs Harbour, had eloquently and scathingly exposed the inadequacy of hiring initiatives.[13] A second-year history and journalism student at the University of Western Ontario, she attacked the federal government for supporting the Panarctic Oil project, a consortium of twenty petroleum and mining companies that controlled forty-four million acres of the North believed to hold oil and gas, about sixty-three percent of total Arctic land. Ottawa had invested nine million dollars for a forty-five percent interest.

She said benefits touted for the Eskimos had not materialized, pointing out that fewer than ten native men had jobs with the Panarctic deal. "All their equipment, all their workers, are brought in from the south. They just don't even know or care that my people want jobs. The government brings in young punks who have personal hang-ups a mile long, bigoted

---

[13] Robert Johnston, "The Girl From the North 'You Think We're a Nigger in a Parka'." *The Toronto Star,* October 5, 1968

and stupid, and these snot-nosed kids tell my people how to live their lives.

"I don't wish to alarm you, but the facts are that the federal government is doing exactly to my people . . . what the whites have done to the Negroes of the United States . . . They are making us into service-class people or slaves—take your choice. The way things are going, what they are really doing, regardless of what they're trying to do, is to make us into a kind of new nigger with a parka.

"The government of Canada through its information services, convinces the Canadian public that we Eskimos are too stupid to run our own affairs. They are the best propaganda merchants since Goebbels was let loose in Nazi Germany."

She accused the news media of accepting the government view that "the rape of the North" is good for the Eskimo. "The thing that knocks me out is that at no time did the news media . . . ever use their heads. They were content to live on the press handouts of a slick, highly paid and thoroughly competent information services department."

Three years later, Jean Chrétien was still fighting the same battle. He said that every time he raised the issue of hiring Northerners with a particular industry group he always got the same response, "Yes, we will take on any Northerner who comes to us for a job—and this is the catch—provided that he is fully trained and willing to accept the job on the same terms and conditions as a southern Canadian, and provided he is as productive as a southern Canadian."[14] He was now warning northern industries, including government agencies, to hire more northern natives or face the possibility of government-imposed quotas, even as his own department continued to hire predominantly from southern Canada.

I challenged Hodgson, "Why shouldn't Northerners be given the first opportunity for all jobs? Why not hire a local Northerner, let her gain the experience and grow into the job?" Already I had had success with our clerical and printing staff, all hired locally. Some were aboriginal, others were Métis or white, but all were from the North. They had some experience but were also learning on the job, and I couldn't have asked for more enthusiastic employees who did superb work.

Hodgson didn't want to continue the discussion. "Let me change the

---

[14] Ben Tierney, "Hire Natives, North Industry Warned", *Edmonton Journal*, October 8, 1971

subject. Let's stop producing those rinky-dink annual reports. They look as if they're lifted from some accountant's file. I want the next one to be a hard-cover book, full of colour photos and stories about life in the North. People will keep them on bookshelves. You can sell them. Over the years they'll become collectors' items. We'll be the only operation in Canada to produce an annual report as a hardcover book."

"Okay."

"Sure. Full colour. Lots of glossy pictures and a full-colour glossy dust jacket!"

I was anxious to revisit the employment issue. "I'm also going to establish an interpreter corps." With three Eskimo dialects and seven Indian languages, trained interpreters would make it much easier to communicate. "They can translate government literature and press releases." The full support of the members of the Territorial Council, who had spoken of the need to preserve northern languages and culture, was almost assured. Bryan Pearson, council-lor for the Eastern Arctic, had first proposed the idea of an interpreter corps, so he would be a strong proponent.

"How much is this going to cost?"

"Whatever. It'll be worth it. I'm thinking of a full year's training program, twelve months, alternating between two weeks in the classroom and a week or two in the field." Interpreters would be paid between $9,400 and $11,900 annually, a fair salary. I intended to run a training course every year for the next several years. Trainees would visit various areas of the North, including work camps like Hire North, a project to clear the highway extension right-of-way north of Fort Simpson. We would arrange a week on a military ship in the High Arctic, a trip to Ottawa to experience the House of Commons interpreter operation, and a visit to the United Nations in New York to view their interpreter system.

"They'll have to master English from a practical standpoint, the buzzwords and acronyms that bureaucrats use and perfect their aboriginal languages. And of course, we'll train them in public speaking. No other department is doing this, and my department, with the native information officers and interpreters, can set an example. Why else are we here, but to make life better for Northerners and provide them with employment opportunities?"

To my surprise, Hodgson nodded in agreement said, "Do it!"

The Interpreter Corps attracted over a hundred applicants from throughout the Northwest Territories—from the Eastern, Central and Western Arctic and throughout the Mackenzie Valley. Each of the northern languages and dialects were represented. Few, if any, of the applicants had graduated from high school. That was irrelevant to me. We selected candidates who were keen, spoke decent English and performed well during interviews. What they lacked in education they would make up in enthusiasm. The first crew of twelve were all young, the oldest being twenty-nine. They became a group to be proud of, future leaders of the North.

In the Public Affairs Bureau we established two information officer positions, one for the Eskimo side and one for the Indian. Our first hire was John Pudnak from Baker Lake, a brilliant individual who proved unsuited for life in a large community like Yellowknife; we transferred him back to Baker Lake and hired Peter Ernerk, a smart, gregarious and well-rounded individual with a great sense of humour. Peter was typical of the young people we were hiring—he was born in an igloo, had grown up on the land in and around Coral Harbour and spent much of his time on the land, taught the ways of the Eskimo by his father. Peter created *Tukisiviksat*, a newspaper in the Eskimo language. He also accompanied Hodgson and me on our travels through the Eastern and High Arctic areas.

The information officer for the Indian languages was Ray Sonfrere, son of the chief of the Hay River reserve, the only reservation in the Northwest Territories. Ray was a quiet, dedicated and intelligent worker who published *Goinseday*. Both Ernerk and Sonfrere proved to be valuable employees who were frequently called on by Hodgson and other executives to provide advice on some aspect of culture or language.

We later hired John Amagoalik as the information officer for the Eastern Arctic, based in Frobisher Bay, while James Arvaluk served the Keewatin from Churchill, Manitoba.

We also established locally operated radio stations in remote communities not serviced by the CBC Northern Service broadcasting from Yellowknife, Inuvik and Frobisher Bay. I received funding from Council to provide equipment in a half-dozen communities that, in turn, provided the manpower. Audiotapes, both in English and the local language, containing news about government activities and Territorial Council matters, were prepared by

Ernerk and Sonfrere and sent to the communities on a weekly basis, but the responsibility for the operation and content lay with the people themselves. Our success eventually spurred the CBC to expand their repeater stations, fulfilling their mandate and allowing us to redirect our funding to other areas.

27

TREATY DAY IN RAINBOW VALLEY

JULY 1972

HODGSON SAT DOWN IN MY office and proclaimed that the fun was going out of his job. He excelled at setting in motion ideas like Project Surname and the Arctic Winter Games but preferred to hand daily administration over to his directors. Now he was being worn down by the opposition of the Indian Brotherhood, the Territorial Council's demand for more authority and the conflicting mandates he had received from the federal government—introduce representative government for all Northerners while recognizing the unique needs of treaty Indians.

In April, Tony Belcourt, President of the Native Council of Canada, had leaked Hodgson's letter recommending that Chrétien provide direct funding to band councils in addition to funding the Indian Brotherhood. *Native Press* had published it on April 4 under a headline that read "Letter Shows Commissioner Against Native Leaders." Hodgson had been particularly angry that "that dirty bastard" Belcourt had denounced Hodgson's "colonial attitude," alleging that he didn't want native people to have money to organize.

In response, Chrétien issued a policy statement that supported Hodgson while confirming that a new Indian Agent would be posted to Yellowknife to deal directly with the 6,700 treaty Indians of the Northwest Territories. In addition, an advisory committee on northern development would be established to improve coordination between departments and agencies involved in the North. To his great satisfaction, Hodgson was appointed chairman and could now scrutinize all federal activity in the North, a mandate that included water, power, transportation, land, justice and health.

Today Hodgson was in a testy mood. "What's that man Ross doing about next year's annual report?" he asked.

"Nothing," I said, shrugging my shoulders. Last year's report had only been released the month before. Normally we wouldn't start the next publication for another three months.

"Get him in here!"

"He's not here. He's at the print shop."

"I want to work on a theme."

"He's in the middle of interviewing potential employees for printer positions, over in the Keewatin building." I was rattled by Hodgson's tone. "I don't think I can get him on the phone. I'll send someone over to get him."

He shook his head. "Forget it. Develop a theme. Have it to me next week. Plan ahead!" He stood up and marched out. I was taken aback by such uncharacteristic surliness—my department had the resources to fulfil his ambitions and I had learned not to block his promotional ideas. I worked hard, supported him fully and made myself indispensable. In turn, he supported me and defended me from criticism from whatever quarter it would come, be it Council members or the public.

I grabbed my car keys and drove down to Old Town to clear my head. It was a hot July day and warm air breezed through the windows. The sky was crystal clear and the lake shimmered with every disturbance of the supply barges and float planes. I felt better already.

I parked my car at the top of a rise. Below, the road unfurled between the straggle of gaily painted houses of Rainbow Valley. It was Treaty Day and the new Indian Agent, Wally Gryba, was handling payments.

The treaties promised $5 to each individual Indian person, $25 for the chief and $15 for each headman, plus equipment such as twine for nets and ammunition. There was also the promise the government would take care of their medical, educational and economic needs. In return the federal government presumed the Indians gave the Crown all their rights, titles and privileges to the land. Now the federal government had resumed the time-honoured tradition of handing out the annual gratuity and the free medical tests when the Indian people returned to the community from the winter's hunting and trapping. The scene below would be replicated in twenty-seven communities throughout the Mackenzie Valley.

Men and women lined up before a plywood table where an RCMP officer in ceremonial scarlet sat next to the Indian Agent. After signing his or her name, or marking the perfunctory X before the Indian Agent, the applicant would move along to the paymaster, who doled out the $5 bill from a huge stack of cash. From there they stepped into a makeshift medical clinic housed in a panel truck where they stood on a scale, underwent body measurements, received a chest X-ray to check for tuberculosis and then blew into a device that measured their lung capacity. In the background, government staff from the territorial game department doled out wild meat that had been shot by native hunters during the winter and stored in government freezers.

The adults stood or sat passively as they awaited their turn at the table. Children raced hither and yon in a frenzy of sound and motion. It was a festival of sorts, a celebration of the one time of year when all band members, hunters or home-dwellers, returned to their hearth for rest and renewal. There would be two days of hand games, checkers and tea dances.

After the last in line had gone past the Indian Agent, I walked over and introduced myself. "I'm Jake Ootes," I said, extending my hand. "Director of Information for the territorial government."

"Wally Gryba. I'm the Indian Agent for the Northwest Territories, as you probably gathered."

Gryba was a slender man, gentlemanly, with black hair and a trim moustache. He was smoking a cigarette with a holder, a holdover of a bygone era. "The last Indian Agent didn't know what to do with the records when the feds pulled out a couple of years ago. So he burned them. I have to start from scratch." Gryba didn't seem terribly upset; he was obviously the kind of person who would roll with whatever life threw at him. The Indian people would respect him.

"You've had some interesting times," Gryba said. "I had a thorough briefing before I was sent up here. But I think things are going to be easier from here on—for you people at least."

"How so?"

"I get the impression the Indians will be turning all their attention to the federal government. You guys are off the hook. I met with Mr. Washie yesterday—he's extremely unhappy with the department in Ottawa. Look, I'm hot and thirsty. How about we get a pop?"

Gryba pulled off his tie and slung his jacket over one shoulder as we walked across to the medical van. He stepped inside and opened the door of a tiny refrigerator installed to transport blood, reaching for a couple of soft drinks.

We took them across the road and up onto a rocky headland overlooking the entrance to Back Bay, where a slight breeze kept the mosquitoes at bay.

"From what I hear, the Brotherhood won't be paying much attention to your territorial programs anymore. It's got bigger fish to fry. The big push is for a settlement of the land ownership, and that's between the Indians and the federal government."

Gryba was right. In May, the Brotherhood had announced that it wouldn't allow the construction of a highway through the Mackenzie Valley until land rights were settled. In fact, it wanted a moratorium on all development, including a proposed gas pipeline from Prudhoe Bay.

"Now that the feds are taking responsibility for the treaties again, why is the Brotherhood so upset with Ottawa?"

"They're pulling back from their commitment. In its first year of operation the Brotherhood received $30,000 from Indian Affairs. This year it's been cut to a measly $4,000." Gryba placed another cigarette in the holder and lit it with a small silver lighter. "Mr. Washie said the Brotherhood's proposal for a $70,000 radio telephone network linking communities in the valley has been refused. So has a request for a mobile videotape unit, and a Brotherhood proposal for community development has been sitting in Ottawa for more than a year without getting any action.

"He's especially annoyed because Secretary of State funding for the Brotherhood's newspaper and radio program has been cut off entirely this year. He's had to lay off half of his thirteen people and divert money from office expenses just to keep things going. And another application for an Opportunity for Youth grant has been refused."

I gave out a low whistle of surprise.

Gryba continued. "Now that Hodgson oversees all federal programs, he approves funding, and of course he isn't going to endorse anything he thinks duplicates services already being provided by the territorial government. So the Brotherhood is turning away from that kind of activity and concentrating on treaty issues."

"Perhaps that's the way it should have been all along," I said.

Gryba nodded as he looked out across the waves. "Even that won't be easy. I understand the Minister is about to pick one of his officials to begin discussions with individual bands about a land settlement. That's the last thing the

Brotherhood wants—to have the government deal with chiefs and bands, and not with its negotiators. The Brotherhood runs the risk of becoming irrelevant, and Washie knows that."

Gryba had just described the strategy advocated by Hodgson to rein in the Brotherhood by giving funding to individual band councils.

"So what do you think of our Mr. Washie?" I asked.

"Oh, I'm impressed by him," Gryba said. "He's genuine, and he's got the grace a lot of Dogribs from Rae have, a dignity. He's thoughtful."

A single-engine float plane taxied out to the head of Back Bay, turned and now revved its engine, making enough of a rumble to interrupt our discussion. When the plane was airborne, Gryba continued. "He's under a lot of strain. I hear he was pretty surprised to become leader of the Brotherhood, because of his age and so on.

"I have a lot of respect for Jimmy because of the times he finds himself in. He is doing a remarkable job."

Gryba's impressions matched mine. While Washie was a thorn in our sides, I respected his role and responsibilities.

Gryba continued, "Washie has convictions, but this is such a turbulent time, like doing the Nahanni rapids with one paddle. Some of his advisors don't help him much. Something he has to put up with—and we'll see a lot of this around the North in the coming years—is the hordes of professional white advisors that flock into situations like this. There's no doubt that many people see an underprivileged group struggling to be heard, and they're there faster than flies. Washie's got some of the best white minds in Canada working in his office, and they're dreaming up more programs, more ways to hire staff and spend money than he can keep track of. It gets to the point where you can't stop it. They write speeches and he reads them; they write reports and he delivers them to Ottawa.

"The Minister thinks it's becoming an industry, that these people don't care about the natives. It's true that native leaders take help where they can find it, but they control it. The lawyers are never allowed to forget they are working for native people. There is always enough horsepower among the chiefs at the meetings to remind people of that. They can see that by using these resources there is some forward motion and the government is starting to pay attention."

"Hodgson is concerned about the heavy-duty left-wing involvement. He sees instant experts flowing into the North who don't live here and have little likelihood of ever doing so."

"The Minister is very aware of the radical element. There is comprehensive surveillance of everyone involved, me included. Dossiers are kept on everyone. The RCMP keeps very close tabs on who talks to who. The concern is that some of these shoot-em-up people will infiltrate and have a negative effect on what's been happening. It's to the credit of the Indian leaders that nowhere is there even a small twitch of talking guns.

"I think the leadership knows what's happening, because some of these advisors would have been under surveillance even before coming north. Washie seems radical because he's pushed. I would think that anybody with less balls would buckle after a year of that."

DESPITE HIS IMPATIENCE WITH ADMINISTRATION, Hodgson continued to enthusiastically seek publicity for the North. By 1972, he and the Northwest Territories were the subject of myriad newspaper articles, magazine columns, opinion pieces, radio and television news shows. *Executive Magazine* labelled Hodgson "The Arctic's Super Executive"[15] and the *Calgary Herald* proclaimed "Northlands Commissioner Unique in Canada."[16] Invitations to speak flowed in from across southern Canada and I continued to travel with him. We now travelled by Learjet, cruising at 450 miles per hour.

In November Hodgson addressed three hundred business executives, including several top oil and gas people doing exploration work in the North, at Toronto's Canadian Club. His topic was "The North of the Future."

He used the opportunity to highlight some of his successes, reminding his audience that the people in the North had gone from the stone age to the jet age in one generation. The number of applications to establish settlement and hamlet councils had rapidly increased. The Housing Corporation was providing housing more in keeping with local needs. Most communities now had bulk fuel tanks, reducing the price of gasoline from four dollars a gallon to sixty or seventy-five cents. Airstrips were being built. The Interpreter Corps, a first in Canada, was now providing translation at meetings with local officials.

---

[15] Michael Cope, *Executive Magazine*, January 1969
[16] Jim Stott, "Cross Between Premier and Santa Claus. Northland's Commissioner Unique in Canada", *Calgary Herald*, August 23, 1969

An alcohol education program had been developed; my department had contributed a series of four comic books called *Captain Alcohol*.

He talked about significant improvements to services a Toronto audience would take for granted. Dick and Jane textbooks had been replaced by ones that made more sense to northern children. The Anik satellite now provided phone service to places like Pangnirtung, Igloolik and Resolute , and television would soon be available in most Northern communities.

Hodgson also expressed concern about all the instant experts flowing into the North—researchers, study groups, consultants, anthropologists, sociologists, planners, analysts and economists who only recently discovered the North. He also maintained that investment in the North "should be encouraged rather than slighted and, by some people, condemned,"[17] a response to NDP leader David Lewis' criticism of a proposed gas pipeline from Canada's Arctic to the United States. His overall message was that, "Canada's North can no longer stand as a monument to the past, despite complaints from opponents of development."

---

[17] "Hodgson Urges Arctic Development", *Toronto Star*, November 7, 1972

NOVEMBER 1973

A GOVERNMENT EMPLOYEE ON HIS way to work found a briefcase on the road and took it to the RCMP detachment. Inside were a handgun and papers belonging to the American Indian Movement.

We had been introduced to AIM some months before, during the siege at Wounded Knee. We had followed the television coverage courtesy of a newly introduced CBC service that worked the same way as movie reels— four hours of programming was taped each day in Edmonton, shipped to Yellowknife by truck and rebroadcast over a local channel one week later. It was canned TV, but a new treat for us in Yellowknife.

The coverage had featured young Indians with defiant faces and frayed jackets in a parched community in South Dakota—the Lakota Sioux village of Wounded Knee where, on December 29, 1890, at least 150 Indians, mostly old men, women and children, had been killed by US troops. Now about two hundred AIM supporters and ten hostages were surrounded by ninety law enforcement officers. Led by AIM national director Dennis Banks and local activist Russell Means, the group sought to redress a series of injustices and had a "complete commitment to die if necessary."[18]

Barb said, "It doesn't surprise me, this happening in the United States. The Indians there are crowded onto reservations, and they got a rotten deal. I just hope that kind of violence doesn't spread here."

"Wally Gryba, the Indian Agent, told me there are a lot of shit disturbers, including white radicals, to help foment the situation here." On March 20, the *Edmonton Journal* had reported that eight Indians from the Edmonton area left to join the siege at Wounded Knee. We didn't know if any native people from the Northwest Territories had made a similar journey.

The Wounded Knee occupation lasted seventy-one days and resulted in a

[18] "Alberta Group Off to Wounded Knee", *Edmonton Journal,* March 20, 1973

number of bloody gun battles involving police officers, US marshals and FBI agents. and ended with a signed pact between the United States government and the Indians. Many of the Indian activists were arrested but Dennis Banks escaped with several others. They became fugitives.

Eight months later we were shocked to discover they were in Yellowknife. It made us realize that radicalism and violence could become a reality in the North, even though indigenous groups were successfully working within the existing legal framework.

At the same time AIM was occupying Wounded Knee, Chief Francois Paulette of Fort Smith had filed a caveat with the Territorial Registrar of Land Titles on his own behalf and as a representative of the Indian people and Indian bands of the Northwest Territories. It listed sixteen names, all chiefs of their respective communities, who claimed an interest in over 400,000 square miles of the Northwest Territories, maintaining that Treaties 8 and 11 had not extinguished their territorial rights.

The stakes in this battle over treaty claims and aboriginal rights were the highest ever in Canadian courts. The federal government stood to lose natural resource and development revenue, especially important in light of the proposed $4 billion Mackenzie Valley pipeline. For the Indians, the stakes were equally significant. If they failed, the whole push to bring Ottawa to the negotiating table could be set back for years. For Hodgson and the territorial government, a caveat would seriously impair the growth and development of towns and hamlets throughout the Western Arctic.

The Crown's position was that the Supreme Court of the Northwest Territories, headed by Justice W.G. Morrow, could only rule on whether the caveat could be filed; the merits of the claim were for the federal court to decide. Morrow took issue, stating this was "an unwarranted attack by the executive of the Canadian Government upon the integrity and independence of the Superior Court of the Northwest Territories . . . I am certain that this is the first time in the history of Canadian jurisprudence, the first time since Confederation, when one superior court judge has been under attack by another superior court judge of equal status."

In September of 1973, Morrow upheld the native position, affirming that the caveators were owners of the lands in question. I had driven to Old Town to hear what Father Fumoleau had to say.

"Yes. It's an important ruling. The Brotherhood's pursuit of the legal approach rather than violence is significant," Fumoleau smiled. "Violence never was an option for the Brotherhood. There are plenty of hotheads who feel lots of frustration, but now they've learned that the legal system and the art of negotiation hold promise of action. The Dene are not a violent people."

The priest motioned for me to sit and offered tea. "Many times the Dene have felt let down. But perhaps we are starting to see progress. Now Morrow has ruled the Dene do have aboriginal rights to the land. The federal government will appeal, but this decision gives the Dene a moral victory and the courage that comes from being in the right. I think legal action and negotiation will forever replace bloodshed. And don't forget the Dene's basic philosophy—we've been here ten thousand years already, so we can easily wait out a few white intruders."

"You told me once that the Dene weren't acquisitive. But now they're pursuing ownership of the land."

"It's still true. They will tell you nobody owns the land, the land owns them. They mean there's a special relationship of mutual support that doesn't involve ownership or obligation. And that relationship can't exist if the land's ability to support them is extinguished by industrial development. That's why they need title, so that they can control the pace and extent of development. The only way a living culture can survive is by gaining some control over the outside forces that threaten it.

"The American Indians were cheated and rejected and killed in a systematic pogrom to settle the country with white farmers. The Dene have been cheated and rejected too, but you could say they escaped the extermination carried out in the States. Still, they're aware and articulate that their way of life could be in jeopardy. Would you fight for your way of life?"

NOW THAT AIM WAS IN the North, it was important to ensure that activism did not become militancy. RCMP Inspector Hugh Feagan and Wally Gryba promptly met with Hodgson.[19]

"We have been aware for some time that Dennis Banks, the head of the

---

[19] While I did not attend this meeting, I subsequently received reports of it from both Feagan and Hodgson

American Indian Movement, accompanied by several others, came to Canada after the Wounded Knee incident," Feagan said. "First to Manitoba and then to Alberta. Our Security Service people from K Division in Edmonton are here with a special team to keep a watch on them.

"With Banks is fellow activist Leonard Peltier, their wives and children." Peltier was on the FBI's Ten Most Wanted list. "They're fugitives and want to get as far from civilization as they can. While on the run in southern Canada they must have heard about the NWT Brotherhood. We just don't know what will happen next."

"What's your take on this, Wally?" asked Hodgson. Gryba took the cigarette holder from his mouth and said, "I got a phone call at four this morning from James Washie. He wanted to talk to me real bad. He came right over to my place, and I can tell you, he was very agitated and surprised by their visit. He had returned from a trip to the communities and at the float plane base he received a message to phone home. His wife said they had visitors, but she couldn't talk. At home he saw the South Dakota license plates and knew right away it was AIM. Inside he was greeted by the group, all dressed up in their war bonnets, beads and formal dress.

"These guys have a pretty wild reputation. Anyway, Washie's concerned about what they'll do to the Brotherhood's image. I believe him when he says neither he nor the Brotherhood invited Banks and party to come."

"So you don't think this is the start of some violent campaign by the Brotherhood?" Hodgson asked.

"Not a chance. Washie hates the idea of them hiding out in his house. He talks big sometimes, but he has no intention of turning to violence."

Hodgson sat silent, turning the information over in his mind.

"How do we get them to leave?" Hodgson asked.

"The less press the better," Feagan said. "We think they're just resting up and will likely leave of their own accord if no one spooks them. But if we push too hard or the general public knows they're here, they're liable to cause us trouble. All I want for now is to keep a close eye on them."

Hodgson rapped his pencil on the desk, allowing his mind to consider all the possibilities. "Why can't you just pick them up and send them back to South Dakota?"

Feagan shook his head. "They haven't committed an extraditable offence and they haven't caused us any trouble. What I want for now is to find a site our special security people can use to keep Washie's house under twenty-four-hour surveillance."

"I've got just the place," Hodgson said. "Take the penthouse on top of the high-rise. That'll give you a bird's-eye view of everything. You can practically see into Washie's living room!" The penthouse in the Fraser Tower was owned by the territorial government to provide secure and private accommodation for VIPs. The first to use the suite were Queen Elizabeth, Prince Philip and Princess Anne in 1970. "And I agree, tell your people to go easy on the situation."

LATER THAT MONTH, I WENT to the RCMP barracks where Feagan told me that Banks and party had moved out to Rae Lakes, a tiny Indian settlement about a hundred miles northwest of Yellowknife, only accessible by float plane. "We have a paid informant, a woman, who is providing us information, so we know what's going on. They've told the local people not to go anywhere and ordered the priest not to talk about them to anyone outside. But word did get out. The priest and the local chief are very concerned."

"Odd place to hide," I said. "In a small Indian village. Why didn't they go to Montreal or somewhere like that?"

"Who knows?" Feagan replied. "We've got to handle this just right. We don't need an incident that might blow into a standoff. It's better if they leave quietly and on their own. After all, they haven't broken our laws so far. I don't really want to force the situation unless they do."

"But they've threatened the priest and no doubt Washie."

Feagan remained calm. "The word from the community is they would leave the North tomorrow if they had the money to get out."

"Gryba's the Indian Agent! Get him to buy their tickets."

"Gryba isn't allowed to use his budget for such things."

"What about the Commissioner?" I said. "He'll come up with something." Feagan called Hodgson who said, "Get them to Yellowknife. I'll pay for their tickets back south. Let's get this over with!"

Feagan called in Corporal Mel Pelletier who was working with the Security Services team from Edmonton. "Charter a civilian single Otter. Get some of the guys dressed up in fishing gear and go to Rae Lakes. Bring them back to

Yellowknife. Be quiet and gentle. We don't want any trouble. We just want them out." Thankfully, the RCMP members successfully handled the departure of Banks and company from the community of Rae Lakes and then out of the North. But our sense of complacency, that "it couldn't happen here," was shaken.

SHORTLY AFTER BANKS' DEPARTURE, HODGSON summoned me to his house, something that had not happened for some time. As we lived only a block away, Hodgson used to invite us over for dinner or for drinks on the spur of the moment. But recently I'd sensed that I was falling out of favour.

I was shocked when I arrived. "What are you doing with a gun?"

"Goddam it," he shook his head. Despite his rough, tough former union boss persona, Hodgson rarely swore. "I got a death threat in the mail." Hodgson held up the Winchester automatic, one of the limited edition rifles manufactured for the Centennial. "Anyone who comes after me better be ready to stare this baby down! And I'm keeping her loaded!"

I couldn't believe it. "Who from?"

"Don't know. I gave the note to Hugh Feagan. He figures it might be from some white agitator in Fort McPherson 'cause I'm scheduled to visit there soon."

"What about cancelling until the RCMP can figure out who it came from?"

"I'm not going to hide from some radical yahoo! I already told Feagan I'm going."

"And?"

"He said I should take along a uniformed officer. He wants me to walk around with an armed guard. I don't want any of that crap!"

Hodgson once told me, "I'm always ready to give advice, but I don't take it too well." That was clear to me now.

"I'm not going to act like a scared rabbit every time someone says 'boo.' If I take a Mountie in uniform it's like saying I don't trust anyone. I'm taking Glen Warner. He just retired from the force and can carry a sidearm. He can come along in his civvies. Lyle Trimble will be with us as well. It's his constituency. He's also an ex-Mountie and can probably carry a gun. Besides, he'll only have to make one of his hellfire and brimstone speeches and he'll scare all the malcontents away."

"Why the death threat? Is somebody still upset about your letter to Chrétien?"

"Some lunatic likely wants to make a statement. Like the guy who blew up the courthouse in Hay River." Some years before a bomb had been detonated at the Hay River courthouse and the perpetrator had never been caught. "They're all dim-witted disturbers."

HODGSON FLEW INTO FORT MACPHERSON[20] on November 24. As Hodgson stepped off the plane, he was met by the Chief of Fort McPherson and a team of leaping, panting dogs. Not wishing to offend, he accepted the ride into town while the others, including his unofficial bodyguards, travelled by truck.

After a meeting with the settlement council, the party proceeded to the school for the community meeting, accompanied by what appeared to be the whole population of Fort McPherson. When Hodgson rose to speak, he was joined by a member of my department's Interpreter Corps—the bright and smiling Susan Husky, who provided simultaneous interpretation in Loucheux and English.

Fort McPherson's settlement council was grudgingly accepted and sparingly supported by the residents. But Hodgson wanted them to take the next step. "Maybe Fort McPherson would like to become a hamlet, like Tuktoyaktuk. It is my job to hand over more and more administration to the communities.

"Today there are twenty-three settlement councils and nine hamlets in the Northwest Territories. Each hamlet has its own administrator and the elected chairman and council members tell the administrator how to run the community. The chairman and council of a settlement council like yours can only advise the administrator what to do."

When he finished, a man asked, "Why are you pushing your settlement council on us? We have a chief, and it is he who should be respected, not a white man's council."

"We think every settlement should have a council which represents everyone, not just treaty Indians," Hodgson replied, picking up a sheaf of papers. "Listen to what your council has asked me to provide for Fort McPherson."

---

[20] I did not accompany Hodgson on this trip. Glen Warner related the experience to me in detail and it was later confirmed by Hodgson himself.

He read off the list, whacking it with one hand as he rattled off each item: "Somewhere for the adult educator to work; closure of the old school; enlargement of the new school; new facilities for the post office; a new town hall and fire hall; better laundry and shower facilities; wider roads; better municipal equipment; a new community freezer; docking facilities for canoes; dorm supervisors for the old folks and a liquor store."

The audience leaned forward. "My government doesn't have the money to take care of all these things. But—and you should realize the value of this—I will help you draw up a detailed proposal to obtain some money, and also help you strengthen your own community government so that one day you can solve these things yourselves."

He sat down, letting the council chairman call for questions. Despite the tension, Hodgson appeared confident. Glen Warner and Lyle Trimble remained on full alert.

There was discussion about the proposed Mackenzie Valley pipeline. Someone asked, "What is this gas? Is it gasoline?"

"No. It's natural gas." When the audience still seemed confused, Hodgson added, "It's like a fart." There was silence followed by thunderous laughter.

"What about the caribou? What will we eat when the pipeline scares away all the caribou?"

"You don't know that the pipeline will scare anything away," Hodgson said.

"Why is it that you white men from Yellowknife come in here and tell us what's good for us?" asked one man. "If we're the majority, why are we listening to you? I don't see no Indian being made commissioner. I don't see no Indian getting any of these fancy government jobs!"

Hodgson stood to respond as a man who appeared to have been drinking staggered to his feet, knocking over the chair he'd been sitting on. He was a large man, his dirty face made more threatening by the shadow of a grimy baseball hat. He halted after a few steps and said, "I got something to say!" Warner and Trimble perked up like guard dogs.

"You tell me my kids have to have an education to get jobs, then you tell me there ain't no jobs for them to do. You say you got to change us, but our life don't get no better." He paused to totter. "It gets worse."

The man staggered forward another few feet. He was waving his finger now. "There's another thing. How much does it cost to buy flour at the Hudson's

THE ART OF NEGOTIATION

Bay store here? You tell me why we're being ripped off like this!" He stood and glared at Hodgson, hands deep in his pockets, amid a hubbub of approval.

"No man is perfect, and no government is perfect," Hodgson said in a calm but loud voice. "You must know that. Anyone who thinks otherwise is dreaming. Can't you see that's why I'm trying to help you build a system in which everyone has a say in how the community is run? I don't want your lives to be run by men who live far away! This way, if you don't like the price of flour, you can set up your own store."

The speaker lurched forward, his focus solely on Hodgson. Trimble's knuckles gripped the edge of the table. Warner had one hand in his pocket, poised for action. When he reached the table, the man gave Hodgson one of the biggest surprises of his life.

He pulled one meaty fist out of his pocket, held it open and shouted, "Put her there, Commissioner! You're not so bad!"

29

LEAP OF FAITH

DECEMBER 1974–FEBRUARY 1975

I HAD GOTTEN INTO THE habit of visiting the Miners' Mess to catch up on the gossip of the day. It had been renovated several times over the years but the regulars never changed. They still sat at the same tables talking about politics and hockey.

I greeted "Coffee-Bob" Olexin who ran the local taxi company and Chuck Vaydik, the mining expeditor. James Wah-Shee sat by himself at a corner table. Some months before he had changed the southern spelling of his name, imposed at residential school, to the phonetic spelling of his traditional Dogrib name—Wah-Shee, meaning Man from Martin Mountain.

"Can I join you?" I asked Wah-Shee.

He nodded and we drank our coffee in silence. After a minute or so he said, "You look like hell. The Kwaterowsky scandal keeping you awake at night?"

In September, CBC news reporter Whit Fraser had broadcast a story that Paul Kwaterowsky, Superintendent of Game, had been involved in illegal hunts.[21] Kwaterowsky implied that Hodgson, who readily admitted issuing complimentary scientific licenses to promote sports hunting, had condoned his behaviour. Sid Hancock, the former Director of Local Government and newly appointed Assistant Commissioner, had looked into the whole mess at Hodgson's direction. He had concluded that Kwaterowsky had done nothing illegal but that his conduct "showed a marked lack of judgment."[22] The Federation of Natives North of Sixty, formed six months previously with James Wah-Shee as President, was furious and had called on Jean Chrétien to uphold their hunting, fishing and trapping rights, guaranteed by both tradition and treaty.

"Hodgson transferred him to my staff. Bit of a comedown for the man.

---

[21] Whit Fraser, "Game Situation", *The National*, CBC News, September 12, 1974
[22] S.W. Hancock, "Report of an Inquiry into Alleged Illegal Hunts." Report to the Commissioner of the Northwest Territories, September 20, 1974

But he's surviving." I had assigned Kwaterowsky to coordinate Prince Charles' territorial tour scheduled for April, another of Hodgson's glamour projects.

"Hodgson should have fired him. There's no way the man should be letting rich white men from Germany come over here and hunt protected wildlife."

Wah-Shee wasn't the only one surprised Hodgson hadn't fired the former game superintendent. But he had refused to make a public sacrifice of a long-service employee. I shrugged. "Not my decision to make."

He took a sip of coffee. "I'm thinking of running in the next election."

"For Council?" I was surprised. "But your position has always been that the Brotherhood is the only legitimate voice of your people."

Wah-Shee smiled, enjoying my confusion. "Think about it," he said. "We'll have to come to terms with the territorial government at some point, and one way to deal with it is to take it over.

"Some in the Brotherhood—mostly the younger, wilder ones—say I'm moving too fast in coming to terms with your system, maybe selling out. But the longer we avoid coming to terms with the territorial institutions the more we'll miss out on the chance to have a say in what happens to us."

This had always been Hodgson's goal, but we never expected the challenge to be taken up by the President of the Indian Brotherhood.

"We have to deal with these issues from strength," Wah-Shee continued. "Not on the good graces of whoever we're negotiating with. So one way to deal with it is to control Council, have it become a forum for everyone, not just the white viewpoint but also the aboriginal. Look at the Eskimos, they've never had any problem dealing with the Council."

I couldn't have agreed more. "It's a good idea to get involved. The timing is right and it's a good strategy."

"The chiefs want to wait, they believe that the time is not right, but the longer we wait the more opportunities we miss. Times are changing, we've got to keep up with it. Some of the chiefs think they can change the whole direction of the territorial government without having to participate in it, just by forcing the government's hand and by separate negotiations with federal officials. But I can see that's never going to work."

"One man won't change the way Council works. Hodgson still holds the power."

"There'll be others like me. The councillors are compelled to represent the interests of aboriginals and non-aboriginals. It's an opportunity to create a better working environment so that we all have common interests. We live in the same communities. So we've got to find a means where we work together and build trust and sit down and understand where aboriginal and non-aboriginal people are coming from. It has taken years and years to come together. It's a leap of faith by both parties."

Wah-Shee had brought the Indian Brotherhood significant prominence and credibility. He would be influential.

"Actually, when I decided to do it, my staff revolted against me, locked me out of my office. They had a big meeting. Thought I was selling out the Dene interests but I said no way . . . I think the whole thing is evolving. I'm determined to run anyway."

I remained silent, waiting for further explanation.

"Eventually all the aboriginal people will get involved in the Territorial Council anyway. The institution is already established, the financial system is incorporated and the means of making legislation and consultation is already there. If you say you don't want to be involved, then who's going to look after your interests? I have to deal with this now, but I'm paying the price for it."

"So who locked you out? Your advisors?"

"Primarily the consultants and staff. I guess they want to create a new political system for the North. I told them that it was rather unrealistic."

"How did you become President of the Brotherhood anyway? You were so young."

"When they were forming the Brotherhood, Chief Bruneau and councillors in Rae approached my father and mother." Wah-Shee's father was a shaman, his mother a medicine woman. "It was the traditional way to talk to them before me. I had just finished Grade 12 and was making application to go to university, so they approached my parents and said, 'We want your son to work for us.' I was only twenty. I said. 'What do they want?' 'Well, they want you to run for President of the Indian Brotherhood that's representing the twenty-six communities of the NWT.' I said, 'I don't know anything about it.' My father said, 'They'll teach you.' Most of the chiefs and councillors at that time were over sixty-five and some were in their seventies and eighties. I took a lot of direction from the Elders, and I would tell them where I thought we could go. I was learning a lot more than I was giving back to the

Elders at that time. It was an eye-opener and a challenge. From there I learned and learned—and I am still learning today."

I asked about his school years. He had attended residential school at Fort Resolution and later Grandin Hall in Fort Smith.

"Tell me about the AIM visitors. They showed up unannounced?" I asked.

"I was aware that AIM was establishing chapters in southern Canada. But I never met any of them in Canada or in the US. I've never been to Wounded Knee in my life . . . They told me who they were and they wanted to be under my protection and requested to be my guests. They wanted to go hunting and fishing and I said no problem. You can hunt and fish.

"I indicated to them when they first arrived at my place that the Indians in the North have treaties and that we are the ones who are going to control negotiations and work things out. I made it quite clear to them that I did not want any of the aboriginal groups from the US or even southern Canada to come over here and hold demonstrations or anything like that.

"I was totally caught by surprise and knew that if this whole thing was made public it could undermine the initiatives that we had been working on with the Indian Brotherhood. They might say the Indian Brotherhood recruited a revolutionary group. I wasn't really interested in getting into any of that.

"The next morning I got a call from the RCMP . . . They said you know the FBI is all upset about fugitives. I was harbouring them. I didn't even know who they were, and so they wanted to know if I had specifically gotten in touch with them before. Did I know them and how did they know where I lived? I said hell if I know . . . I never told any of my staff these guys from AIM had arrived because it really had nothing to do with the Indian Brotherhood."

ON MAY 1, 1975, WE stood to attention in the banquet room of the Explorer Hotel, as the RCMP member shouldered the ornate territorial mace, his boots crashing onto the floor of the Council chamber. Behind the Mountie marched Binx, in his black cloak, the Legal Advisor, and then the Assistant Clerk. But Hodgson, who for eight years had marched behind the mace to the front of the chamber, now stood with the rest of the civil servants off to one side.

The Northwest Territories Act, recently revised by the federal government, had finally made the Commissioner just another bureaucrat. The federal government continued to maintain sovereignty over northern resources and still provided funding for education, economic development, housing, and local government. But the Commissioner would no longer preside over Council sessions; he had been replaced by the long-coveted Executive Council. It was a huge step forward, a significant day,

The Territorial election held in early March had resulted in a Canadian first—the first elected government body in the country dominated by native members. Six Eskimos, two Indians and one Métis had been elected to the fifteen-member Council; the appointed members were gone. In seven years, native people had worked their way into the governing system.

James Wah-Shee had been elected by acclamation. The other Indian member was George Barnaby, who had come up through the ranks as settlement secretary of Fort Good Hope. William Lafferty was a Métis journalist from Fort Simpson. The Eskimo members were Ludy Pudluk, settlement manager of Grise Fiord; Peter Ernerk, who had worked in my department, representing Rankin Inlet; Bill Lyall, a businessman from Cambridge Bay; John Steen, a businessman from Tuktoyaktuk; Mark Evaluarjuk, president of an Eskimo co-operative in Igloolik; and Ipeelee Kilabuk, a labourer, hunter and trapper from Pangnirtung.

White members were now a minority and included incumbents David Searle, Bryan Pearson, Tom Butters and Don Stewart. Dave Nickerson, a mining engineer from Yellowknife, and Arnold McCallum, a Fort Smith schoolteacher, were the new members.

"Welcome to the lower ranks," I whispered in Hodgson's ear. He nodded and smiled without replying.

After the mace was placed on its green velvet cushions, the Clerk read the prayer and then asked, "Is it the wish of the Legislature to now proceed with the election of a Speaker?"

A ripple of anticipation flowed around the room. This was like signing the order to cut off the king's head. Once the North had a Speaker, the Commissioner would formally lose his control of the law-making process.

The members held their hands high to show assent. Bryan Pearson stroked his goatee, looked at the paper on his desk and rose to his feet. "Mr. Clerk, I move, seconded by the Honourable Member for Mackenzie Liard, that Mr. David H. Searle of the electoral district of Yellowknife do take the chair in this House as Speaker." A unanimous vote in favour of the motion was followed by a tumult of applause and desk thumping. Searle beamed broadly as he moved to the chair and turned to face his colleagues. "I am very pleased on behalf of this House to officially declare this Legislative Assembly in session. May I say while I am on my feet how extremely honoured I am to have this first office, and how I will attempt to continue the proceedings in the tradition of dignity that has hitherto been done by our Commissioner."

He bowed ceremoniously in Hodgson's direction, who stood and bowed deeply in return.

Searle spoke again. "Mr. Clerk, would you kindly determine whether Mr. Commissioner is available and wishes to address this House?"

"Yes, Mr. Speaker, I shall."

With an air of pride and purpose, Hodgson was escorted to the podium where he spoke extemporaneously. "Collectively, we in the Territories have come a long way, in a very, very short time, particularly when you remember that just ten years ago appointed members to Council outnumbered the elected members, that our capital was in Ottawa and that we had few territorial public servants.

"I am sure none of us are under any illusions that it is going to be clear sailing from here on for the rest of the journey. We have a long way to go with a new ship and, like any other similar situation, a lot of it is trial and error." He looked up at the audience as if seeking a nod or two of approval. "It will take some time to get used to it, but if all those involved dedicate themselves to the principle and make it work, and give support to the new Council structure, then I believe that territorial residents will be assured that this is indeed a forward step along the path to responsible government."

Hodgson paused. Members and guests rewarded him with a round of applause. He smiled and continued. "I first joined Council as an appointed member in 1964. Then I became the first full-time Deputy Commissioner in 1965 and then, when I became Commissioner in 1967, I lost my vote—but I retained the right to speak. I can see now that I will have to be pretty quick around here when I get this right, or I will lose even that!"

The members thumped their desks, enjoying Hodgson's sense of humour and the truth of his words. Then he was again serious. "I have had the privilege of participating through twenty-eight sessions of Council. So, I think I have some feeling and some understanding for the history and problems and the difficulties and challenges that you are going to face over this next four years.

"We, as the administration, will give you all the support that we can give you. We know the difficulties that we find ourselves in, because the Council on the one hand may feel strongly about various things, and on the other hand other people with responsibilities in the North may feel just as strongly in a different way. Go slow, and give everyone the opportunity of stating first-hand their feelings . . .

"The biggest lesson I have learned is that what the people want most of all is to be consulted and to be listened to. What they want is the opportunity to hold on to those traditions and the past or culture they want to hold on to, not what you and me want them to hold to, but what they want to hold to. For this reason it is going to take a certain amount of experimentation on all our parts before we're going to be able to truly say that we have reached the proper system, the ultimate system, for this vast territory.

"If we do this, if we listen and not try and do everything at once, all at the same time, that when we do things we tackle it and do it well, and finish it, then I think that we would not have to look back and say that we wish we had been able to do more.

"No one can ask more of a person than that he give his all, and that he give his loyalty, and be prepared to work day and night for the people of these Territories."

In his reply to the Commissioner's opening address, James Wah-Shee was magnanimous. "I would like to express my appreciation for all the efforts and all the work that the Commissioner of the Territories has done for a number of years . . . I, as an individual member of this Council, do not necessarily agree with all the events that have taken place, nor am I that critical to the extent that I can say that we were unhappy, totally unhappy, with the situation. I think what happens from here on is really important.

"I think that we have a number of good people here who believe in team-work and doing everything we can to the benefit of the people of the North . . . Thank you Mr. Speaker."

As well as appointing the Speaker, Council appointed Peter Ernerk and Arnold McCallum to the Executive Committee, the first ministers of the government of the Northwest Territories. Ernerk became the equivalent of cabinet minister responsible for social development, McCallum for education. The Executive Committee was still chaired by Hodgson and included the Deputy Commissioner and two Assistant Commissioners; it continued to control much of the Council's agenda by vetting any proposed legislation. It would be another five years before the renamed Legislative Assembly would appoint a Premier and form a consensus government, the first in Canada.

AT THE CLOSE OF THE session Hodgson and I walked back to the Laing Building.

"How's the new baby?"

"People look at me dubiously when I tell them we brought Luke home from the hospital on a sleigh in an orange crate at -40 in a howling windstorm. But it's true. Healthy start for sure. No doubt he'll grow like a weed."

"Everything's changing so fast," Hodgson said. "Gene and Lynne are growing up so quickly, and now you and Barb have a son. The North is growing up too. Look at today's Council session.

"The North of the next ten years is the North we could never have envisaged a decade ago. Native kids will be educated, native people will settle land claims, strengthen their band councils, form their own corporations and move easily into government. There'll be better transportation, new airports, telephone service everywhere, better housing and better communications. The Anik satellite has already brought live television. It'll be an exciting time. Mind you, not the exciting time you and I have gone through."

Hodgson, who had just turned fifty-one, appeared to have aged twenty years since we first arrived in the North. "Is the excitement still there for you? You're a builder, an innovator. You like to get things started, dream up grand projects, and then let the John Parkers of this world run them."

"What do you mean?"

"When you asked me to put out *News of the North* so many years ago, I knew eventually I wanted to own my own newspaper. I wasn't ready then, not enough experience. Under your wing I've learned a lot—how to stand on my own two feet, how to get others to help achieve my goals, how to persist when the odds seem unbeatable."

I needed to tell him my intentions. "You've been my teacher, and I couldn't have wished for a better one. But the time has come for me to move on. It's the seven-year itch."

"Where?" A response I hadn't expected.

"I've lined up a newspaper in Alberta."

To my surprise he slapped me on the back. "Well good for you, Jacobee! I knew you'd do that someday. You have that spark of imagination and determination so many people are missing—it shows in their lives. I'm happy for you and pleased to know I've helped along the way."

My decision had been thoroughly thought out. Hodgson would depart within two to three years, completing his ten-year commitment. As his right-hand man, I would have a hard time developing a relationship with a new Commissioner, likely John Parker. Besides, I was tired after seven years of attending community meetings in drafty, smoke-filled halls complete with late nights, terrible food, freezing temperatures and blisteringly hot, dry rooms, uncomfortable beds and snoring roommates.

I was proud of my accomplishments, but I had been promoted as high as I could go and the thought of becoming a worn-out, disenchanted civil servant bothered me. I had seen too many stay in the job too long. A functioning Information Department was now in place and would do well with an efficient administrator. "It's best to quit while ahead," I said.

Hodgson replied, "You implying it's time for me to quit too?"

"Who am I to say? You've done what you came here to do."

"You know it's not the fun it used to be," he said with frankness. "It's all different now and changing faster every day. But I'm not excess baggage yet. I promised ten years, two to go. One day history will talk about the person who brought government to the North, and I hope they'll acknowledge that I made a contribution. Building democracy for Northerners should be worth some mention in the history books. If I've done nothing else, I've put the Northwest Territories on the map!"

When we reached Hodgson's office, he grabbed a roll of blueprints and spread them on the conference table. "A northern museum," he exclaimed. "Our very own. The feds have been carting off all our artifacts to Ottawa for years. Ha! I'll fix them! Can't call it a museum though. Ottawa says territories aren't allowed to build them."

It had been a long time since I'd seen him this excited. "It'll face onto

Frame Lake, with lots of concrete on the outside, lots of natural timber on the inside. We're going to build right on top of the rock formation, let the floor rise and fall with ramps. What do you think?"

"Looks kind of cold and hard on the outside," I said. "But that's the North, isn't it? The secret to its success will be how you'll design the inside."

"Cold and hard, with unexpected flashes of life!"

"Now you'll have somewhere to put all those artifacts you've collected over the years. What will it cost?"

"I haven't put the money together, but I will. Never fear! You can't tell me a territory larger than India shouldn't have its own museum. I only need six million dollars. Prince Charles said he will come to open it! So I'll christen it the Prince of Wales Northern Heritage Centre. Then it's not a museum."

The recent visit of Prince Charles had provided the future king with a firsthand look at a frontier land and its people and had given Hodgson an opportunity to build a close connection with Buckingham Palace. Greeted as *Ataniup Irninga*, (the Big Boss' Son), the Prince took in a seal-skinning contest, drove his own dog team, dove under the sea ice of the Arctic Ocean, raced his snowmobile, munched on caribou steak and even accepted a snack of raw seal liver, which he called "an acquired taste not unlike caviar." On the final day, Hodgson had shown him the site of the proposed museum and asked the Prince if he could name it in his honour.

"THIS WILL BRIGHTEN YOUR DAY," I said the next morning, sliding a *Globe and Mail* newspaper towards Hodgson. "Scott Young has written a column about you.[23] He tears a strip off of Ed Broadbent for his reaction to the dinner for the Prince of Wales."

The royal tour had concluded in Yellowknife with a black-tie dinner attended by several hundred northern citizens, the vast majority of whom were white. Ignoring the fact that other functions on the Prince's tour had focused on indigenous culture, Ed Broadbent, the NDP parliamentary leader, had called for Hodgson's removal. It was a remarkable criticism of someone who had been a key supporter of the NDP in its formative years.

"Broadbent should spend a bit of time up here," I said. "There are a lot of issues and concerns Ottawa-based politicians should be concerned about that are much more urgent than the Yellowknife dinner guest list."

[23] Scott Young, "Basic Rights for Northerners", *Globe and Mail*, May 2, 1975

I read the article aloud: "This tall, affable man with a labour union background has an odd job, running the Territories as a representative of Ottawa, but knowing that the best legacy he can give to the Territories is the kind of confidence and self-esteem that will help make full self-government a success when it comes, as it must eventually.

"He does that part of his job admirably. What visiting reporters first see is a sort of obliging PR man for the North. When they look closer there is much more—a man who seems to be genuinely welcomed by native leaders wherever he goes through the North, who seeks their counsel, and very rarely is the target for their criticism.

"If there was an election in the NWT and Hodgson ran, I think he'd be hard to beat, whichever party he ran for."

Part Five

FAREWELL

30
RECOGNITION

NINETEEN MONTHS AFTER I LEFT the North, a vicious February blizzard was roaring along the streets of Fort Saskatchewan, Alberta. The press had had so many problems we were hours late getting the run finished.

"What?" I yelled above the roar of the press as David Holehouse, my editor manager, yelled in my ear.

"Ethel," he shouted, "says the women won't stay late. They're going home." If Ethel's crew didn't stay to stuff the various sections together, we wouldn't get the newspapers on the newsstands on time.

"Here!" I yelled back. "Here's fifty bucks. Get some pizza, enough for everybody. We can't let the papers come out a day late!"

The back door blew open and Barb bustled in with our son, Luke, in her arms. "Turn on the radio!" Barb said. "CBC has a program on Hodgson, starting in a few minutes."

We went into the paste-up shop. ". . . received the civil service's highest honour today," the announcer said. "Stuart Hodgson was presented the Public Service of Canada 1976 Award for Outstanding Achievement and $5,000 by Governor General Jules Leger. After the presentation, an address was given by Prime Minister Trudeau."[24]

I said, "Good for you, Commissioner, you deserve it, dammit!"

We sat on a pair of stools hunched up close to the radio to hear Trudeau's voice. "An Inuit once met Stu and asked him: 'Do you mind if I name the baby after you, sir?' And I guess that Stuart, feeling that Stuart was not such a bad name, said 'First class.' Whereupon she said, 'Very well, I will call him Umingmak.' Which, and my pronunciation may not be too good, means muskox in Eskimo. And now that is Stuart's nickname. The muskox is a

---

[24] "Transcript of the Prime Minister's Remarks at the Outstanding Achievement Award Presentation, Government House, Ottawa", Pierre Elliot Trudeau, February 9, 1977

symbol of strength, a symbol of authority, and it is reputed to be an animal which has very, very good eyesight. And I think these three characteristics, as the Inuit very well saw, apply eminently to our distinguished guest of honour."

I knew Hodgson would be extremely flattered.

The Prime Minister continued, "He is a man of great strength and endurance, always on the move. I think the first time I've ever seen him stand still for long, Your Excellency, was this afternoon when he was listening to the well-deserved tribute. But a territory of a million and a quarter square miles covering, I think, something like two-fifths of Canada's land space, has fifty-odd communities that Stuart has had to visit or wanted to visit at least once a year and many several times; an incredible number of hours logged in flying—something like a hundred thousand miles a year—this obviously requires a man of great courage, great stamina and great strength. And this has shown not only in his travels but in the dedication and force with which he attacked, tackled the very difficult job of decentralizing to the North the government of the North.

"A second characteristic is that of authority. And there again, one who has travelled with Stu in the North, and there are many, because a large part of his efforts has been to make people see and understand the North, have seen the way in which Stuart Hodgson when he arrives in the North really brings authority with him . . . When he arrives, the government arrives.

"Perhaps the most typical incident was when once we were flying from one point to another and Stu just said: 'Well, there seems to be some dog-sleds down there, let's land.' And it was some remote bay, snow-covered bay in Bathurst Inlet; and sure enough we landed, and there was this family of Eskimos who invited us into their snow-covered tent under the snowbank and invited us in for some tea, George Hakongak, some name like that, I remember the first name was George.

"And after the greetings and tea and so on, George went out and came back with a little parcel which he very delicately unwrapped and he was talking, and I didn't understand what he was saying but it was a little Eskimo carving that he had done and he was preparing to present it to, I supposed, the important person . . . and I was stretching out my hand when he gave it to Stuart Hodgson!

"Many instances like that have shown the way Stuart Hodgson has tackled his job. Whether it be opening the Winter Games or having royalty tour the North, or putting another dint in the Franklin Probe or really solving school problems or making decisions which had to do with social questions, there has been that authority . . . with the paradox that Stu brought his authority to the North and left it there."

After all those years when it seemed no one noticed what Hodgson was doing, nor cared, it was a real boost to hear the country's Prime Minister give the man the recognition he deserved.

Trudeau continued, "His is one of the most successful efforts of decentralizing the Canadian government and bringing the government of the North closer to the people, making sure their needs and their desires were met. And I think in this he has been superbly aided by the third characteristic of the muskox: one of having tremendous eyesight. He sees the North. He sees the changing . . . He sees the human beings in a state of evolution. And perhaps more important even than that, he has helped us see the North. He has helped the rest of Canada, in many cases the rest of the world, see the tremendous potential of this great part of Canada and see the tremendous value of the people who live in the North, the Eskimos and the Indians.

"And I am absolutely delighted to be able on this occasion to say, on behalf of the government of Canada, how proud we are that this great Canadian has been sought out by the committee of the Outstanding Achievement Award to receive this honour today. It is ten years since Lester Pearson instituted this honour and I want to congratulate the selection committee for having made such a superb choice."

31

THE LAST HURRAH

APRIL 1979

TWO YEARS LATER A GILT-EDGED invitation summoned us to Yellowknife for the opening of Hodgson's pride and joy, the Prince of Wales Northern Heritage Centre, to be followed by an evening banquet honouring Prince Charles. Hodgson had beaten all the odds, and Ottawa's bureaucracy, to get his beloved museum built, among the most stunning in all of Canada, according to those who'd seen the finished product.

Barb, Luke and I flew out of Edmonton on one of Pacific Western Airlines' stubby 737 jets. "Jake!" someone called. It was David Searle, seated across the aisle.

"You know Stu did a hell of a lot for the North," he said, "but his time's over. The last year or two he's been in the way of everything we've been trying to do. He built a fine government but then I think he had trouble letting go. And his obsession with medals and monuments has become a mania.

"He sent one of his senior people down to Salt Lake City with a motorhome to pick up a portrait of Prince Charles he commissioned for the banquet. Wasn't even finished, and it's so huge it wouldn't fit through the banquet room doors—the Public Works people had to take the doors off and chip away at the wall until it would go in. And, as soon as the Prince leaves, they'll be doing it all again to move it to the museum."

We laughed; it was quintessential Hodgson.

"Things have changed drastically in the North," Searle said. "After the election this year, we'll have twenty-two members of the Legislative Assembly and seven cabinet ministers. The budget is $282 million. There are thirteen thousand kids in school now, twice what there were in the early '60s. We've had nineteen communities reach hamlet status, with two more ready to go. Things are just a whole lot more developed these days."

"I hope the members remember who made a lot of that progress happen."

"No one is knocking what Stu did for the North," Searle said. "But take a look when you see him. It's like he put everything he had into the job, and it's just about drained him dry. This will be his final fling."

ON APRIL 3, A CROWD of about two hundred people gathered outside the Prince of Wales Northern Heritage Centre. The grey concrete structure with the rounded barrel-shaped roof glowed under the wan light, and the stern, straight lines of the upper superstructure gave the place a durable, proud look.

Winds gusted up to twenty miles per hour and the -23 temperature eventually penetrated the warmest of parkas. Shivering Boy Scouts and Girl Guides lined a walkway leading to the broad cement steps of the main entrance. A podium and several chairs had been set up, along with a ribbon for Prince Charles to cut.

Finally, the official party arrived. Hodgson, wearing his red duffle parka over a dark business suit, stepped from one of the vehicles. He was still a big man but didn't tower the way I remembered. I was struck by how much he had aged. He was only fifty-five, but his hair had greyed severely about the ears, as had his eyebrows and most of his moustache. He wore thick-rimmed glasses now, but his smile was just as wide, just as proud. He stepped forward and opened the door of the car bearing Prince Charles. Dressed in an Inuit-made parka and rubber snowmobile boots with felt liners, the Prince stopped in his tracks when he beheld the magnificence of the building.

Aware the crowd had been waiting for some time, Hugh Faulkner, the new Minister of Indian Affairs and Northern Development, was quick to get to the microphone. "The Prince's presence here today is a sign of the Royal Family's interest in Canada as well as a tribute to Commissioner Hodgson's endeavours in the Northwest Territories." He then introduced Prince Charles.

"This is not a day for making speeches," said the Prince. "My vocal chords have frozen up, so I will not be talking for long. I will say that after three visits in nine years, I feel I know the Northwest Territories better than any other part of Canada. I can remember, on my last visit, when Commissioner Hodgson showed me this site, which was nothing more than a hole in the ground. I am honoured and pleased it should be named after me."

With that he snipped the ribbon and led the way into the majestic building, followed by a crowd of frozen subjects. I watched the knot of dignitaries from a distance, noticing how Hodgson carried himself, how he gestured and spoke to his guests. He'd absorbed some of the essence of royalty over the last twelve years and his subjects played along, deferring to him and looking up to him as he strolled into his granite palace, even as they secretly cursed his omnipotence.

Tea and bannock were served after the Prince presented the museum with a limited edition sword commemorating his mother's coronation and an 18th century naval telescope. It was then that Hodgson noticed me in the crowd.

I was pleased that he would do so, but blurted out, "What the hell are you doing, leaving the Prince?"

"He'll be fine!" Without missing a beat he talked to me as though I had never left. "I'm ready to go, Jacobee. You and I had some good times. But it's not a little government anymore, where one person can call all the shots and do whatever he wants. The North has grown up, and it's ready to make its own decisions."

"What will you do now?" A media report had suggested Hodgson might be the next Governor General.

"Trudeau is to appoint me as Chairman of the International Joint Commission to settle border disputes between Canada and the United States. It will keep me out of mischief."

The official party went off to see the exhibits, escorted by museum director Robert Janes, while we commoners wandered the halls. I felt a twinge of loss, a loss of status, now that I was no longer close to Hodgson. Barb and I flowed with the crowd, revelling in sights and smells that attested to the reality of the Eskimo, Indian, Métis, and other Northerners' place in history. To think we'd been proud of our 100th anniversary celebration in 1970; the Indian and Eskimo civilizations went back thousands of years.

They were not called Indian and Eskimo anymore. As the Council had become the Legislative Assembly of the Northwest Territories, so too had the Mackenzie Valley Indians became more commonly referred to by their aboriginal name of Dene. The Eskimos were now referred to as Inuit while those in the Western Arctic were known as Inuvialuit. Moves were also underway to have native place names officially reinstated.

"So what d'ya say to all this, Jake Ootes?" said a voice behind me. I turned to face Charles Lynch, senior columnist with Southam News Services. Lynch liked Hodgson.

"This is all just fabulous," Lynch said, waving his hand and twirling it in a circle. "No wonder Faulkner calls him the Emperor of the North. The guy couldn't even build a normal museum, could he? I mean, a nice little museum would have done just fine for the North. But this is Hodgson, same as always, showing that any time you go a little beyond what's reasonable, what's expected, you reach what he calls first class."

"I think it's a fitting symbol of all the things Hodgson has given the North," I said. "A lot of them you can't see, but they're there—like the government, the sense of unity, a definition for the world of what a Northerner is."

THE NORTHERN LIGHTS DANCED AS Barb and I entered the glittering interior of the Explorer Hotel where 320 guests were dressed in black tie, mess kit, or native dress—James Wah-Shee's challenge had brought about a permanent change in the way invitations were worded. Chandeliers illuminated a red banner bearing the Prince of Wales' crest behind the head table; heavy maroon drapes covered the monumental painting. I was immensely flattered by our seats directly in front of the Prince, the best in the house.

On the stroke of 7:45, RCMP Sergeant Ray James marched to the podium and announced that a special painting in honour of the Prince of Wales would be unveiled by the artist, Arnold Friberg. To the rousing fanfare of the Princess Patricia's Canadian Light Infantry Band, Friberg stepped forward, perfectly erect and proud, as two Mounties drew back the drapes.

It was an awe-inspiring painting, seven feet high and as wide, of the Prince as Colonel of the Welsh Guards standing with Centennial, an enormous and magnificent horse presented to The Queen by the RCMP during their centennial year of 1973. The Prince stood in front of the beast, one hand raised to hold reins that would be painted in when Friberg was allowed to complete his work.

Sergeant James then loudly announced, "Ladies and gentlemen, please stand for His Royal Highness, Charles, the Prince of Wales." Prince Charles led the head table procession into the room. We remained on our feet as Sergeant James led the singing of "O Canada."

The two-and-a-half-hour event passed flawlessly and I marvelled at the way Hodgson had turned his job into a gateway to fame, status, respect and power. Twelve years earlier he and I sat in a tiny house eating corn cobs straight out of the can. Now he was hosting the man who would be King of England.

After liqueurs and cigars, the Commissioner stood. "Your Highness," he said, turning to the Prince, who also rose. "It's difficult for me to put into words how much I and the people of the Northwest Territories appreciate your presence tonight, and any night, here in the North. I would like to present you with this on behalf of the 46,000 people of the Northwest Territories and hope you will return to the North to use it." Applause filled the banquet room as the Prince opened a polished rectangular wooden box and held high a fly-fishing rod. The lights dimmed and a spotlight focussed on the PPCLI Band which played "God Bless the Prince of Wales."

It was a fitting and moving end to the evening, to Hodgson's reign. The Yellowknife Scottish Pipe Band entered the room and, with the PPCLI Band for accompaniment, played "Amazing Grace." Spontaneously, people stood to applaud, drowning out the sound of the band. We were here to honour the Prince of Wales, but all in the room were really applauding Hodgson.

THREE DAYS LATER, THE SOUNDS of "Tunes of Glory" droned up into the clear April sky as a lone bagpiper played at the foot of the Grumman Gulfstream aircraft at the Yellowknife Airport. A brisk wind nudged the bagpipes' tassels and picked at the familiar blue carpet that would take Hodgson out of the North.

Hodgson turned and gave a last wave to the hundred or more well-wishers clustered on the tarmac. He'd finished a final tour of the northern communities, attended a party thrown by approximately five hundred of his headquarters staff and made what he said was his first visit to a northern bar. Now it was time for him to go.

Bob Gauchie, the errant pilot who had survived on a plane load of fish for fifty-eight days in the Arctic wilderness and who had been so happy to have Hodgson named Commissioner in 1967, said, "There's only one thing anyone need say about Stu Hodgson. He cared. You don't know how much that means to people who lived up here before he came north."

Army and Air Cadets formed an honour guard as Hodgson walked under the territorial and polar bear flags. I was overcome with nostalgia. The guy had looked after me as if he were my father. What Syd Thompson, Air Marshal

Campbell and Art Laing had been to Hodgson, he was to me. He had taken a liking to me when I was young and struggling in Ottawa and had taught me many things of value, passed on the strength of his philosophy and even some of his mannerisms. I felt grateful to have worked alongside him and even more grateful for having become a Northerner.

Ever the showman, Hodgson turned while he was still within earshot of the crowd. The pipes stilled. "Think of it like a herd of muskox," he cried out. "Like I tell my Eskimo friends, when the muskox leader gets old, it's time for him to go off by himself. It's time for me to go off by myself and let the younger ones take over. I'm still a muskox, but my horns aren't as sharp as they were. The only difference between me and a muskox is that when I go out, I take my mate with me."

A roar of approval went up from the crowd. "Long live Stu the First," shouted one of the onlookers, and others took up the chant. Hodgson grinned as he waved, one arm around a tearful Pearl. It was his final moment in the northern limelight.

EPILOGUE

HODGSON DID SOMETHING VITALLY IMPORTANT and significant for Canada. Elected officials now hold the reins of power at all levels and the role of commissioner is largely ceremonial. His greatest legacy was turning political and administrative power over to the people of the North.

While ongoing and significant challenges remain, communities have moved into the modern era with scheduled airlines as well as telephone, radio and television services provided to the farthest corners of the North. Perishable foods are regularly available in most communities. Children are no longer sent away for primary schooling. Housing, water and sanitation services have improved, as have health care and social services.

I was privileged to experience the North's transition firsthand. After Barb and I divorced, I sold my community newspapers in Alberta and moved back to the Northwest Territories to develop *Above and Beyond,* an in-flight magazine for a northern airline. In 1995, I was elected as a member of the Northwest Territories Legislature for Yellowknife Centre and, during my second term, was honoured to serve as Minister responsible for Education, Culture and Employment. I saw the home of the legislature move from the dowdy Elks Hall to the Explorer Hotel, the Yellowknife Inn, and then to one of Canada's most impressive legislative buildings, which opened in 1993.

During my time in the legislature, the map of the North changed dramatically. On April 1, 1999, the Northwest Territories was divided and the new territory of Nunavut was established, thanks in large part to the efforts of John Amagoalik, my former information officer. Peter Ernerk, now Peter Irniq, also one of my former information officers, became its second commissioner.

After leaving the North, Hodgson chaired the International Joint Commission where he settled twenty-one long-standing disputes between Canada and the United States. He then became Chairman of the British Columbia Ferry Corporation and went on to head BC Transit. Until his retirement in 2005 he also served as a Canadian Citizenship Judge.

Stuart Milton Hodgson passed away on December 18, 2015, in Vancouver, thirty-five years after he left the North. He was ninety-one. On March 21, 2017, some of Umingmak's ashes were scattered on Beechy Island in the High Arctic, next to the cairn dedicated to Arctic Explorer Sir John Franklin. It was a fitting tribute.

ACKNOWLEDGEMENTS

I am indebted and grateful to the following people who provided assistance, information and encouragement:

Barbara Ootes for putting up with me, while providing a supportive home life. David Holehouse, a dear friend and skilled journalist, who understood what I wanted to accomplish when I first conceived this book. He spent numerous weekends assisting me with research and editorial input. Catherine Pellerin for her fabulous editing which provided magic results, and for acting as my official agent, which resulted in the publication of this book. Lynn Duncan and Kilmeny Jane Denny of Tidewater Press for believing in *Umingmak*.

I am grateful to both Peter Irniq and James Wah-Shee for their valuable input. Peter provided Inuktitut translation and James spent time with me sharing his memories of the Indian Brotherhood era. I also appreciate the assistance that I received from the following individuals: Robin Weber, Tiffany Champagne and Rebecca Mahler at the Prince of Wales Northern Heritage Centre Archives; Lisc Daley at the Northwest Territories Legislative Library; Nunavut Senator Dennis Patterson and staff member, Julie Armstrong. My appreciation also extends to Don Waite for the screening of photographs and to Yacub Adam for his advice, support and encouragement.

Personal interviews were conducted by David Holehouse and me with the following individuals: Bent Sivertz, Caroline Anawak, Dale Eckleson, David Searle, Daryl Brown, Hugh Feagan, Rae Parker, René Fumoleau, Syd Thompson, Wally Gryba, Kay Vaydik, and Joyce Jarmen. I also relied on the Debates of the Northwest Territories.

Summer 1969, Bay Chimo on the Arctic Coast

ABOUT THE AUTHOR

JAKE OOTES IS A FORMER reporter who was Hodgson's executive assistant and then Director of the Territorial Department of Information, responsible for all government public affairs and communications. In 1995, Ootes was elected to the Legislative Assembly of the Northwest Territories and later appointed Minister of Education, Culture and Employment.

After he retired from politics in 2004, he and his wife, Margaret Baile, established and now operate Celista Estate Winery in British Columbia. A risk taken and never regretted. He can be contacted at jakeootes@gmail.com or through www.celistawine.com.

INDEX

A

Adams, Willie 217
AIM. *See* American Indian Movement
Air Marshal. *See* Campbell, Hugh
Aklavik 52, 177, 217, 239
Alexander, Colin 51, 57
Amagoalik, John 256, 297
American Indian Movement 265, 268
Anawak, Caroline 299. *See also* Pickles, Caroline; *See also* Washie, Caroline
Angulalik, Stephen 211
Arctic Bay 75, 108, 109, 111–112
Arctic Circle Club 91–94
Arctic Ocean 80, 283
Arctic Winter Games 158, 165, 195, 197, 203, 204, 205, 206, 258
Arrowmaker, Chief 251, 252
Arvaluk, James 256

B

Baffin Island 15, 52, 56, 75, 86, 108, 111, 115, 125, 129, 134
Baird, Irene 8, 74
Baker Lake 204, 256
Baker, Pete 3, 4, 27, 28, 199, 204, 256
Banks, Dennis 265, 266, 267
Banks Island 226
Barber, Lloyd 53
Barnaby, Antoine 236
Barnaby, George 278
Belcher Islands 52, 134–138, 139, 142
Belcourt, Tony 258
Bird, Ed 241, 249
Blondin, Georgina 17, 164, 235. *See also* Pryde, Georgina
Broadbent, Ed 283
Brotherhood. *See* Indian Brotherhood of the Northwest Territories
Brown, Daryl 77–83, 84, 89, 93–97, 99, 113–115, 123, 125, 129–146, 299
Bruneau, James 64–68, 167–170, 173, 179, 276
Butters, Tom 217, 278

C

Cambridge Bay 79, 123, 204, 211, 278
Campbell, Hugh 3, 36, 53, 79, 97–98, 100, 115, 124, 130, 134, 137, 146, 161, 165, 194, 217, 233, 295

Canadian Broadcasting Corporation 35, 37, 51, 54, 55, 78, 79, 90, 160, 161, 188, 196, 201, 202, 210, 236, 256, 257, 265, 274, 287
Canadian National Telecommunications 74
Cape Dorset 55, 134
Caribou Queen 25, 26, 198
Carney, Pat 79–82, 94, 97, 98, 102, 124, 129–130, 141–145
Carpenter, Mary 253
Carrothers Commission xvi, 3, 160, 161, 184, 185, 187, 189, 190, 193, 228
Cazon, Baptiste 240
Cazon, Dolly 236, 237
CBC. *See* Canadian Broadcasting Corporation
Charles, the Prince of Wales 206–209, 275, 283, 290–293
Charlo, Alec 239
Chrétien, Jean 70, 72, 91, 98, 143, 159, 160, 166, 172, 179, 181, 183–191, 196, 206, 208, 210, 241, 248, 251, 252, 254, 258, 274
Churchill 14, 17, 18, 79, 203, 256
Cloughley, Maurice and Katie 82, 84, 86, 87, 109
Clyde River 123–129, 136, 137
Committee for Original Peoples Entitlements 226, 229, 236, 250
Company of Young Canadians 170, 171
COPE. *See* Committee for Original Peoples Entitlements
Coppermine 203, 213, 217, 221, 226
Coral Harbour 134, 256
Côté, Ernest 5
Council of the Northwest Territories 7, 49, 54, 111, 158–161, 248. *See also* Territorial Council
Courier, Erma 8, 9, 10, 16, 31, 35, 167, 248, 251
Cournoyea, Nellie 250
Cowan, Ed 79, 80, 85, 100, 100–104, 124, 125, 137, 142–144
Cressnan, Doug 125, 126, 127, 128, 129
CYC. *See* Company of Young Canadians

D

Davies, Dave 131
Davies, Mary-Ellen 80, 82, 89, 92, 92–94, 93, 130, 138
Day, Bev 17, 19, 23, 40
Day, Gordy 17, 20, 40
Decker, Dennis 91, 94
Dettah 46, 174, 251
Doornbos, Tom 23, 29, 54, 60

E

Eckleson, Dale 26, 44, 299
Elks Hall 24, 25, 44, 48–51, 158, 183, 198, 297
Ellesmere Island 56, 79, 80, 85

Ernerk, Peter 256, 278, 280, 297. *See also* Irniq, Peter
Esau, Peter 226
Evaluarjuk, Mark 278
Explorer Hotel 277, 293

F

Fairbrother, Mark 53
Faulkner, Hugh 291, 293
Feagan, Hugh 267–270, 299
Federation of Natives North of Sixty 274
Football, Virginia 103, 236, 237
Fort Good Hope 174, 236, 278
Fort McPherson 53, 196, 239, 270, 271
Fort Norman 239
Fort Rae 63, 64, 167–176, 179, 212, 217, 219, 234–237
Fort Resolution 171, 172, 277
Fort Simpson 53, 157, 187, 217, 229, 236, 237, 240, 255, 278
Fort Smith 4, 27, 172, 173, 211, 217, 236, 237, 241, 266, 277, 278
Fournier, Jean 91, 94, 98, 103, 124, 146, 166, 252
Francis, Tadit 239
Fraser, Whit 269, 274
Friberg, Arnold 293
Friesen, Dave 183, 188
Frobisher Bay 35, 42, 91, 256
Fumoleau, René 174–181, 266, 267, 299

G

Gauchie, Robert (Bob) 7, 9, 53, 123, 294
Gibson, Gordon 53, 199
Gilchrist, Bertha 16, 17, 40, 45, 46
Gilchrist, Clarence (Gillie) 16, 17, 30, 40, 48, 78, 155, 234
Gillie, Bernard 16, 40, 41, 154–156
Gon, Andrew 240
Governor General xi, 163, 165, 195, 206, 210
Great Bear Lake 3, 18
Great Slave Lake 3, 18, 45, 52, 74, 171, 177, 178
Grise Fiord 79–93, 98, 108, 109, 110, 112, 115, 116, 133, 134, 136, 144, 278
Gryba, Wally 259–262, 265–269, 299

H

Hakongak, George 204, 288
Hall Beach 134
Hancock, Sid 157, 197, 207, 274
Harris, Florence 236, 237
Harvey, Ross 132, 214

Leger, Jules 287
Legislative Assembly 160, 279, 281, 290, 292. *See also* Council of the Northwest
 Territories
Leishman, Harry 167–171
Louyine, Doris 236, 237
Lyall, Bill 278
Lynch, Charles 12, 292, 293

M

Mackenzie Highway 30, 48, 63
Mackenzie River 46, 52, 59, 69, 113, 211, 234
Mackenzie Valley 18, 56, 174, 177, 178, 179, 197, 203, 204, 256, 259, 261, 266,
 272, 292
Martindale, Cyril 17, 19, 23, 24, 25, 26, 40, 41, 48
McCallum, Arnold 278, 280, 281
Means, Russell 265
Meyers, Bill 51, 55, 56
Michael, Simonie 52, 91, 94, 109, 111, 125, 127, 128, 131, 208
Michener, Nora 163, 208
Michener, Roland 206, 208
Monaghan, Bill 79, 81, 84, 97, 130, 134, 135, 145, 146
Morgan, Bill 156
Morrow, William 227, 266, 267

N

National Indian Brotherhood 236, 241, 245
Native Council of Canada 258
N'dilo 174. *See also* Rainbow Valley
New Democratic Party (NDP) 5, 104, 264, 283
News of the North 4, 12, 13, 21, 33, 41, 48, 51, 281
Nickerson, Dave 278
Nixon, Harry 53, 183, 198
Northwest Territories
 Area Administrators of 74, 76, 82
  Cloughley, Maurice and Katie 82, 84, 86, 87, 109
  Cressnan, Doug 125, 126, 127, 128, 129
  Davies, Dave 131
  Kempt, Bill 109, 110, 113
  Pilot, Bob and Lois 115, 116, 121, 124
  Sieber, Ernie and Patricia 141, 143
 Council of 3, 7, 49, 54, 111, 158, 248. *See also* Territorial Council
 flag of 55
 mace of 50, 53, 55, 183, 188, 277, 278
Norwegian, Louis 239

O

Okpik, Abe 156, 157
Ootes, Barb 43, 48, 63, 151–154, 162–165, 179, 179–180, 180, 197–201, 252, 265, 281, 287, 290, 292, 293, 297
Ootes, Luke 281, 287, 290
Orange, Bud 20, 230

P

Pangnirtung 129, 130, 131, 133, 134, 264, 278
Parker, John 3, 19, 27, 29, 53, 78, 155, 169, 193, 282
Parker, Rae 31, 32, 113, 152, 299
Paulette Caveat 266
Pearson, Bryan 217, 255, 278
Pearson, Lester xv, 16, 70, 166, 289
Pedersen, Lena 217, 221–222, 222, 224, 225
Pelletier, Mel 269
Pelly Bay 204
Peltier, Leonard 268
Peters, Omer 236
Petrigo, Walter 79, 84, 94, 94–97, 97, 121, 124, 133, 142, 205
Phipps, Weldy 92, 115, 217
Pickles, Caroline 170–171, 200–201, 299. *See also* Washie, Caroline; *See also* Anawak, Caroline
Pilot, Bob and Lois 115, 116, 121, 124
Pine Point 157, 187, 245
Pond Inlet 76, 86, 91, 115, 118, 119, 124
Porritt, Bobby 3, 4, 5, 6
Port Burwell 134
Port Harrison 86
Prince of Wales. *See* Charles, the Prince of Wales
Prince of Wales Northern Heritage Centre 283, 290–291
Princess Anne 206, 208, 209, 269
Project Surname 157, 258
Pryde, Duncan 51, 52, 56, 153, 164, 191, 204
Pryde, Georgina 17, 164, 164–165, 235–239
Pudluk, Ludy 278
Pudnak, John 256

Q

Queen Elizabeth xi, 49, 50, 55, 165, 179, 183, 189, 195, 206–214, 269, 293

R

Rabesca, James 170, 217, 219–220, 220, 224, 225
Rae Lakes 240, 269, 270
Rainbow Valley 46, 174, 258–259, 259. *See also* N'dilo